Ecology, Environment And Tourism

For

Bachelor of Tourism [(BTS), (DTS), (CTS)]

Useful For

IGNOU, KSOU (Karnataka), Bihar University (Muzaffarpur), Nalanda University, Jamia Millia Islamia, Vardhman Mahaveer Open University (Kota), Uttarakhand Open University, Kurukshetra University, Seva Sadan's College of Education (Maharashtra), Lalit Narayan Mithila University, Andhra University, Pt. Sunderlal Sharma (Open) University (Bilaspur), Annamalai University, Bangalore University, Bharathiar University, Bharathidasan University, HP University, Centre for distance and open learning, Kakatiya University (Andhra Pradesh), KOU (Rajasthan), MPBOU (MP), MDU (Haryana), Punjab University, Tamilnadu Open University, Sri Padmavati Mahila Visvavidyalayam (Andhra Pradesh), Sri Venkateswara University (Andhra Pradesh), UCSDE (Kerala), University of Jammu, YCMOU, Rajasthan University, UPRTOU, Kalyani University, Banaras Hindu University (BHU) and all other Indian Universities.

We use Recycled Paper

GULLYBABA PUBLISHING HOUSE PVT. LTD.

ISO 9001 & ISO 14001 CERTIFIED CO.

Published by:

GullyBaba Publishing House Pvt. Ltd.

Regd. Office:
2525/193, 1st Floor, Onkar Nagar-A,
Tri Nagar, Delhi-110035
(From Kanhaiya Nagar Metro Station Towards Old Bus Stand)
Call: 9991112299, 9312235086
WhatsApp: 9350849407

Branch Office:
1A/2A, 20, Hari Sadan,
Ansari Road, Daryaganj,
New Delhi-110002
Ph.011-45794768
Call & WhatsApp:
8130521616,8130511234

E-mail: hello@gullybaba.com, **Website**:GullyBaba.com

New Edition

ISBN: 978-93-81638-61-3

Author: Gullybaba.com Panel

Preface

This book is mainly targeted for the exam of Ecology, Environment and Tourism for all Universities. It has been introduced in market after seeing the huge demand of ready to grasp material for exams with high level of quality, and its un-availability in market. We the GullyBaba Publishing House took a step ahead to publish the quality material focusing on exams at the same time giving you indepth knowledge about the subject.

GPH Book is the pioneer effort that provides a unique methodology so as to perform better in exams. If your goal is to attain higher grade use this powerful study tool independently or along with your text.

On the Web : ***www.gullybaba.com*** *is the vital resource for your exams acting as catalyst to boost up your preparation. Now you can access us on the net through* ***www.doeacconline.com, www.ignouonline.com, and www.astrologyeverywhere.com.***

Feedback about the book can be sent at **ts05writers@gullybaba.com.**

Constructive criticism is always welcome as it will add to our knowledge. You can email at ts05@gullybaba.com.

New Delhi

Topics Covered

Block : 6 Policy and Infrastructure

Unit : 18 Tourism Policy and Its Impacts
Unit : 19 Infrastructure
Unit : 20 Environmental Degradation and Tourism
Unit : 21 Acts and Laws
Unit : 22 Polities of Environment

Block : 7 Pressures and Thresholds

Unit : 23 Identifying Pressures and Understanding Thresholds
Unit : 24 Host/Local Population
Unit : 25 Visitor Behaviour

Block : 8 Environmental Impacts-1

Unit : 26 Vegetation and Wildlife
Unit : 27 Mountains

Block : 9 Environmental Impacts-2

Unit : 28 Wetlands
Unit : 29 Islands and Beaches
Unit : 30 Sports -Adventure, Golf, Water
Unit : 31 Hotels and Resorts

Question Papers

Environment - An Introduction

Q1. Define ecology and environment. What is an environmental factors?

Ans. Ecology is the scientific study of the distribution and abundance of life and the interactions between organisms and their environment. The environment of an organism includes physical properties, which can be described as the sum of local abiotic factors such as insolation (sunlight), climate, and geology, and biotic factors, which are other organisms that share its habitat.

The word "ecology" is often used more loosely in such terms as social ecology and deep ecology and in common parlance as a synonym for the natural environment or environmentalism. Likewise "ecologic" or "ecological" is often taken in the sense of environmentally friendly.

The term ecology or *oekologie* was coined by the German biologist Ernst Haeckel in 1866, when he defined it as "the comprehensive science of the relationship of the organism to the environment." Haeckel did not elaborate on the concept, and the first significant textbook on the subject (together with the first university course) was written by the Danish botanist, Eugenius Warming. For this early work, Warming is often identified as the founder of ecology.

Environment

The surroundings. The *natural environment* includes the nature of the living space (sea or land, soil or water), the chemical constituents and physical properties of the living space, the climate, and the assortment of other organisms present. The *phenomenal environment* includes changes and modifications of the natural environment made by man. The effect of the environment on man is modified, in part, by the way the environment is perceived, and human geographers distinguish this – the *subjective environment* – from the *objective environment* – the real world as it is. The objective environment is of less importance to the individual than his or her perceived image of it. A division may also be made between the *built environment* and the *social environment* which is made up of the various fields of economic, social, and political interactions.

Simmons (Geography 85) integrates the sub-categories above by describing the 'many layers' of environment as 'something more like a double helix of mind and matter, whose gyre seems to be ever-widening, spinning unpredictable combinations of society and economy into the main space, but also throwing off minor gyres, which might be short-lived but might equally be the germs of the main arms of the future...at any one moment we can slice through the whole and think about the layers that are discernible to our minds, conscious though we are that to try to freeze such processes inevitably robs them of some of their life and that, like Peer Gynt, the existence, let alone the discovery, of a heart is a bit unlikely.'

Environmental factor

In epidemiology, **environmental factors** are those determinants of disease that are not transmitted genetically. Apart from the true monogenic genetic disorders, environmental factors may determine the development of disease in those genetically predisposed to a particular condition. Stress, physical and mental abuse, Diet, exposure to toxins, pathogens, radiation and chemicals found in almost all personal care products and household cleaners are common environmental factors that determine a large segment of non-hereditary disease. Environmental Factors affect business as well. I.E. interest rates, prices of oil, the weather. If a disease process is concluded to be the result of a combination of genetic and *environmental factor* influences, its etiological origin can be referred to as having a multifactorial pattern.

Q2. Write in brief about followings:

(1) Atmosphere **(2) Soil**

(3) Temperature

Ans. (1) Atmosphere – The **Earth's atmosphere** is a layer of gases surrounding the planet Earth that is retained by the Earth's gravity. It contains roughly (by molar content/volume) 78.08% nitrogen, 20.95% oxygen, 0.93% argon, 0.038% carbon dioxide, trace amounts of other gases, and a variable amount (average around 1%) of water vapor. This mixture of gases is commonly known as **air**. The atmosphere protects life on Earth by absorbing ultraviolet solar radiation and reducing temperature extremes between day and night.

There is no definite boundary between the atmosphere and outer space. It slowly becomes thinner and fades into space. Three quarters of the atmosphere's mass is within 11 km of the planetary surface. In the United States, people who travel above an altitude of 80.5 km (50 statute miles) are designated astronauts. An altitude of 120 km (~75 miles or 400,000 ft) marks the boundary where atmospheric effects become noticeable during re-entry. The Kármán line, at 100 km (62 miles or 328,000 ft), is also frequently regarded as the boundary between atmosphere and outer space.

Composition of dry atmosphere, by volume	
ppmv: parts per million by volume	
Gas	**Volume**
Nitrogen (N_2)	780,840 ppmv (78.084%)
Oxygen (O_2)	209,460 ppmv (20.946%)
Argon (Ar)	9,340 ppmv (0.9340%)
Carbon dioxide (CO_2)	383 ppmv (0.0383%)
Neon (Ne)	18.18 ppmv (0.001818%)
Helium (He)	5.24 ppmv (0.000524%)
Methane (CH_4)	1.745 ppmv (0.0001745%)
Krypton (Kr)	1.14 ppmv (0.000114%)
Hydrogen (H_2)	0.55 ppmv (0.000055%)
Not included in above dry atmosphere:	
Water vapor (H_2O)	~0.40% over full atmosphere, typically 1% to 4% near surface

Minor components of air not listed above include	
Gas	**Volume**
Nitrogen (N_2)	0.3 ppmv (0.00005%)
xenon	0.09 ppmv ($9x10^{-6}$%)
ozone	0.0 to 0.07 ppmv (0%-$7x10^{-6}$%)
nitrogen dioxide	0.02 ppmv ($2x10^{-6}$%)
iodine	0.01 ppmv ($1x10^{-6}$%)
carbon monoxide	trace
ammonia	trace

The mean molar mass of air is 28.97 g/mol. The composition figures above are by volume-fraction (V%), which for ideal gases is equal to mole-fraction (that is, fraction of total molecules). By contrast, *mass-fraction* abundances of gases, particularly for gases with significantly different molecular (molar) mass from that of air will differ from those by volume. For example, in air, helium is 5.2 ppm by *volume-fraction* and *mole-fraction*, but only about $(4/29) \times 5.2$ ppm = 0.72 ppm by *mass-fraction.*

Nitrification is the biological oxidation of ammonia with oxygen into nitrite followed by the oxidation of these nitrites into nitrates. Degradation of ammonia to nitrite is usually the rate limiting step of nitrification. Nitrification is an important step in the nitrogen cycle in soil. This process was discovered by the Russian microbiologist, Sergei Winogradsky.

The oxidation of ammonia into nitrite is performed by two groups of organisms, ammonia oxidizing bacteria and ammonia oxidizing archaea. Ammonia oxidizing bacteria can be found among the â- and ã-proteobacteria. In soils the most studied ammonia oxidizing bacteria belong to the genera *Nitrosomonas* and *Nitrosococcus*. Although in soils ammonia oxidation occurs by both bacteria and archaea in harsher environments like oceans ammonia oxidation is dominated by archaea. The second step (oxidation of nitrite into nitrate) is (mainly) done by bacteria of the genus *Nitrobacter*. Both steps are producing energy to be coupled to ATP synthesis. Nitrifying organisms are chemoautotrophs, and use carbon dioxide as their carbon source for growth.

Nitrification also plays an important role in the removal of nitrogen from municipal wastewater. The conventional removal is nitrification, followed by denitrification. The cost of this process resides mainly in aeration (bringing oxygen in the reactor) and the addition of an external carbon source (e.g. methanol) for the denitrification.

In most environments both organisms are found together, yielding nitrate as the final product. It is possible however to design systems in which selectively nitrite is formed (the *Sharon process*).

Together with ammonification, nitrification forms a mineralization process which refers to the complete decomposition of organic material, with the release of available nitrogen compounds. This replenishes the nitrogen cycle.

(2) Soil – SOIL may be defined as a thin layer of earth's crust which serves as a natural medium for growth of plants. It is the unconsolidated mineral matter that has been subjected to, and influenced by, genetic and environmental factors— parent material, climate, organisms and topography all acting over a period of time. Soil differs from the parent material in the morphological, physical , chemical and biological properties. Also, soils differ among themselves in some or all the properties, depending on the differences in the genetic and environmental factors. Thus some soils are red, some are black; some are deep and some are shallow; some are coarse textured and some are fine-textured. They serve as a reservoir of nutrients and water for crops, provide mechanical anchorage and favourable tilth. The components of soil are mineral matter, organic matter, water and air, the proportions of which vary and which together form a system for plant growth.

Soil profile. It is a vertical section of soil through all its horizons and extends upto the parent materials. A study of soil profile is important both from the standpoint of soil formation and soil development (pedology) and crop husbandry(edaphology). In deep soils the soil profile may be studied upto one metre and a quarter and in others upto the parent material. The layers (horizons) in the soil profile which vary in thickness may be distinguished from the morphological characteristics which include colour, texture, structure, etc. Generally, the profile consists of 3 mineral horizons 'A', 'B' and 'C'.

The 'A' horizon may consist of sub-horizons richer in organic matter intimately mixed with mineral matter 'A', the horizon that has lost clay, iron or aluminium with the resultant concentration of quartz (A_2—eluvial horizon) or an intermediate or transitional horizon.

The 'B' horizon is below the 'A' horizon showing dominant features of concentration of clay, iron, aluminium of humus alone or in combination.

The 'C' horizon excludes the bedrock from which 'A' and 'B' horizons are presumed to have been formed. The 'C' horizon is itself little affected by pedogenic processes. It is the layer of consolidated bedrock which, upon weathering, may be presumed to have given rise to the 'C' horizon above.

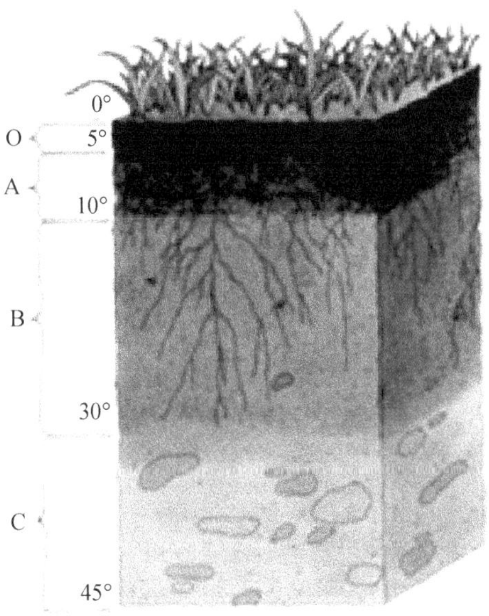

Not all the profiles show the sequence mentioned above. Profiles developed *in situ* under intense pedogenic processes over a sufficient period shoe the presence of the horizons 'A', 'B' and 'C'. Since the formation of soil and the development of profile are dependant on the genetic and environmental factors which vary considerably within and between regions, variations in horizon are frequent and common. Thus, for example, the soils developed in a recent flood plain may have only AC profile without any A_2, whereas those in the red and laterite soils area may have 'A_1', 'B_2' and 'C'. In some forest soils organic layers may also be found on the surface above 'A'. It will be beyond scope of this brief chapter to deal at length the nomenclature, implication and significance of horizons. It may be mentioned that a study of morphology of the soil profile gives a clear expression of the influence of the pedological processes involved.

(3) Temperature-All living organisms are influenced by temperature. Most organisms survive within a narrow temperature range. Infact, each species tends to have its own range of temperature within which it can function normally. If temperature is less or more than this range, its functioning is affected and even survival becomes difficult. The range of temperature, in which an organisms can survive is known as **'tolerance limit'**. For any physiological activity, there is minimum, maximum and optimum temperature. **Minimum temperature is that on which the activity starts, maximum beyond which activity is not possible and optimum at which it is at its highest pace**. Relatively few organisms survive body temperatures above 45°C. Some of the organisms develop physiological and behavioral adaptations to withstand extremes of temperature. If you visit the deserts of Rajasthan, you will see that the flora is completely different from other regions. There are many morphological changes in the leaf, stem and other parts of the plants growing in deserts. Similarly, animals of the desert live inside burrows to avoid the intense heat. Migration of birds from cold regions towards warmer regions in winters and back to their colder habitats in summers is an another example of adaptation to temperature. There are a number of species of mammals that undertake such migration to avoid extreme cold or heat. On the other hand many species that are not capable of migration to avoid extremes in temperature enter physiologically dormant states. For example, polar bears can live in freezing temperature, but hibernate in extreme winters.

Q3. What do you understand by green house effect?

Ans. The greenhouse effect is the rise in temperature that the Earth experiences because certain gases in the atmosphere (water vapor, carbon dioxide, nitrous oxide, and methane, for example) trap energy from the sun. Without these gases, heat would escape back into space and Earth's average temperature would be about 60°F colder. Because of how they warm our world, these gases are referred to as greenhouse gases.

Most greenhouses look like a small glass house. Greenhouses are used to grow plants, especially in the winter. Greenhouses work by trapping heat from the sun. The glass panels of the greenhouse let in light but keep heat from escaping. This causes the greenhouse to heat up, much like the inside of a car parked in sunlight, and keeps the plants warm enough to live in the winter.

Earth's atmosphere is all around us. It is the air that we breathe. Greenhouse gases in the atmosphere behave much like the glass panes in a greenhouse.

Sunlight enters the Earth's atmosphere, passing through the blanket of greenhouse gases. As it reaches the Earth's surface, land, water, and biosphere absorb the sunlight's energy. Once absorbed, this energy is sent back into the atmosphere. Some of the energy passes back into space, but much of it remains trapped in the atmosphere by the greenhouse gases, causing our world to heat up.

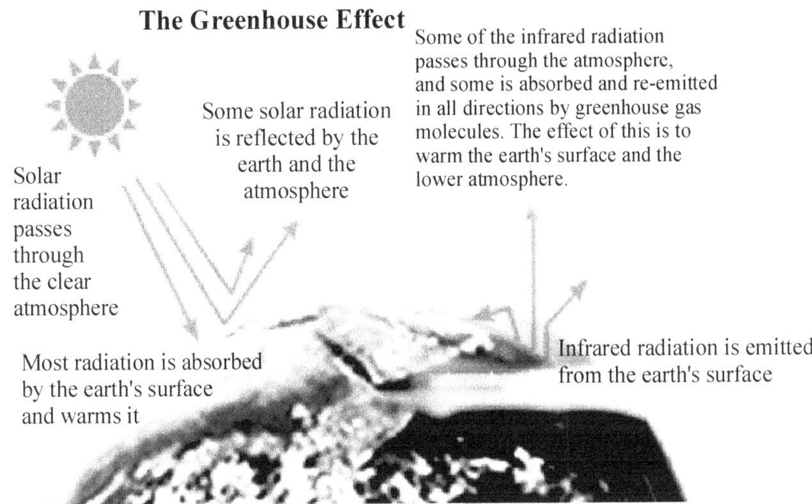

The greenhouse effect is important. Without the greenhouse effect, the Earth would not be warm enough for humans to live. But if the greenhouse effect becomes stronger, it could makes the Earth warmer than usual. Even a little extra warming may cause problems for humans, plants and animals.

Q4. What is an ecosystem? List some biotic and abiotic factors in an ecosystem. [June 2008, Q1, Dec 2007, Q1]

Ans. Within all species, individuals interact with each other – feeding together, mating together, and living together. Some species have a pecking order as well, and each individual has a role to play within it.

However, it is not only individuals within a species that interact. Different species of animals interact with each other all the time. For instance, animals eat other animals through their interactions in a food web. But plants are included in this web as well as they, too, are eaten by animals.

What would happen if the weather were really cold all the time? Well, not all species of animals, plants and bacteria would be able to survive. What differences are there between species who live in the Rocky Mountains and those who inhabit the Sahara desert? Landscape also determines where plants and animals might live. But what, exactly, is an ecosystem? An ecosystem is a geographical area of a variable size where plants, animals, the landscape and the climate all interact together.

The whole earth's surface can be described by a series of interconnected ecosystems. All living beings form and are part of ecosystems. They are diverse and always changing. Within an ecosystem, all aspects of the environment (both living things and their non-living settings) interact and affect one another. Every species affects the lives of those around them.

A small ecosystem in the boreal forest might look something like this: in the summertime, trees in forests (that produce oxygen used by living things through photosynthesis) lower the temperature in the forest for communities in the hot summer months. In turn, some members of the communities will probably feed upon the tree to gain nourishment, thus affecting or stunting the tree's growth.

Different areas in the world house different ecosystems. For example, you won't find an elephant or a tropical rainforest in Alberta! The different world ecological units are called biomes and they each have different flora, fauna, landscapes and weather patterns. An ecosystem is not the same thing as a biome. A biome is a large unit that is home to many different ecosystems. Within Alberta, there are six different biomes that each have their own specific flora and fauna distribution. These regions are: Grassland, Parkland, Boreal Forest, Foothill, Rocky Mountain and the Canadian Shield, all indicated on the map of Alberta's Regions.

Biotic and abiotic factors are interrelated. If one factor is changed or removed, it impacts the availability of other resources within the system. Biotic and abiotic factors combine to create a system or more precisely, an ecosystem. An ecosystem is a community of living and nonliving things considered as a unit.

Biotic Factors : Biotic, meaning of or related to life, are living factors. Plants, animals, fungi, protist and bacteria are all biotic or living factors.

Abiotic Factors : Abiotic, meaning not alive, are nonliving factors that affect living organisms. Environmental factors such habitat (pond, lake, ocean, desert, mountain) or weather such as temperature, cloud cover, rain, snow, hurricanes, etc. are abiotic factors.

Q5. What do you understand by food chain? What are the two major types of food chain?

Ans. Food chains describe the feeding relationships between species within an ecosystem. Organisms are connected to the organisms they consume by arrows representing the direction of biomass transfer. It also shows you how the energy from the producer is given to the consumer. Typically a food chain or food web refers to a graph where only connections are recorded, and a food network or ecosystem network refers to a network where the connections are given weights representing the quantity of nutrients or energy being transferred.

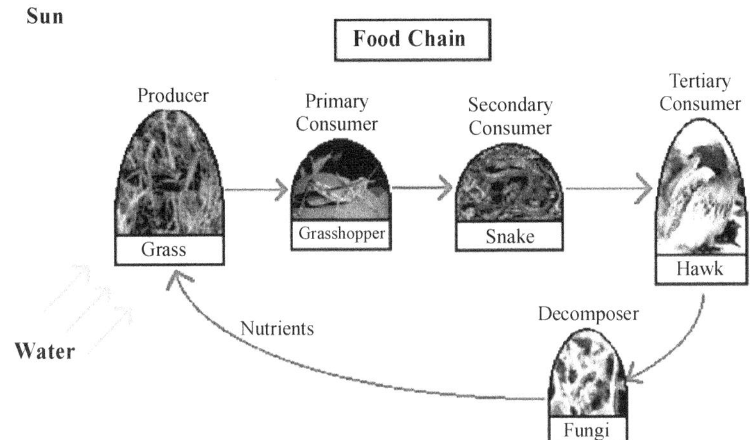

There are two kinds of food chains - **grazing food chains** and **detritus food chains**. Grazing food chains derive their energy directly from the sun. These are the chains that we are familiar with because we can see them and because they are more frequently described in articles about energy flow through food chains. However, think about the enormous amount of dead matter (leaves especially) that accumulate on a forest's floor or the large amount of dead plants that wind up on the bottom of lakes and ponds each year. This dead matter (**detritus**) is rich in energy and nutrients. Decomposers and detritivores obtain their nutrients and energy from this resource as opposed to the sun. All the organisms feeding on the detritus are part of the **detritus food chain** (rarely mentioned or illustrated in children's books on food chains). Those feeding directly on the detritus are **primary detritus feeders** and those preying on these organisms are **secondary detritus feeders**. In nature, the two types of food chains mix as organisms from one chain feed on those from the other food chain.

a. Grazing food Chain

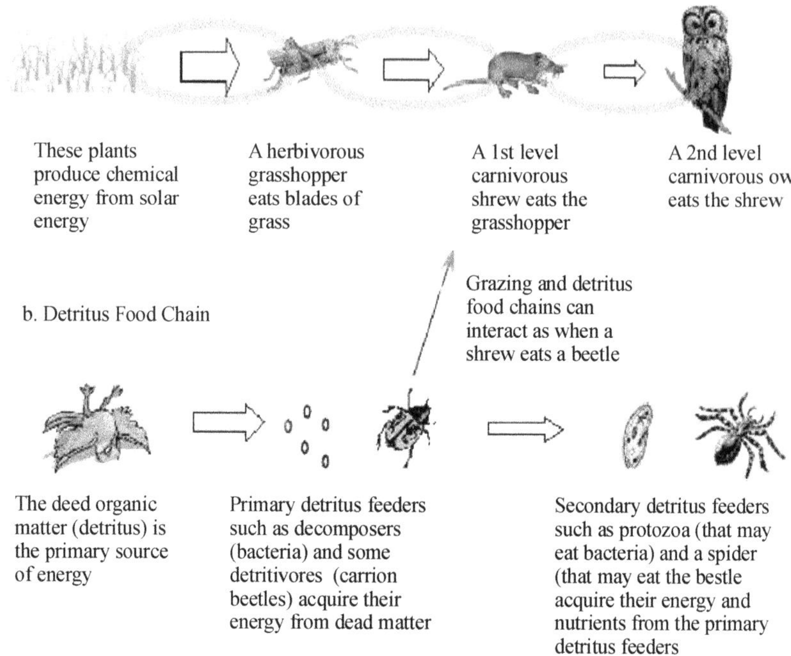

Q6. Define food web. How do food webs different from food chain?

Ans. A **food web** extends the *food chain* concept from a simple linear pathway to a complex network of interactions. The earliest food webs were published by Victor Summerhayes and Charles Elton in 1923 and Hardy in 1924. Summerhayes and Elton's (right) depicted the interactions of plants, animals and bacteria on Bear Island, Norway, while Hardy's food web showed the interactions of herring and plankton in the North Sea.

The direct steps as shown in the food chain example above seldom reflect reality. This web makes it possible to show much bigger animals (like a seal) eating very small organisms (like plankton). Food sources of most species in an ecosystem are much more diverse, resulting in a complex *web* of relationships as shown in the figure on the right. In this figure, the grouping of Algae - Protozoa - Oligochaeta - Northern Eider - Arctic Fox is a *chain*; the whole complex network is a *food web*.

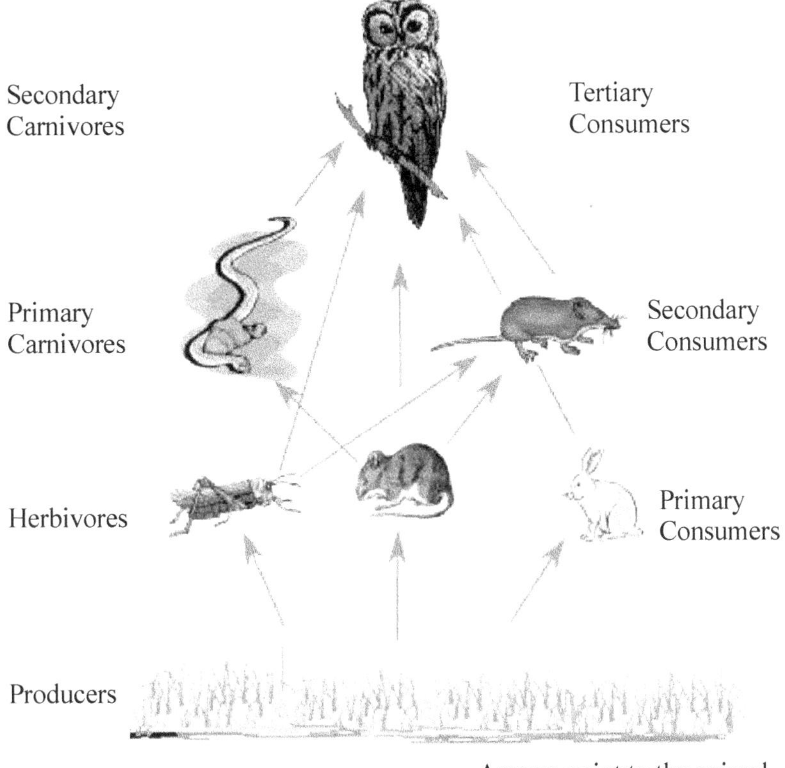

Arrows point to the animal doing the eating (predator)

Q7. What do you understand by ecological pyramid?

Ans. An **Ecological Pyramid** (or **Trophic pyramid**) is a graphical representation designed to show the biomass or productivity at each trophic level in a given ecosystem. Biomass pyramids show the abundance or biomass of organisms at each trophic level, while productivity pyramids show the production or turn-over in biomass. Ecological Pyramids begin with producers on the bottom and proceed through the various trophic levels, the highest of which is on top.

Ecological pyramids are graphical representations of the number of individuals in different nutritional levels. For example, the plant-insect-bird-hawk food chain can be represented as an ecological pyramid. Plants absorb energy from the sun, the insects eat the plants, the birds eat the insects, and the hawks eat the birds. Hence, the energy of the sun has been transferred from the sun to the tissues of the hawk. Since the number of individuals in each level *usually* decreases, the resulting diagram looks like a pyramid.

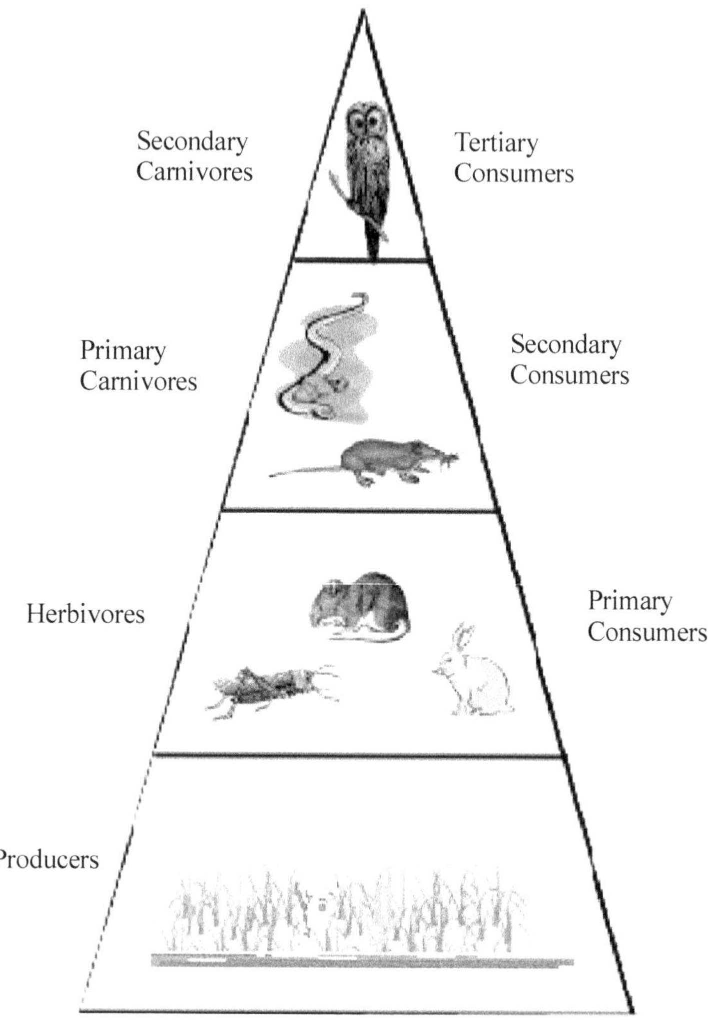

Q8. Why the ecological issues are being important for the tourism industry? [June 2008, Q1, Dec 2007, Q1]

Ans. Tourism is gaining importance amongst the various human activities in the modern world. So much so that today, the tourism industry is fast emerging as a major economic force both at national as well as at the international level. You may be wondering, why we are suddenly talking on the entirely different issue. Well, this is the central theme of this course, which we begin to directly discuss with you from now on. The environmental basics that you have studied so far, should set you to start analyzing the activities of Tourism Industry vis-a-vis the environment. After all what tourism is about? Tourism is an umbrella term for all the relationships and phenomena associated with public traveling and visiting different parts of the country/world with certain specific objectives. Tourism involves two key interactive components – the tourists and the environment. However benign the objectives of a tourist may be, it does exert certain amount of pressure on the local environment. How? Imagine, a small group of tourists visits and spends a number of days in a certain area, with a simple aim to watch the beautiful landscape and the wildlife. The bare minimum tourists needs, accommodation, transport facilities and service infrastructure need to be taken care of. All these activities alongwith the behaviour of tourists, do exert certain pressure on the environment. Our attempt, therefore, should be to anticipate such likely pressures and leave enough scope for the environment to recover and regain the original status after the tourists moved out from that site. You should realize that this should not remain at the philosophical level only, but it should generate a deep environmental concern in you. The interaction between tourism and environment should be viewed as an important consideration in designing conservation and protection of the delicate balance of the nature. When we say so it does not mean that for the first time any attention is being paid to this aspect. People associated with the tourism enterprises have felt some of these problems in the past and many tourist impact studies have been conducted. Such studies have highlighted the adverse consequences of tourism related activities on the environment. The damage levels were recorded but the processes by which damage occurs have been rarely identified. Another weakness of such investigations is that usually a single environmental component of a tourist spot has been examined, ignoring the relationships and interdependences of the components for taking a comprehensive view of the total environment. In nutshell, most of these studies are reactionary, that is, after the event analysis. The following five examples would bring out this point very clearly to you. These examples, taken from different situations sum up the adverse after-effects of some tourism related activities and are based on substantial data which we have not deliberately included here.

- The use of off road vehicles in sensitive ecosystems such as dunes is damaging.
- Wildlife observation by tourists disturbs the feeding and breeding of animals and birds.
- Wastes discarded by tourists, at sites visited get accumulated in huge amounts over the years. In some places, situation has come to a pass where it is posing grave danger to the very existence of that area as a tourist spot.
- In the seaside tourist resorts the untreated raw sewage from the tourist accommodation is discharged into the sea thereby adversely affecting

the marine life and communities existing on shores and nearby areas.

- Excursions and carelessly conducted educational trips involve uprooting and collection of rare or important plants by tourists and trampling of vegetation resulting in avoidable loss of biodiversity.

There is no death of impressively documented examples conveying the same message. All these remain locked in books, papers or technical journals only. In future too, many such instances may add on to the existing list to make it even longer. Since tourism is almost certain to become a major sector in international trade in the years to come, a central review of the impact of tourism on environment is urgently required. **A proper ecologically responsive planning and management is needed to take care of such problems. Sensitization of the people related to tourism industry has to be the key component of the approach which need to be incorporated at each and every level in tourism enterprises.** If we all—the tourists and the tourism corporates are conscious of the likely impact of their each and every activity on the environment, the safeguard measures would be automatically implemented without effort. Any beginning, even at a small scale, would only permeate and spread to the global scale!

Q9. Define the term Biome and Ecotone. [June 2008, Q2]

Ans. BIOME – A **biome** is a climatically and geographically defined area of ecologically similar communities of plants, animals, and soil organisms, often referred to as ecosystems. Biomes are defined based on factors such as plant structures (such as trees, shrubs, and grasses), leaf types (such as broadleaf and needleleaf), plant spacing (forest, woodland, savanna), and climate. Unlike ecozones, biomes are not defined by genetic, taxonomic, or historical similarities. Biomes are often identified with particular patterns of ecological succession and climax vegetation. The biodiversity characteristic of each biome, especially the diversity of fauna and subdominant plant forms, is a function of abiotic factors and the biomass productivity of the dominant vegetation. Species diversity tends to be higher in terrestrial biomes with higher net primary productivity, moisture availability, and temperature.

Biomes are often given local names. For example, a Temperate grassland or shrubland biome is known commonly as *steppe* in central Asia, *prairie* in North America, and *pampas* in South America. Tropical grasslands are known as *savanna* in Australia as well as Southern Africa where in Afrikaans it is known as *veldt*. Sometimes an entire biome may be targeted for protection, especially under an individual nation's Biodiversity Action Plan.

Ecotone- An **ecotone** is a transition area between two adjacent ecological communities (ecosystems). It may appear on the ground as a gradual blending of the two communities across a broad area, or it may manifest itself as a sharp boundary line.

Changes in the physical environment may produce a sharp boundary, as in the example of the interface between areas of forest and cleared land. Elsewhere, a more gradually blended interface area will be found, where species from each community will be found together as well as unique local species. Mountain ranges often create such ecotones, due to the wide variety of climatic conditions experienced on their slopes. They may also provide a boundary between species due to the obstructive nature of their terrain; Mont Ventoux in France is a good example, marking the boundary between the flora and fauna of northern and southern France. Most wetlands are ecotones.

Ecotones are particularly significant for mobile animals, as they can exploit more than one set of habitats within a short distance. This can produce an edge effect along the boundary line, with the area displaying a greater than usual diversity of species. The phenomenon of increased variety of plants and as well as animals at the community junction is called **Edge effect** and is essentially due to a wider range of suitable environmental condition. The word was coined from a combination of *eco*(logy) plus *-tone*, from the Greek *tonos* or tension – in other words, a place where ecologies are in tension.

Q10. Write a short note on followings:
(1) Deserts **(2) Tundra**
(3) Tropical Rain Forest

Ans. (1) Deserts : Deserts cover about one fifth of the Earth's surface and occur where rainfall is less than 50 cm/year. Although most deserts, such as the Sahara of North Africa and the deserts of the southwestern U.S., Mexico, and Australia, occur at low latitudes, another kind of desert, cold deserts, occur in the basin and range area of Utah and Nevada and in parts of western Asia. Most deserts have a considerable amount of specialized vegetation, as well as specialized vertebrate and invertebrate animals. Soils often have abundant nutrients because they need only water to become very productive and have little or no organic matter. Disturbances are common in the form of occasional fires or cold weather, and sudden, infrequent, but intense rains that cause flooding. There are relatively few large mammals in deserts because most are not capable of storing sufficient water and withstanding the heat. Deserts often provide little shelter from the sun for large animals. The dominant animals of warm deserts are non-mammalian vertebrates, such as reptiles. Mammals are usually small, like the kangaroo mice of North American deserts.

Desert biomes can be classified according to several characteristics. There are four major types of deserts :

- Hot and dry
- Semiarid

- Coastal
- Cold

Sand dunes in Death Valley National Monument, California.

(2) Tundra : Tundra is the coldest of all the biomes. Tundra comes from the Finnish word tunturi, meaning treeless plain. It is noted for its frost-molded landscapes, extremely low temperatures, little precipitation, poor nutrients, and short growing seasons. Dead organic material functions as a nutrient pool. The two major nutrients are nitrogen and phosphorus. Nitrogen is created by biological fixation, and phosphorus is created by precipitation.

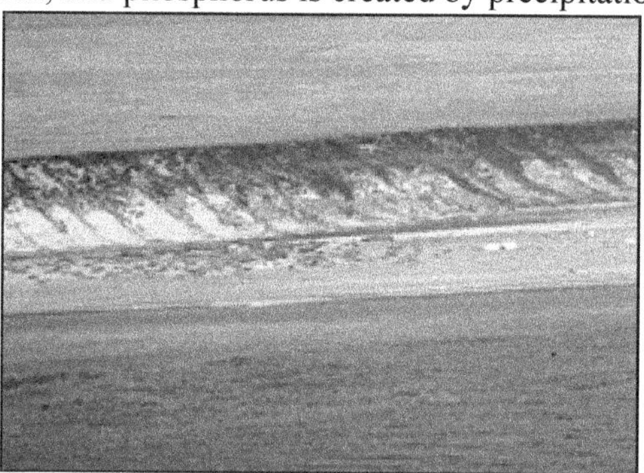

Tundra along the Colville River, Alaska

Characteristics of tundra include :

1. Extremely cold climate
2. Low biotic diversity
3. Simple vegetation structure
4. Limitation of drainage

5. Short season of growth and reproduction

6. Energy and nutrients in the form of dead organic material

7. Large population oscillations

(3) Tropical Rain Forest : The tropical rainforests of the world are located in the green areas. The tropical rainforest is the richest source of life on earth. It is a treasure chest of plant and animal life. Tropical means close to the equator. The equator is an imaginary belt which circles the earth and divides it into two halves. Near the equator, the sun shines directly on the earth. The areas directly above and below the equator are called the tropics and are always warm and humid, much like summertime.

Most tropical rain forests are located on the continents of Central and South America, Africa, Asia and Australia. The largest tropical rain forest in the world is the Amazon Rain Forest in South America. The world's largest river, the Amazon, flows through it. Much of this rain forest is in the country of Brazil. The seasons do not change in the tropical rain forest. It has been hot and wet for millions of years. The average temperature year-round is about 80 degrees. The tropical rain forest is the wettest place on earth. It rains every day. In one year it may rain about 100 to 400 inches. This means that 9 to 30 feet of rain may fall each year. The heat and moisture in the rainforest cause plants and animals to rot quickly once they have died. This is called decay. When things decay, all the rich nutrients are recycled back into the soil to feed the roots of other plants. Rain forests even recycle their rain! As water evaporates from the forest back into the air, it forms clouds above the canopy. Later, the clouds will rain once again over the forest. Scientists think destroying rainforests makes our earth warmer. This is called the Greenhouse Effect and is not good. Without rainforests, we will have less rain. This will harm the trees and plants that help to keep the air we breathe clean. Our earth could become very dry and barren, like a desert.

Q11. Define fresh water biomes and marine biomes.[Dec 2008, Q10(i)]

Ans. The freshwater biome : Freshwater is defined as having a low salt concentration — usually less than 1%. Plants and animals in freshwater regions are adjusted to the low salt content and would not be able to survive in areas of high salt concentration (i.e., ocean). There are different types of freshwater regions :

(1) Ponds and lakes **(2)** Streams and rivers

(3) Wetlands

(1) Ponds and lakes : These regions range in size from just a few square meters to thousands of square kilometers. Scattered throughout the earth, several are remnants from the Pleistocene glaciation. Many ponds are seasonal, lasting just a couple of months (such as sessile pools) while lakes may exist for hundreds of years or more. Ponds and lakes may have limited species diversity since they are often isolated from one another and from other water sources like rivers and oceans. Lakes and ponds are divided into three different "zones" which are usually determined by depth and distance from the shoreline.

The topmost zone near the shore of a lake or pond is the *littoral zone.* This zone is the warmest since it is shallow and can absorb more of the Sun's heat. It sustains a fairly diverse community, which can include several species of algae (like diatoms), rooted and floating aquatic plants, grazing snails, clams, insects, crustaceans, fishes, and amphibians. In the case of the insects, such as dragonflies and midges, only the egg and larvae stages are found in this zone. The vegetation and animals living in the littoral zone are food for other creatures such as turtles, snakes, and ducks. The near-surface open water surrounded by the littoral zone is the *limnetic zone*. The limnetic zone is well-lighted (like the littoral zone) and is dominated by plankton, both phytoplankton and zooplankton. Plankton are small organisms that play a crucial role in the food chain. Without aquatic plankton, there would be few living organisms in the world, and certainly no humans. A variety of freshwater fish also occupy this zone.

Plankton have short life spans – when they die, they fall into the deep-water part of the lake/pond, the *profundal zone*. This zone is much colder and denser than the other two. Little light penetrates all the way through the limnetic zone into the profundal zone. The fauna are heterotrophs, meaning that they eat dead organisms and use oxygen for cellular respiration. Temperature varies in ponds and lakes seasonally. During the summer, the temperature can range from 4° C near the bottom to 22° C at the top. During the winter, the temperature at the bottom can be 4° C while the top is 0° C (ice). In between the two layers, there is a narrow zone called the thermocline where the temperature of the water changes rapidly. During the spring and fall seasons, there is a mixing of the top and bottom layers, usually due to winds, which results in a uniform water temperature of around 4° C. This mixing also circulates oxygen throughout the lake. Of course there are many lakes and ponds that do not freeze during the winter, thus the top layer would be a little warmer.

(2) Streams and rivers : These are bodies of flowing water moving in one direction. Streams and rivers can be found everywhere – they get their starts at headwaters, which may be springs, snowmelt or even lakes, and then travel all the way to their mouths, usually another water channel or the ocean. The characteristics of a river or stream change during the journey from the source to the mouth. The temperature is cooler at the source than it is at the mouth. The water is also clearer, has higher oxygen levels, and freshwater fish such as trout and heterotrophs can be found there. Towards the middle part of the stream/river, the width increases, as does species diversity —

numerous aquatic green plants and algae can be found. Toward the mouth of the river/stream, the water becomes murky from all the sediments that it has picked up upstream, decreasing the amount of light that can penetrate through the water. Since there is less light, there is less diversity of flora, and because of the lower oxygen levels, fish that require less oxygen, such as catfish and carp, can be found.

From left: McArthur-Burney Falls State Park, California; trout; Green River, Utah; Brooks River, Alaska.

(3) Wetlands : Wetlands are areas of standing water that support aquatic plants. Marshes, swamps, and bogs are all considered wetlands. Plant species adapted to the very moist and humid conditions are called hydrophytes. These include pond lilies, cattails, sedges, tamarack, and black spruce. Marsh flora also include such species as cypress and gum. Wetlands have the highest species diversity of all ecosystems. Many species of amphibians, reptiles, birds (such as ducks and waders), and furbearers can be found in the wetlands. Wetlands are not considered freshwater ecosystems as there are some, such as salt marshes, that have high salt concentrations — these support different species of animals, such as shrimp, shellfish, and various grasses.

The marine biome : Marine regions cover about three-fourths of the Earth's surface and include oceans, coral reefs, and estuaries. Marine algae supply much of the world's oxygen and take in a huge amount of atmospheric carbon dioxide. The evaporation of the seawater provides rainwater for the land.

Oceans

Coral reefs

Estuaries

Oceans

The largest of all the ecosystems, oceans are very large bodies of water that dominate the Earth's surface. Like ponds and lakes, the ocean regions are separated into separate zones: intertidal, pelagic, abyssal, and benthic. All four zones have a great diversity of species. Some say that the ocean contains the richest diversity of species even though it contains fewer species than there are on land.

The intertidal zone is where the ocean meets the land – sometimes it is submerged and at other times exposed, as waves and tides come in and out.

Because of this, the communities are constantly changing. On rocky coasts, the zone is stratified vertically. Where only the highest tides reach, there are only a few species of algae and mollusks. In those areas usually submerged during high tide, there is a more diverse array of algae and small animals, such as herbivorous snails, crabs, sea stars, and small fishes. At the bottom of the intertidal zone, which is only exposed during the lowest tides, many invertebrates, fishes, and seaweed can be found. The intertidal zone on sandier shores is not as stratified as in the rocky areas. Waves keep mud and sand constantly moving, thus very few algae and plants can establish themselves – the fauna include worms, clams, predatory crustaceans, crabs, and shorebirds.

The pelagic zone includes those waters further from the land, basically the open ocean. The pelagic zone is generally cold though it is hard to give a general temperature range since, just like ponds and lakes, there is thermal stratification with a constant mixing of warm and cold ocean currents. The flora in the pelagic zone include surface seaweeds. The fauna include many species of fish and some mammals, such as whales and dolphins. Many feed on the abundant plankton. The benthic zone is the area below the pelagic zone, but does not include the very deepest parts of the ocean (see abyssal zone below). The bottom of the zone consists of sand, slit, and/or dead organisms. Here temperature decreases as depth increases toward the abyssal zone, since light cannot penetrate through the deeper water. Flora are represented primarily by seaweed while the fauna, since it is very nutrient-rich, include all sorts of bacteria, fungi, sponges, sea anemones, worms, sea stars, and fishes.

The deep ocean is the abyssal zone. The water in this region is very cold (around 3° C), highly pressured, high in oxygen content, but low in nutritional content. The abyssal zone supports many species of invertebrates and fishes. Mid-ocean ridges (spreading zones between tectonic plates), often with hydrothermal vents, are found in the abyssal zones along the ocean floors. Chemosynthetic bacteria thrive near these vents because of the large amounts of hydrogen sulfide and other minerals they emit. These bacteria are thus the start of the food web as they are eaten by invertebrates and fishes.

From left: reef life in the Gulf of Aqaba, Red Sea; a reef at Fanning Island atoll in the central Pacific; a reef in the Florida Keys National Marine Sanctuary.

Coral reefs : Coral reefs are widely distributed in warm shallow waters.

They can be found as barriers along continents (e.g., the Great Barrier Reef off Australia), fringing islands, and atolls. Naturally, the dominant organisms in coral reefs are corals. Corals are interesting since they consist of both algae (zooanthellae) and tissues of animal polyp. Since reef waters tend to be nutritionally poor, corals obtain nutrients through the algae via photosynthesis and also by extending tentacles to obtain plankton from the water. Besides corals, the fauna include several species of microorganisms, invertebrates, fishes, sea urchins, octopuses, and sea stars.

Estuaries : Estuaries are areas where freshwater streams or rivers merge with the ocean. This mixing of waters with such different salt concentrations creates a very interesting and unique ecosystem. Microflora like algae, and macroflora, such as seaweeds, marsh grasses, and mangrove trees (only in the tropics), can be found here. Estuaries support a diverse fauna, including a variety of worms, oysters, crabs, and waterfow.

Q12. Discuss about the major biomes of India.

Ans. India is the seventh largest country in the world and Asia's second largest nation with an area of 3,287,263 square km. The Indian mainland stretches from 8 4' to 37 6' N latitude and from 68 7' to 97 25' E longitude. It has a land frontier of some 15,200 kms and a coastline of 7,516 km (Government of India, 1985). India's northern frontiers are with Xizang (Tibet) in the Peoples Republic of China, Nepal and Bhutan. In the north-west, India borders on Pakistan; in the north-east, China and Burma; and in the east, Burma. The southern peninsula extends into the tropical waters of the Indian Ocean with the Bay of Bengal lying to the south-east and the Arabian Sea to the south-west. For administrative purposes India is divided into 24 states and 7 union territories. The country is home to around 846 million people, about 16% of the World's population (1990 figures).

Physically the massive country is divided into four relatively well defined regions - the Himalayan mountains, the Gangetic river plains, the southern (Deccan) plateau, and the islands of Lakshadweep, Andaman and Nicobar. The Himalayas in the far north include some of the highest peaks in the world. The highest mountain in the Indian Himalayas is Khanjunga (8586 m) which is located in Sikkim on the border with Nepal. To the south of the main Himalayan massif lie the Lesser Himalaya, rising to 3,600- 4,600 m, and represented by the Pir Panjal in Kashmir and Dhaula dhar in Himachal Pradesh. Further south, flanking the Indo-Gangetic Plain, are the Siwaliks which rise to 900-1,500 m.

The northern plains of India stretch from Assam in the east to the Punjab in the west (a distance of 2,400 km), extending south to terminate in the saline swamplands of the Rann of Kachchh (Kutch), in the state of Gujarat. Some of the largest rivers in India including the Ganga (Ganges), Ghaghara,

Brahmaputra, and the Yamuna flow across this region. The delta area of these rivers is located at the head of the Bay of Bengal, partly in the Indian state of west Bengal but mostly in Bangladesh. The plains are remarkably homogenous topographically: for hundreds of kilometres the only perceptible relief is formed by floodplain bluffs, minor natural levees and hollows known as 'spill patterns', and the belts of ravines formed by gully erosion along some of the larger rivers. In this zone, variation in relief does not exceed 300 m (FAO/UNEP, 1981) but the uniform flatness conceals a great deal of pedological variety. The agriculturally productive alluvial silts and clays of the Ganga-Brahmaputra delta in north-eastern India, for example, contrast strongly with the comparatively sterile sands of the Thar Desert which is located at the western extremity of the Indian part of the plains in the state of Rajasthan.

The climate of India is dominated by the Asiatic monsoon, most importantly by rains from the south-west between June and October, and drier winds from the north between December and February. From March to May the climate is dry and hot.

Wetlands : India has a rich variety of wetland habitats. The total area of wetlands (excluding rivers) in India is 58,286,000ha, or 18.4% of the country, 70% of which comprises areas under paddy cultivation. A total of 1,193 wetlands, covering an area of about 3,904,543 ha, were recorded in a preliminary inventory coordinated by the Department of Science and Technology, of which 572 were natural (Scott, 1989). India's most important wetland areas are-Chilka Lake (Orissa) and Keoladeo National Park (Bharatpur) - have been designated under the Convention of Wetlands of International Importance (Ramsar Convention) as being especially significant waterfowl habitats. The country's wetlands are generally differentiated by region into eight categories (Scott, 1989): the reservoirs of the Deccan Plateau in the south, together with the lagoons and the other wetlands of the southern west coast; the vast saline expanses of Rajasthan, Gujarat and the gulf of Kachchh; freshwater lakes and reservoirs from Gujarat eastwards through Rajasthan (Kaeoladeo Ghana National park) and Madhya Pradesh; the delta wetlands and lagoons of India's east coast (Chilka Lake); the freshwater marshes of the Gangetic Plain; the floodplain of the Brahmaputra; the marshes and swamps in the hills of north-east India and the Himalayan foothills; the lakes and rivers of the montane region of Kashmir and Ladakh; and the mangroves and other wetlands of the island arcs of the Andamans and Nicobars.

Forests : India possesses a distinct identity, not only because of its geography, history and culture but also because of the great diversity of its natural ecosystems. The panorama of Indian forests ranges from evergreen tropical rain forests in the Andaman and Nicobar Islands, the Western Ghats, and the north-eastern states, to dry alpine scrub high in the Himalaya to the north. Between the two extremes, the country has semi-evergreen rain forests, deciduous monsoon forests, thorn forests, subtropical pine forests in the lower montane zone and temperate montane forests (Lal, 1989). One of the most important tropical forests classifications was developed for Greater India (Champion, 1936) and later republished for present-day India (Champion and Seth, 1968). This approach has proved to have wide application outside India. In it 16 major forests types are recognised, subdivided into 221 minor types. Structure, physiognomy and floristics are all used as characters to define the types.

The main areas of tropical forest are found in the Andaman and Nicobar Islands; the Western Ghats, which fringe the Arabian Sea coastline of peninsular India; and the greater Assam region in the north-east. Small remnants of rain forest are found in Orissa state. Semi-evergreen rain forest is more extensive than the evergreen formation partly because evergreen forests tend to degrade to semi-evergreen with human interference. There are substantial differences in both the flora and fauna between the three major rain forest regions (IUCN, 1986; Rodges and Panwar, 1988).

The Western Ghats Monsoon forests occur both on the western (coastal) margins of the ghats and on the eastern side where there is less rainfall.. These forests contain several tree species of great commercial significance (e.g. Indian rosewood *Dalbergia latifolia*, Malabar Kino *Pterocarpus marsupium*, teak and *Terminalia crenulata*), but they have now been cleared from many areas. In the rain forests there is an enormous number of tree species. At least 60 percent of the trees of the upper canopy are of species which individually contribute not more than one percent of the total number. Clumps of bamboo occur along streams or in poorly drained hollows throughout the evergreen and semi-evergreen forests of south-west India, probably in areas once cleared for shifting agriculture.

The tropical vegetation of north-east India (which includes the states of Assam, Nagaland, Manipur, Mizoram, Tripura and Meghalaya as well as the plain regions of Arunachal Pradesh) typically occurs at elevations up to 900 m. It embraces evergreen and semi-evergreen rain forests, moist deciduous monsoon forests, riparian forests, swamps and grasslands. Evergreen rain forests are found in the Assam Valley, the foothills of the eastern Himalayas and the lower parts of the Naga Hills, Meghalaya, Mizoram, and Manipur where the rain fall exceeds 2300 mm per annum. In the Assam Valley the giant *Dipterocarpus macrocarpus* and *Shorea assamica* occur singly, occasionally attaining a girth of up to 7 m and a height of up to 50 m. The monsoon forests are mainly moist sal *Shorea robusta* forests, which occur widely in this region (IUCN, 1991).

The Andamans and Nicobar islands have tropical evergreen rain forests and tropical semi-evergreen rainforests as well as tropical monsoon moist monsoon forests (IUCN, 1986). The tropical evergreen rain forest is only slightly less grand in stature and rich in species than on the mainland. The dominant species is *Dipterocarpus grandiflorus* in hilly areas, while *Dipterocarpus kerrii* is dominant on some islands in the southern parts of the archipelago. The monsoon forests of the Andamans are dominated by *Pterocarpus dalbergioides* and *Terminalia* spp.

Q13. Define community. What are the major characteristics of community?

Ans. Within an ecosystem, each living being or an organism has a place, an actual area in which it resides. This space including all the factors within it is the organism's **habitat**. An organism does not exist in isolation but has dynamic interaction with other organisms as well as with the abiotic environment. Each organism plays a specific role in an ecosystem which is referred to as its **niche**. A niche includes parameters like food, space, temperature, water and appropriate conditions for mating. It also includes the organism's behaviour and the ways in which this behaviour changes with different seasons and at different times of the day. To put it in simple terms, habitat refers to the actual physical site occupied by an organism or its address whereas niche is related to its profession.

The interactions among organisms within ecosystems are varied. These can be at two level – at the level of populations and at the level of community. Before we go deeper into these interactions, first let us understand the ecological meanings of a population, a community and an ecosystem and see how these are related. Individuals of the same species constitute a population. Populations of different species of plants and animals inhabiting and sharing resources of an area are collectively called a biotic community or simply a community. A community together with its surrounding non-living environment is called an ecosystem.

Community Characteristics :

(1) Productivity : The word productivity is derived from production which refers to the production of biomass. We know that the production of biomass is a manifestation of energy storage-transfer reactions. All the organisms after the first tropic level, obtain their energy and nutrient requirements from lower trophic levels.

A community's productivity is measured as the rate of production of biomass. Productivity is dependent on physical factors like climate, air, water currents, soil type, land forms and altitude or depth. The variation in the productivity in different communities is due to the variation in the above mentioned factors. Generally speaking, the average productivity of terrestrial ecosystems is higher than the marine ecosystems, except shallow coastal waters which are highly productive. Oceans cover about 71 percent of the earth's surface, still the average marine productivity is less than 25 percent of average terrestrial productivity.

(2) Diversity : A community consists of a variety of species of plants and animals. This 'variety' is referred to as 'diversity' and is also known as 'species diversity' of the community. To know the species diversity of a community, one has to determine the number of different species present in an ecosystem. Species diversity is dependent on three variables: the number of **different species** in the community; the **number of individuals in each species**; and **total number of individuals** in a community.

(3) Resilience : You might have noticed that if there are some natural disturbances, the communities 'recover' to their original state after a period of time. This capacity of a community to recover from any kind of disturbance is known as resilience. In nature, the physical environment poses continuous challenge to the life forms with disturbances of various kinds. For example, consider weather conditions which are seldom same for a few days at a stretch or for that matter even during one day. There are daily changes in temperature, wind velocity and its direction. Besides the natural disturbances, the human factor also inflicts minor perturbations to major disruptions in the communities. How? Think of a situation when an area with thick natural vegetation is cleared for construction purposes. This onslaught may be too severe for the community to recover back. Consider another situation, where a large tree in a forest had fell resulting in the formation of a vacant area. After a span of time, the natural growth of plants of various kinds 'seals' this gap. This recovery reflects the community's resilience, i.e., the inherent tendency of the community to attain a dynamic equilibrium. To say it in ecological terms, **homeostasis** is inbuilt in community resilience. Homeostasis means inherent capacity of a system to revert back to normal state after perturbation.

Q14. In what manner stratification is related to diversity?

Ans. Stratification is a distinctive feature of a community. The dictionary meaning of the term is 'the arrangement in state or layers'. In context of a community, it means how the life forms are arranged in a vertical order. Stratification of a community is determined largely by the life forms of plants – their size, branching pattern and leaves. **Light** is the crucial factor that governs the vertical structure of a plant community which in fact provides a physical structure or a framework for accommodating different animal species.

Communities have characteristic stratification patterns. For example, a well developed forest ecosystem may have upto 7 or 8 strata which can be differentiated into **canopy; understory; shrub; herb** or **ground layer; forest floor; root layer** and the **soil strata**. The **vines, epiphytes** and **parasites** represent separate strata. The canopy, which is the primary site for capturing the solar energy has the major influence on the structure and life of the rest of the forest. In an open canopy forest considerable amount of sunlight reaches the lower layers and the forest floor. As a result, the understory trees, shrub and the herbaceous ground layer are well developed. In a closed canopy forest enough sunlight is not available to the underlying substrata. In such a situation the understory trees, shrub and herbaceous layer are poorly developed. In addition to light, **soil moisture** is another factor that influences stratification. The herb layer, particularly depends on soil moisture conditions. Other factors, such as **the slope, density of the overstory** that vary from place to place in a forest, also influence the nature of the herb layer.

The lowest, aerial layer of the forest is the forest floor. It is the site where the important process of forest litter decomposition takes place and nutrients are released for nutrient cycle. The status of this layer is dependent on all the above factors. A forest having, all the well-developed strata, generates a vast amount of litter making the forest floor also an immensely active stratum.

The degree of vertical stratification has a profound influence on the diversity of animal life in the community. A strong correlation exists between the foliage height diversity and bird species diversity. In the places having increased vertical stratification, there is increased availability of resources and living space; which favours a certain degree of specialization. The grasslands with their two strata, hold about 6 or 7 species of birds, all ground nesters. On the other hand, a well stratified forest may support 35 or more species, occupying different strata according to their specializations. The stratification and partitioning of resources are two important and mutually dependent dimensions of a community.

Aquatic ecosystems like lakes and oceans too exhibit stratification. Their stratification pattern is determined by **light, temperature** and **oxygen regimes**. A well-stratified lake usually has the following layers. First, is a layer of freely circulating surface water, the **epilimnion**. Since light is available in plenty, therefore, it is dominated by plants. It is the chief site of photosynthesis. The second layer, the **metalimnion**, is characterized by thermocline, i.e., a steep and rapid decline in temperature. Besides the presence of few, plant species adapted to low light, decomposition is most active in this layer. The third layer, the **hypolimnion**, is a deep, cold and dense layer of water, often with low amount of dissolved oxygen. Next, is a layer of **bottom mud**.

What is common in the community stratification in terrestrial and aquatic ecosystems? They both possess an **autotrophic layer** concentrated where light is available in plenty. You may recall that the autotrophic layer harvests solar energy and manufactures food from simple substances. In forest this layer is largely confined to the canopy layer, in grasslands, in the herb or the ground layer and in lakes and seas in the upper layers of water. Along with autotrophic layer there is also a **heterotrophic layer**. The strata constituting this layer obtain their food from the autotrophs, transfer energy and circulates matter by means of herbivory, predation and decomposition.

Q15. What is the meaning and importance of biodiversity?

[June 2006, Q2]

Ans. Biodiversity is the variety and differences among living organisms from all sources, including terrestrial, marine, and other aquatic ecosystems and the ecological complexes of which they are a part. This includes genetic diversity within and between species and of ecosystems. Thus, in essence, biodiversity represents all life. India is one of the mega biodiversity centres in the world and has two of the world's 18 'biodiversity hotspots' located in the Western Ghats and in the Eastern Himalayas (Myers 1999). The forest cover in these areas is very dense and diverse and of pristine beauty, and incredible biodiversity.

Importance of Biodiversity : It is no exaggeration to say that biodiversity is just as important as oxygen and water for sustaining life. Think of any sphere of life, be it health, food, clothing, aesthetics, industry, sports or recreation – each one is linked to either the wild or domesticated component of biodiversity.

Even in today's high-tech society where most things can be synthesized in laboratories, a good percentage of modern medicines prescribed are of biotic origin. Numerous life saving drugs have been isolated from flowering plants. Quinine from the cinchona tree, is used to treat malaria; digitalis from foxglove plant is used to treat chronic heart trouble; the morphine and cocaine from the poppy and coca shrubs respectively are used to reduce pain. Many other forms of drugs extracted from plants are used to treat leukemia, several forms of tumorous cancers and several heart ailments. A recent exciting find is total. It is a chemical extracted from the bark of yew tree. Taxol has been found very effective in treatment of ovarian cancer, as it specifically targets and kills the cancerous cells without harming the normal cells.

In addition to plants, microorganisms too have been widely used in the manufacture of medicines. More than 3000 antibiotics have been extracted from microorganisms. We all are familiar with the important antibiotics – Penicillin and Tetracycline. Another product of microorganisms, i.e., Cyclosporin, was developed from a soil fungus. It revolutionised heart and kidney transplant surgery by suppressing immune reactions. Aspirin and many other drugs that are all synthesized, were first discovered in wild.

A large number of wild plant and animal species that exist, could be potential food sources for the future. Most plant species have not been explored so far and their utility remains to be tapped. A large number of human tribals inhabiting remote areas or forests, look to wildlife for most of their proteins. It is estimated that about 30,000 species of plants have edible parts, but 90 percent of the world's food presently comes from just 20 plant species. A recently discovered tropical species – the winged beans, is a potential source of food. Every part of this plant is edible. Its leaves taste like spinach, young pods are like green beans, young seeds like peas, mature seeds like soyabeans and its underground stems are like potatoes and are rich in proteins. Another positive attribute is that it is a fast growing nodule-bearing plant that enriches soil with fixed nitrogen. Such plants and others like them from the wild give hope to feed growing millions.

The value of biodiversity is particularly apparent in agriculture. For generations people have raised a wide range of crops and livestock to stabilize and increase, production. These traditional practices have evolved genetically different strains of crop plants which are now being abandoned in favour of newer high-yield strains. Unfortunately these high yielding strains are genetically homogeneous and have a narrow genetic base and are highly vulnerable to insect pests and various diseases. The predominant strain of rice grown in Asia, for instance was devastated by a virus, but one wild strain from India had genes for resistance. Through intensive breeding a resistant hybrid was created which is now widely grown. This example clearly shows the importance of **genetic diversity** or the **genepools** for promoting and ensuring high agricultural yield.

Industries also use a wide variety of plant and animal products and thus benefit from a rich diversity of species. As many as 2,000 plant species throughout the world are known for their economic importance. The building, furniture and paper making industries use more than one hundred different species of trees. Cotton, flax, hemp, jute and agave provide fibre for manufacture of textile, ropes and other articles. Natural substances from a wide variety of plant species are used in the manufacture of rubber, dyes, tanning agents, perfumes, resins, gums, oils, insecticides and other products. Thus no sphere of life remains untouched by biodiversity. Even the diverse human cultures are linked to biodiversity.

The living environment has been an important factor in the development and shaping of human cultures. We all know that humans too influence their environment. Thus, diverse environmental conditions 'created' have been significantly important in the development of diverse cultures. Coming back to the point or linkage between culture and biodiversity, though the cultures differ from one another in diverse ways, but all revolve around biodiversity.

That 'biodiversity' is very important for human survival and sustenance was known to man since he descended on this earth and started practising agriculture and domesticating animals to fulfill his needs. Thus engaged certain strictures for the use, sharing and conservation of these biological resources. With the passage of time and further development of human society, these structures gradually became deeply 'ingrained values' of human cultures. The importance of biodiversity is reflected in various ways in different cultures: in religious beliefs, land-management practices, crop-selection and diet, art, music, social structure and even language. Indeed the variety of life is the backdrop against which many cultures have flourished or vanished!

Q16. What are the main causes of biodiversity loss. [Dec 2007, Q2]

Ans. The world biological diversity is a vast and undervalued resource. It comprises every form of life, from the smallest microbe to the largest animal, and the ecosystems of which they are part.

The number of species on Earth has been variously estimated to be between 10 and 100 million, although only 1.7 million of them have been described so far. To date, the loss of biodiversity is greater that at any time in the past. Some 100 species are being lost every day. Even the most insignificant-seeming species can play a crucial role in the ecosystem to which it belongs. We simply do not know what we are throwing away. Forest ecosystems are among those facing the most severe biodiversity loss.

Causes of Biodiversity Loss

Although biodiversity, in essence, has to do with genes, species and ecosystems, it is also related to issues far beyond the confines of biology. Understanding the threats to biodiversity and offering solutions to them necessitates insights from the socio-economic and applied sciences.

The major source of the recent interest in diversity of life on earth arises from the feeling of a rapid decline in biodiversity. Extinction of species is part of an evolutionary process. However, during recent times, extinction rates are ten to a hundred times higher than during pre-human times. The main causes for this loss of biodiversity are :

(a) The loss of habitats. Table 1 provides data on human disturbance of habitats on a worldwide scale. The data show the significant impact of human activity on world ecosystems. For example, in Europe, only 15% of the continent is classified as "undisturbed", which is the lowest percentage world-wide. Loss of tropical forest is the most highly published aspect of this. Elsewhere, rivers are impounded, coral reefs destroyed by dynamite, and natural grasslands are ploughed.

	Total area (km^2)	% undisturbed[1]	% partially disturbed[2]	% human dominated[3]
Europe	5 759 321	15.6	19.6	64.9
Asia	53 311 557	43.5	27.0	29.5
Africa	33 985 316	48.9	35.8	15.4
North America	26 179 907	56.3	18.8	24.9
South America	20 120 346	62.5	22.5	15.1
Australia	9 487 262	62.3	25.8	12.0
Antarctica	13 208 983	100.0	0.0	0.0
World	162 052 691			

(b) The introduction of exotic species. Many are accidental, as with noxious weeds and insect pests. Others are deliberate. Foxes, rabbits and cats, which were taken to Australia aboard European ships, have decimated Australia's indigenous wildlife. In freshwater, the stocking of exotic fish for sport, or (rarely) for food, has caused at least 18 extinctions of fish species in North American rivers. Catastrophic changes in the fish biodiversity of Lake Victoria (East Africa) resulted from the introduction of Nile perch. Eucalyptus, which is indigenous in Australia, has been introduced in many tropical and subtropical regions in the world, where the tree merely behaves as a pest.

(c) Over-harvesting by (illegal) hunting, and the systematic cutting of wood for heating purposes, or charcoal production, are other reasons for biodiversity loss. The use of medicinal plants might illustrate this point. In the semi-arid rural area of Southern Cochabamba (Bolivia), it was shown that, out of 132 inventoried plants that the local people use for traditional medicinal purposes, 10 were threatened because of their intensive collection.

(d) Lesser-known causes are due to "knock-on" effects. Species that are co-evolved with another, such as plants with specialised insect pollinators, will go extinct if one of the pair goes extinct. When the last passenger pigeon (*Ectopistes migratorius*) died in the early 1990s, so also did two of its obligate parasites, two lice species. Moabi (Baillonella toxisperma) used to be a common tree in West-Africa. The fruits are eaten, cooking oil is extracted from the seeds (karite) and the bark is used for medicinal purposes. For its reproduction, the plant depends on the elephants. Only these animals swallow and disperse the moabi seeds. The impressive reduction of elephants in countries such as the Ivory Coast, Ghana and Benin has had an important impact on the distribution of the tree.

(e) Homogenisation in agriculture and forestry; in particular, industrial agriculture and forestry use a limited number of species. Of the hundreds of species of edible potatoes available in South America, less than 20 are in commercial use in Europe. Although an estimated 7,000 plant species have been collected and cultivated for food, only 30 contribute over 90% of the entire global population's energy needs. The case of the banana (Musa spp.) is illustrative. Bananas are the fourth most important food source in the tropics after rice, wheat and corn. They are cultivated in nearly 120 countries. Farmers use only about 25 edible sterile banana varieties. The number of varieties is diminishing due to the spread of pests and diseases and the deterioration of the resource.

(f) Pollution and global environmental change also threaten the world's biodiversity. Climate changes affect the distribution of species. Plants that two decades ago were only found in Southern Spain currently appear at the foot of the Pyrenees mountains, in the North of the country.

(g) Species Introduction: Species introduction, accidental or intentional, is an important factor in the loss of native biodiversity of an area. The introduced species occasionally being superior competitors, establish and flourish at the expense of the original species. Notwithstanding the sudden changed pressures the original biodiversity is wiped from that area. Examples are many. We take up the example of the bird, Dodo. Dodo lived only in Mauritius – a small island in the Indian Ocean. The Dodo possessed two characteristics that were its eventual undoing; it had no fear of people and therefore, could be easily clubbed to death and it was flightless, so it had to lay its eggs on the ground. The Dodo became extinct by 1681, after the introduction of pigs to the island, who devoured its eggs. The extinction of Dodo may also be analysed in terms of changed habitat conditions due to the introduction of a new species – pigs, to the island. In an ecosystem like an island, both the variety of habitats and the area that comprises each habitat are physically limited. As a result of such constraints, the native animal's, Dodo in this case, ability to adapt to new predators and competitors is often reduced. For example, the habitat may not be large enough or diverse for the prey species (the Dodo) to avoid new predators (the pigs). And the diversity of resources may not be adequate to allow an existing species to coexist with a new competitive species. Hence, the superior competitor survived and the native species perished.

(h) Overexploitation of Plant and Animal Species: Forest, fisheries and wildlife resources have been over-exploited, even to the point of extinction. The Passenger Pigeon aptly exemplifies this situation. Once these were the most abundant birds in North America. They were in such immense numbers that their flocks darkened the sky during migration. Their one such flock alone was 400 km long and had no less than two billion birds! And there used to be as many as 90 nests per tree throughout a forest of about 5 km width and about 67 km length. An immense tonnage of their droppings fertilised the forests where passenger pigeons roosted. This bird, particularly their young ones were a delicacy. Since these were available in plenty, their price too was less. They were selectively hunted, in very large numbers to cover the wastage during transportation. The young ones and adult birds were killed indescriminately. Their rate of reproduction could not cope with the high rate of elimination as a passenger pigeon laid just one egg. The last pigeon – 'Martha' died in Cincimnati Zoo in 1914 and its body is kept in U.S. Natural Museum in Washington. Like the story of Passenger Pigeon, each extinct species carried along its tale of destruction. The human need for food; search for precious commodities (e.g., ivory) and pets; curiosities and collector's items have also impinged on some species.

All these causes have one element in common: they are induced by human activity. This makes human activity the most important source of the current decline in biodiversity. Therefore, understanding the many aspects of human influences on biodiversity, and their underlying driving forces, is of crucial importance for setting priorities and counteracting the current negative trends.

Environment And Conservation Ethics

Q1. Define conservation. Discuss the importance of conservation at present time.

Ans. Conservation is to be understood as the preservation of some level of biodiversity that is essential to the functioning of the ecosystems and the survival of the mankind. We have also to acknowledge, with some degree of confidence, the fact that extinction of a few varieties of life in nature and the consequent loss of biodiversity is not at the centre of the problem. Although we do not equate biodiversity conservation with the complete preservation of all species nor the maintenance of the environmental status quo, we are concerned with the current rates of resource exploitation and habitat modification which may be leading to an excessive bio-diversity loss.

Environmentalists want environmental systems and the diversity of species conserved. But their call is reinforced by many others who have become disillusioned with the course of development. All are threatened by the decay of global life support systems. Historically, people in industrialised countries have not perceived the importance of environmental conservation in the same way as the people in developing countries have done. North Americans, due to their cultural history, have to glorify nature to decry its defilement and to propose "back to – nature" type solution. As a consequence of their colonial history, Third world people have tended to be much more concerned with the social origins and human consequences of environmental degradation. Northern (Developed Countries) environmentalists were shocked in 1972 by the positions taken by the South (Developing countries) at the U.N. Conference on the human environment in Stockholm. Environmental leaders and scientists from North and South have learned from each other since that clash in views through repeated discussions and teamworks in the field. The 1987 report of the **World Commission on Environment and Development** reflects both views. There is a new synthesis arising among world political leaders as well. Among the populace the differences between North and South are diminishing. Northern workers are becoming more politically active with respect to the danger their work has on environments, while Southern people are gaining a broader understanding of the importance of ecological systems and processes for economic development. Therefore, cultural differences still continue to make differences in approaches adopted by North and South on environmental conservation.

Importance of Conservation at the Present Moment: Various developmental activities are rapidly destroying nature and its finely maintained and fragile balance and interdependence created over millions of years. But by destroying nature society is creating a basis for self destruction. The destruction of nature has gathered speed in the last two decades and we are fast heading towards a complete devastation and destruction of ecology. We are not on the brink of disaster; we have already entered the realm of disaster. Man by his thoughtless acts is fast turning the globe into a large garbage heap.

Much of the recent industrialization and agrarian development was ill conceived and continues to be so. Man and society have ruthlessly robbed nature and desertified earth. But the worst crime man and society continue to commit is to deprive the planet of its deep-fresh-cover of dense forests. Precisely those forests that sustain man and all the living beings and provide them with the life giving oxygen. Virtually every state and country is involved in this criminal act – an act against the humanity. Some people do it for profit, others in the name of providing basic necessities of life, still others purely for pleasure.

Q2. What do you understand by ecotourism? [June 2008, Q7]

Ans. Ecotourism, also known as **ecological tourism**, is a form of tourism that appeals to ecologically and socially conscious individuals. Generally speaking, ecotourism focuses on volunteering, personal growth, and learning new ways to live on the planet. It typically involves travel to destinations where flora, fauna, and cultural heritage are the primary attractions.

Responsible ecotourism includes programs that minimize the negative aspects of conventional tourism on the environment and enhance the cultural integrity of local people. Therefore, in addition to evaluating environmental and cultural factors, an integral part of ecotourism is the promotion of recycling, energy efficiency, water conservation, and creation of economic opportunities for the local communities.

Ideally, ecotourism should satisfy several criteria, such as:

- conservation of biological diversity and cultural diversity through ecosystem protection
- promotion of sustainable use of biodiversity, by providing jobs to local populations
- sharing of socio-economic benefits with local communities and indigenous people by having their informed consent and participation in the management of ecotourism enterprises
- tourism to unspoiled natural resources, with minimal impact on the environment being a primary concern.

- minimization of tourism's own environmental impact
- affordability and lack of waste in the form of luxury
- local culture, flora and fauna being the main attractions

For many countries, ecotourism is not simply a marginal activity to finance protection of the environment but is a major industry of the national economy. For example, in Costa Rica, Ecuador, Nepal, Kenya, Madagascar, and Antarctica, ecotourism represents a significant portion of the gross domestic product and economic activity.

The concept of ecotourism is widely misunderstood, and in practice is often used as a marketing tool to promote tourism which is related to nature. This is an especially frequent malpractice in the realm of Jungle tourism. Critics claim that ecotourism as practiced and abused often consists of placing a hotel in a splendid landscape, to the detriment of the ecosystem. According to them, ecotourism must above all sensitize people to the beauty and the fragility of nature. They condemn some operators as "greenwashing" their operations: using the label of "green-friendly", while behaving in environmentally irresponsible ways.

Although academics disagree about who can be classified as an ecotourist and there is precious little statistical data, some estimate that more than five million ecotourists - the majority of the ecotourist population - come from the United States, with others from Western Europe, Canada, and Australia. Currently there are various moves to create national and international ecotourism accrediation programs, although the process is also controversial. Ecotourism certificates have been put in place in Costa Rica, although some critics have dismissed these programs as greenwashing.

Q3. Discuss the impacts of tourism on environment?

Ans. Ecotourism operations occasionally fail to live up to conservation ideals. It is sometimes overlooked that ecotourism is a highly consumer-centered activity, and that environmental conservation is a means to further economic growth. Although ecotourism is intended for small groups, even a modest increase in population, however temporary, puts extra pressure on the local environment and necessitates the development of additional infrastructure and amenities. The construction of water treatment plants, sanitation facilities, and lodges come with the exploitation of non-renewable energy sources and the utilization of already limited local resources. The conversion of natural land to such tourist infrastructure is implicated in deforestation and habitat deterioration of butterflies in Mexico and squirrel monkeys in Costa Rica. In other cases, the environment suffers because local communities are unable to meet the infrastructure demands of ecotourism. The lack of adequate sanitation facilities in many East African parks results in the disposal of campsite sewage in rivers, contaminating the wildlife, livestock, and people who draw drinking water from it.

Aside from environmental degradation with tourist infrastructure, population pressures from ecotourism also leaves behind garbage and pollution associated with the Western lifestyle. Although ecotourists claim to be educationally sophisticated and environmentally concerned, they rarely understand the ecological consequences of their visits and how their day-to-day activities append physical impacts on the environment. As one scientist observes, they "rarely acknowledge how the meals they eat, the toilets they flush, the water they drink, and so on, are all part of broader regional economic and ecological systems they are helping to reconfigure with their very activities." Nor do ecotourists recognize the great consumption of non-renewable energy required to arrive at their destination, which is typically more remote than conventional tourism destinations. For instance, an exotic journey to a place 10,000 kilometers away consumes about 700 liters of fuel per person.

Ecotourism activities are, in of itself, issues in environmental impact because they disturb fauna and flora. Ecotourists believe that because they are only taking pictures and leaving footprints, they keep ecotourism sites pristine, but even harmless sounding activities such as a nature hike can be ecologically destructive. In the Annapurna Circuit in Nepal, ecotourists have worn down the marked trails and created alternate routes, contributing to soil impaction, erosion, and plant damage. Where the ecotourism activity involves wildlife viewing, it can scare away animals, disrupt their feeding and nesting sites or acclimate them to the presence of people. In Kenya, disruption of wildlife observers drive cheetahs off their reserves, increasing the risk of inbreeding and further endangering the species.

Environmental hazards

Unfortunately, industrialization, urbanization, and unsustainable agriculture practices have had all serious effects on the environment. Ecotourism is now also playing a role in this depletion. While the term ecotourism may sound relatively benign, one of its most serious impacts is its consumption of virgin territories (Kamuaro, 2007). These invasions often include deforestation, disruption of ecological life systems and various forms of pollution, all of which contribute to environmental degradation. The number of motor vehicles crossing the park increases as tour drivers search for rare species. The number of roads has disrupted the grass cover which has serious effects on plant and animal species. These areas also have a higher rate of disturbances and invasive species because of all the traffic moving off the beaten path into new undiscovered areas (Kamuaro, 2007). Ecotourism also has an effect on species through the value placed on them. "Certain species have gone from being little known or valued by local people to being highly valued commodities. The commodification of plants may erase their social value and lead to overproduction within protected areas. Local people and their images can also be turned into commodities" (West, 2006). Kamuaro brings up a relatively obvious contradiction, any commercial venture into unspoiled, pristine land with or without the "eco" prefix as a contradiction in terms. To generate revenue you have to have a high number of traffic, tourists, which inevitably means a higher pressure on the environment.

Local people

Most forms of ecotourism are owned by foreign investors and corporations that provide few benefits to local communities. An overwhelming majority of profits are put into the pockets of investors instead of reinvestment into the local economy or environmental protection. The limited numbers of local people who are employed in the economy enter at its lowest level, and are unable to live in tourist areas because of meager wages and a two market system. In some cases, the resentment by local people results in environmental degradation. As a highly publicized case, the Maasai nomads in Kenya killed wildlife in national parks to show aversion to unfair compensation terms and displacement from traditional lands. The lack of economic opportunities for local people also constrains them to degrade the environment as a means of sustenance. The presence of affluent ecotourists encourage the development of destructive markets in wildlife souvenirs, such as the sale of coral trinkets on tropical islands and animal products in Asia, contributing to illegal harvesting and poaching from the environment. In Surinam, sea turtle reserves use a large portion of their budget to guard against these activities.

Displacement of people

One of the most powerful examples of communities being moved in order to create a park is the story of the Masai. About 70% of national parks and game reserves in East Africa are on Masai land (Kamuaro, 2007). The first undesirable impact of tourism was that of the extent of land lost from the Masai culture. Local and national governments took advantage of the Masai's ignorance on the situation and robbed them of huge chunks of grazing land, putting to risk their only socio-economic livelihood. In Kenya the Masai also have not gained any economic benefits. Despite the loss of their land, employment favours better educated workers. Furthermore the investors in this area are not local and have not put profits back into local economy. In some cases game reserves can be created without informing or consulting local people, who come to find out about the situation when an eviction notice is delivered (Kamuaro, 2007). Another source of resentment is the manipulation of the local people by their government. "Eco-tourism works to create simplistic images of local people and their uses and understandings of their surroundings. Through the lens of these simplified images, officials direct policies and projects towards the local people and the local people are blamed if the projects fail" (West, 2006). Clearly tourism as a trade is not empowering the local people who make it rich and satisfying. Instead ecotourism exploits and depletes, particularly in African Masai tribes. It has to be reoriented if it is to be useful to local communities and to become sustainable (Kamuaro, 2007).

Threats to indigenous cultures

Ecotourism often claims that it preserves and "enhances" local cultures. However, evidence shows that with the establishment of protected areas local people have illegally lost their homes, and most often with no compensation (Kamuaro, 2007). Pushing people onto marginal lands with harsh climates, poor soils, lack of water, and infested with livestock and disease does little to enhance livelihoods even when a proportion of ecotourism profits are directed back into the community. The establishment of parks can create harsh survival realities and deprive the people of their traditional use of land and natural resources. Ethnic groups are increasingly being seen as a "backdrop" to the scenery and wildlife. The local people struggle for cultural survival and freedom of cultural expression while being "observed" by tourists. Local indigenous people also have strong resentment towards the change, "Tourism has been allowed to develop with virtually no controls. Too many lodges have been built, too much firewood is being used and no limits are being placed on tourism vehicles. They regularly drive off-track and harass the wildlife. Their vehicle tracks criss-cross the entire Masai Mara. Inevitably the bush is becoming eroded and degraded" (Kamuaro, 2007).

Mismanagement

While governments are typically entrusted with the administration and enforcement of environmental protection, they often lack the commitment or capability to manage ecotourism sites effectively. The regulations for environmental protection may be vaguely defined, costly to implement, hard to enforce, and uncertain in effectiveness. Government regulatory agencies, as political bodies, are susceptible to making decisions that spend budget on politically beneficial but environmentally unproductive projects. Because of prestige and conspicuousness, the construction of an attractive visitor's center at an ecotourism site may take precedence over more pressing environmental concerns like acquiring habitat, protecting endemic species, and removing invasive ones. Finally, influential groups can pressure and sway the interests of the government to their favor. The government and its regulators can become vested in the benefits of the ecotourism industry which they are supposed to regulate, causing restrictive environmental regulations and enforcement to become more lenient.

Management of ecotourism sites by private ecotourism companies offers an alternative to the cost of regulation and deficiency of government agencies.

It is believed that these companies have a self interest in limited environmental degradation, because tourists will pay more for pristine environments, which translates to higher profit. However, theory indicates that this practice is not economically feasible and will fail to manage the environment.

The model of monopolistic competition states that distinctiveness will entail profits, but profits will promote imitation. A company that protects its ecotourism sites is able to charge a premium for the novel experience and pristine environment. But when other companies view the success of this approach, they also enter the market with similar practices, increasing competition and reducing demand. Eventually, the demand will be reduced until the economic profit is zero. A cost-benefit analysis shows that the company bears the cost of environmental protection without receiving the gains. Without economic incentive, the whole premise of self interest through environmental protection is quashed; instead, ecotourism companies will minimize environment related expenses and maximize tourism demand.

The tragedy of the commons offers another model for economic unsustainability from environmental protection, in ecotourism sites utilized by many companies. Although there is a communal incentive to protect the environment, maximizing the benefits in the long run, a company will conclude that it is in their best interest to utilize the ecotourism site beyond its sustainable level. By increasing the number of ecotourists, for instance, a company gains all the economic benefit while paying only a part of the environmental cost. In the same way, a company recognizes that there is no incentive to actively protect the environment; they bear all the costs, while the benefits are shared by all other companies. The result, again, is mismanagement. Taken together, the mobility of foreign investment and lack of economic incentive for environmental protection means that ecotourism companies are disposed to establishing themselves in new sites once their existing one is sufficiently degraded.

Q4. Suggest some possible solution to decrease the environment degradation.

Ans. Regulation and accreditation : Because the regulation of ecotourism is poorly implemented or nonexistent, ecologically destructive greenwashed operations like underwater hotels, helicopter tours, and wildlife theme parks are categorized as ecotourism along with canoeing, camping, photography, and wildlife observation. The failure to acknowledge responsible, low impact ecotourism puts these companies at a competitive disadvantage.

Many environmentalists have argued for a global standard of accreditation, differentiating ecotourism companies based on their level of environmental commitment. A national or international regulatory board would enforce accreditation procedures, with representation from various groups including governments, hotels, tour operators, travel agents, guides, airlines, local authorities, conservation organizations, and non-governmental organizations. The decisions of the board would be sanctioned by governments, so that non-compliant companies would be legally required to disassociate themselves from the use of the ecotourism brand.

Crinion suggests a Green Stars System based on criteria including a management plan, benefit for the local community, small group interaction, education value, and staff training. Ecotourists who consider their choices would be confident of a genuine ecotourism experience when they see the higher star rating. In addition, environmental impact assessments could be used as a form of accreditation. Feasibility is evaluated from a scientific basis, and recommendations could be made to optimally plan infrastructure, set tourist capacity, and manage the ecology. This form of accreditation is more sensitive to site specific conditions.

Guidelines and education

An environmental protection strategy must address the issue of ecotourists removed from the cause-and-effect of their actions on the environment. More initiatives should be carried out to improve their awareness, sensitize them to environmental issues, and care about the places they visit. Tour guides are an obvious and direct medium to communicate awareness. With the confidence of ecotourists and intimate knowledge of the environment, they can actively discuss conservation issues. A tour guide training program in Costa Rica's Tortuguero National Park has helped mitigate negative environmental impacts by providing information and regulating tourists on the parks' beaches used by nesting endangered sea turtles.

Small scale, slow growth and local control

The underdevelopment theory of tourism describes a new form of imperialism by multinational corporations that control ecotourism resources. These corporations finance and profit from the development of large scale ecotourism that causes excessive environmental degradation, loss of traditional culture and way of life, and exploitation of local labor. In Zimbabwe and Nepal's Annapurna region, where underdevelopment is taking place, more than 90 percent of ecotourism revenues are expatriated to the parent countries, and less than 5 percent go into local communities. The lack of sustainability highlights the need for small scale, slow growth, and locally based ecotourism. Local peoples have a vested interest in the well being of their community, and are therefore more accountable to environmental protection than multinational corporations. The lack of control, westernization, adverse impacts to the environment, loss of culture and traditions outweigh the benefits of establishing large scale ecotourism.

The increased contributions of communities to locally managed ecotourism create viable economic opportunities, including high level management positions, and reduce environmental issues associated with poverty and unemployment. Because the ecotourism experience is marketed to a different lifestyle from large scale ecotourism, the development of facilities and infrastructure does not need to conform to corporate Western tourism standards, and can be much simpler and less expensive. There is a greater multiplier effect on the economy, because local products, materials, and labor are used. Profits accrue locally, and import leakages are reduced. However, even this form of tourism may require foreign investment for promotion or start up. When such investments are required, it is crucial for communities for find a company or non-governmental organization that reflects the philosophy of ecotourism; sensitive to their concerns and willing to cooperate at the expense of profit. The basic assumption of the multiplier effect is that the economy starts off with unused resources, for example, that many workers are cyclically unemployed and much of industrial capacity is sitting idle or incompletely utilized. By increasing demand in the economy it is then possible to boost production. If the economy was already at full employment, with only structural, frictional, or other supply-side types of unemployment, any attempt to boost demand would only lead to inflation. For various laissez-faire schools of economics which embrace Say's Law and deny the possibility of Keynesian inefficiency and under-employment of resources, therefore, the multiplier concept is irrelevant or wrong-headed.

As an example, consider the government increasing its expenditure on roads by $1 million, without a corresponding increase in taxation. This sum would go to the road builders, who would hire more workers and distribute the money as wages and profits. The households receiving these incomes will save part of the money and spend the rest on consumer goods. These expenditures in turn will generate more jobs, wages, and profits, and so on with the income and spending circulating around the economy.

The multiplier effect arises because of the induced increases in consumer spending which occur due to the increased incomes – and because of the feedback into increasing business revenues, jobs, and income again. This process does not lead to an economic explosion not only because of the supply-side barriers at potential output (full employment) but because at each "round", the increase in consumer spending is less than the increase in consumer incomes. That is, the marginal propensity to consume (mpc) is less than one, so that each round some extra income goes into saving, leaking out of the cumulative process. Each increase in spending is thus smaller than that of the previous round, preventing an explosion. Ecotourism has to be implemented with care.

Q5. Discuss the concept of nature.

Ans. Nature, in the broadest sense, is equivalent to the **natural world**, **physical universe**, **material world** or **material universe**. "Nature" refers to the phenomena of the physical world, and also to life in general. Manufactured objects and human interaction are not considered part of nature unless qualified in ways such as "human nature" or "the whole of nature". Nature is generally distinguished from the supernatural. It ranges in scale from the subatomic to the galactic.

The word *nature* is derived from the Latin word *natura*, or "the course of things, natural character." *Natura* was a Latin translation of the Greek word *physis*, which originally related to the intrinsic characteristics that plants, animals, and other features of the world develop of their own accord. This is shown in the first written use of the word, in connection with a plant. The concept of nature as a whole, the physical universe, is one of several expansions of the original notion; it began with certain core applications of the word öýóéò by pre-Socratic philosophers, and has steadily gained currency ever since. This usage was confirmed during the advent of modern scientific method in the last several centuries.

Within the various uses of the word today, "nature" may refer to the general realm of various types of living plants and animals, and in some cases to the processes associated with inanimate objects – the way that particular types of things exist and change of their own accord, such as the weather and geology of the Earth, and the matter and energy of which all these things are composed. It is often taken to mean the "natural environment" or wilderness – wild animals, rocks, forest, beaches, and in general those things that have not been substantially altered by human intervention, or which persist despite human intervention. This more traditional concept of natural things which can still be found today implies a distinction between the natural and the artificial, with the latter being understood as that which has been brought into being by a human or human-like consciousness or mind.

The word *nature* means the universe, with all its phenomena. *Natura* was a Latin translation of the Greek word *physis*, which originally related to the intrinsic characteristics that plants, animals, and other features of the world develop of their own accord. The word occurs very early in Greek philosophy, generally in similar senses to those of the modern English word *nature*. This is shown in the first written use of the word, in connection with a plant by Homer. The concept of nature as a whole, the physical universe, is one of several expansions of the original notion. This usage was confirmed during the advent of modern scientific method. Isaac Newton's Philosophiae Naturalis Principia Mathematica (1687), for example, is translated "Mathematical Principles of Natural Philosophy". The etymology of the word "physical" shows its use as a synonym for "natural" in about the mid-15th century.

Q6. How oral traditions perceive the relationship between man and nature?

Ans. Oral traditions form the basic method by which we come to know about the knowledge which has not been codified. They also help us to understand those societies for which we have very limited textual information. Day-to-day human conversation carries the glimpses of ancient past. In oral tradition in India, Environment has been perceived as a living being which breathes, feels, protects, etc. Environment is a friendly entity. Various components of Environment have been given special position, which means a kind consideration was kept in mind for Environmental forces. At times these special considerations were ritualized. The animals and forms are one of the basic component of tales, the oral tradition in India had created. Various attributes of animals were identified and were used as if they are natural characteristics. Plant life provided the base of different stories. It was always kept in mind that human survival was possible only with the conservation of entire flora and fauna. It is also reflected in the religious practices as different animals and plants were worshipped at different times so as to ensure their survival. In the oral tradition the ecological man looks upon nature as a reality of which he is an inseparable part at all levels.

The oral myths do not give man a unique position in so far as his origin is concerned. He is also not in the possession of knowledge automatically. The knowledge, it is generally believed in the oral tradition, came to him from birds and animals. The priests of all creatures were born ahead of human beings. Man is not the creator of knowledge. Cosmic intelligence is the self existent source of all knowledge. In the oral perception of the ancient Indians the world was divided into two halves: the sky and the earth. There also existed a world beyond the sky and another below the earth. the five elements overlap in the formation and so also that of the matter with the other world. This explains how biological and social, both aspects of human life were placed in an integral vision of environment in the ancient Indian oral tradition.

Q7. What is the philosophical explanation of nature?

Ans. The Indian textual tradition conceives Environment as a system with life which has synchronized the complex internationship of numerous living and non-living entities. Even the abiotic world has been perceived as a living creature with a soul. It was a very significant concept as it placed man as equal to every other element of our Environment. The Indian thought greatly emphasizes upon very cordial relationship among all the elements of our world. To highlight the importance of various components of our Environment, various rituals have been institutionalized. These rituals ensured that we treated even the non-living world with great care and maintain a harmony.

For example fire is conceived as messenger of God. Earth has been considered as mother goddess. Sky is worshipped as father. Earth worship manifested itself even in stone worship.

The non-human living world has also been given a very kind attention in Indian philosophic thought. There is a whole tradition of anthropomorphism, where various kinds of plant and animal life have been ascribed special position. The ancient tradition of worship of **Pashupati** Mahadev is one such example.

The tales of **Panchtantra** also highlight the special position which is given to living world. Animals are given human characteristic of not only language but also faculty of feelings and rationality. It tries to give lessons to mankind by highlighting the problems through animal world's characteristics. Different attributes of animals have been identified and are very beautifully utilized in these tales. Cow is worshipped. Trees are worshipped. Various animals are allotted to different Gods & Goddesses as their mode of transportation to highlight their utility and to enhance their position. Indian philosophical thought also highlights the numerous species of flora and fauna and their special position vis-a-vis environment and a Master living creature. This totalistic view is a great achievement of the Indian philosophy.

Q8. Explain the relation between environment and creativity.

Ans. The Indian tradition looks at 'Art' as imbibing three composite aspects, each involved in the other and each orienting the other. The order of priority goes like this;

- the first place is for **pratibha** or inspired vision,
- the second is for **vyutpatta** or studious equipment of the poet, and
- the last being **abhayasa** or assiduous practicing of the technique or craft under the guidance of a master of the art concerned.

It is while explaining the details of the second that the theoreticians find an occasion to take environment into their consideration. The term they use for it is **loka** which means the world in all its infinite variety of living and non-living beings.

In Indian philosophy it is generally believed that each creative act comes from direct contact with **Prakriti** (nature). The language of the artistic manifestation evolves through the visual and audio perceptions of the objects in nature. Even the smallest sprout in nature becomes the artist's greatest joy. In celebrating nature nothing is considered as useless. The art form becomes a living entity, a part of the self, family, village and that way, the whole environment.

The dance of Shiva is a perfect iconographical statement of ecology. His emblems are **Agni** and **deer**. His locks are the forests. He hides within himself **Ganga** (water). His hair adorns the sun and the moon. His garlands are the snakes. He wears the tiger skin. He brings to this world the cosmic rhythm of his **damara** in this incessant process of cyclic creation, degeneration and regeneration and finally of enlightenment. His energy is **Sakti**. Without she he is incomplete. She herself, the daughter of the **Himalayas**, must undergo penance and austerities. The emphasis here is on discipline and austerity, with greater integration of environment.

Q9. Explain traditional Indian way of life.

Ans. Cutting across historical, philosophical debates, the one principle which underlies and provides unity in Indian philosophy as also continuity of vision and perception is the assertion that **Man is only one among all living matter**. Man's life depends upon and is conditioned by all that surrounds him and sustains him, namely, inanimate, mineral and animate, aquatic, vegetative and gaseous life. It is therefore, Man's duty to constantly remind himself of the environment and the ecology.

In the Indian world view, as also of other ancient civilizations and cultures, life on earth emerges from the eternal waters that hold the potency of fires. Perhaps we have not pondered over the significance of the myth. While on surface myth has a dreamlike structure, it's meaning and value lies in it's pointing at the natural phenomenon. Indian science and philosophy and thus culture develop on the postulate of the perpetual movement of **creation, degeneration and regeneration** of the cosmos.

All traditional societies are structured on a four fold control system that order human life, its subsistence and desires. Life is ordered into four successive stages **(ashramas)** from learning and performing to gradual indifference and final withdrawal. Although seemingly opposed in character, these primal desires stand in an organic and interactive relationship to one another. This fourfold ordering of life is called **purusartha**, that is, the making of a cultural person **(purusha)**. At a higher level of consciousness, the cultural person is transformed into a cosmic person **(Purna)**.

Environmental Issues and Tourism Development

Q1. What do you understand by the term 'environment'?

Ans. Environment, is a terminology that comprises all living and non-living things that occur naturally on Earth or some region thereof. This term includes a few key components:

(1) Complete ecological units that function as natural systems without massive human intervention, including all vegetation, animals, microorganisms, rocks, atmosphere and natural phenomena that occur within their boundaries.

(2) Universal natural resources and physical phenomena that lack clear-cut boundaries, such as air, water, and climate, as well as energy, radiation, electric charge, and magnetism, not originating from human activity.

The natural environment is contrasted with the built environment, which comprises the areas and components that are strongly influenced by man. A geographical area is regarded as a natural environment, if the human impact on it is kept under a certain limited level. This level depends on the specific context, and changes in different areas and contexts. The term wilderness, on the other hand, refers to areas without human intervention.

Q2. What do you understand by development? **[June 2008, Q3]**

Ans. You have learnt how the civilizational progress of the humankind interacted with the surrounding natural environment. It is worth appreciating that in it's original conception, the idea of progress was closely allied with the views of moral advance. Progress however, steadily lost its moral direction over the subsequent centuries.

The greatest expansion of human requirements for natural resources followed the **Industrial Revolution** during the latter half of the 18th and first half of the 19th centuries. Man now, consumed enormous quantities of coal. Moreover the agricultural economy of Europe underwent a revolutionary change during the 17th and 18th centuries. This process is also known as the **Agricultural Revolution**. On the one hand, it increased the productivity of the land and on the other, released a substantial section of the population, from the agricultural fold. These people, thrown out of the land, moved to the cities in search of employment. This created extra food requirement, putting more pressure on the agricultural economy. Chemical materials and sophisticated farming implements as well as an input of fuel energy were some of the major consequences of this process. Moreover, because both the demand for luxurious items and the degree of wastefulness were excessive not all consumption of resources was related to the supplying of needs. With this change in attitude a kind of 'democratization' took place. This 'democratization' was manifested in political sphere, social sphere and particularly in relation to the right to exploit the natural resources. Now even common man got access and authority to use the natural resources. This was widely related to their faith in the notion of development, which promised a luxurious life.

By the end of the nineteenth century, the public's belief in progress was institutionalized and the term economic development came into use. The term progress referred to the belief in what was possible while development referred to the conscious process of making it happen. Every step taken forward in any sphere of development added to environmental degradation. Many thoughtful explanations as to why development during the past century has been so environmentally destructive have been forwarded :

(i) Some natural scientists argue that massive environmental destruction is inevitable when human population is growing rapidly.

(ii) Others emphasize that far too many new substances have been introduced into the environment before determining their impacts on other species let alone ourselves.

(iii) Economists argue that the producers and consumers behave in a manner that cannot be sustained because market prices do not include environmental costs, etc.

Beyond these disciplinary explanations, however, there are broader philosophical interpretations of why development and hence modernism has led to the degradation of the environment. We shall, though, not go into those details here. The development which we have achieved has not only disturbed our environment, a complex system, but it has also disturbed the social structure/ human relation which is also a very complex system.

Q3. Why has development been environmentally destructive? [June 2008, Q3]

Ans. The earth is facing an environmental crisis. There is now a worldwide consensus on this. There is little doubt that this crisis can be attributed to the manner in which the industrial and technological development has taken place in the world. The crux of the problem is, that the extent of human reproduction is infinite while the resources of the Earth to support human life are finite. The related problem is that of attitude where 'wants' dectate the life style. Now we shall try to understand the nature and magnitude of this problematic relationship between environment and development.

A full understanding of the challenges facing humanity requires knowledge of the evolution of the roles of technology, population expansions, cultural mores, climate, disease and warfare in changing human attitudes and responses through time. This is especially the case if the past is to be used in more sophisticated ways than as a simplistic analogue of projected future conditions. We also know that assessment of the sensitivity or vulnerability of modern landscapes and ecosystems to future human activities and climate can be greatly improved by knowing the rates and directions of past trajectories in key processes such as land cover, soil erosion and flooding, observing how thresholds have been transgressed and deducing the natural or pre-impact patterns of environmental variability. Already, such knowledge is leading to the improved formulation of resource management strategies.

Human history has traditionally been cast in terms of the rise and fall of great civilizations, wars, specific human achievements, and extreme natural disasters (e.g. earthquakes, floods, plagues). This history tends to leave out, however, the important ecological and climatic context and the less obvious interactions which shaped and mediated these events. Socio-ecological systems are intimately linked in ways that we are only beginning to appreciate. Furthering the research agenda on such systems poses great methodological challenges. Events can be selectively chosen from the past to support almost any theory of historical causation. While puts a range of environmental indicators and historical events together on the same graph, it can show only coincidence, not causation. The causal links are more complex and not self-evident. For example, water availability is related to complex developments resulting from social organization, engineering and climate. While we use the timeline to illustrate the parallels between human and environmental change, the complex web of causation that resulted in the sequence of events depicted cannot be easily represented on such a graph.

Human societies respond to environmental (e.g., climate) signals through multiple pathways including collapse or failure, migration and creative invention through discovery. Extreme drought, for instance, has triggered both social collapse and ingenious management of water through irrigation. Human responses to change may in turn alter feedbacks between climate, ecological, and social systems, producing a complex web of multidirectional connections in time and space. Ensuring appropriate future responses and feedbacks within the human-environment system will depend on our understanding of this past web and how to adapt to future surprises. To develop that understanding, we need to look at multiple time and space scales.

POLLUTION

At millennial timescales different cultural elements (social and political structure, traditional practices, and beliefs, to name a few) enable or constrain responses. Even global-scale events (climate change, major volcanic activity, etc.) do not affect all regions at precisely the same time or with the same intensity. Models (conceptual and computational) of how societal characteristics and environmental conditions affect the resilience of socio-ecological systems are needed. Processes important for the study of resilience, vulnerability, or sustainability include: the degree of rigidity of social, economic, and political networks; the diversity of biophysical resources and of human resourcefulness; the development of complexity, costliness and ineffectiveness in problem-solving; and the cyclical expansion/contraction and geographical shift in the center of accumulation with periodic declines and "dark ages" when external limits to social reproduction are reached. Simple, deterministic relationships between environmental stress, (for example, a climatic event), and social change are inadequate. Organizational, technological and perceptual mechanisms mediate the responses of societies to environmental stress, and there are also time-delays to societal responses.

More recent changes in the human-environment relationship, such as accelerated globalization and global environmental change, have deep roots in humanity's relationship with nature over the past millennium. While we often associate the term "global change" with the greenhouse gas warming evident in the last decade, socio-ecological changes at continental and global scales were put in motion over at least the past 1000 years (e.g. many European landscapes looked much like they do today far earlier than this). Important phenomena include a rise in human population, the strengthening of nation states, the global transfer of inventions and values, the beginning of industrialization and the rise of global communications, and associated with these the dramatic modifications of land use and biodiversity, hydrological and energy flows, and key ecological processes.

The last 1000 year period is also interesting because it's a period when broad swings in temperature as well as clusters of extreme weather events arguably changed the trajectory of history. The fourteenth century in Europe saw the end of the Medieval Warm Period. Particularly during the period from 1315–1317 Western Europe witnessed a combination of rainy autumns, cold springs, and wet summers that led to crop failures and a dramatic slowdown in urban expansion. These early Europeans were further subjected to the last major locust invasion (1338), the "millennium flood" (1342), and the coldest summer of the millennium in 1347. From 1347 to 1350 the "Black Death" devastated populations. The clustering of extreme events in the fourteenth century fundamentally undermined social order and was a key factor in a major wave of anti-Semitic pogroms and systematic discrimination. In the same period, agricultural land was abandoned and forests increased. Many would argue that it also led to the end of the feudal system, improved land and employee rights and, through the enlightenment period, paved the way for the modern age. The Little Ice Age affected food availability in many parts of Europe, leading to the development of technological, economic and political strategies as ways to reduce vulnerability. The exceptional 1788-1795 ENSO event reverberated around the world in places as far afield as the first British colonial settlement in Australia, the Indian monsoon region, Mexico and western Europe. Thus, the present nature and complexity of socio-ecological systems are heavily contingent on the past; we cannot fully understand the present condition without going back centuries or even millennia into the past. An important implication is that societal actions today will reverberate for centuries into the future in climatic and many other ways.

Turning to the more recent past, the 20th century witnessed several sharp changes in the evolution of socio-ecological systems, at both global (two world wars and the Great Depression) and regional (e.g. the failure of Soviet farming, its reliance on grain from the U.S., and subsequent collapse as a polity) discontinuities. Variations in the growth rate of carbon dioxide (CO_2) in the atmosphere occurred in response to both climatic controls over land-atmosphere-ocean fluxes (for example, CO_2 increases more rapidly in El Niño years because of climate effects on terrestrial ecosystems) and political events (the growth rate slowed during the 1970s oil shock and after the breakup of the Soviet Union because of changes in fossil fuel use). The 20th century also marks the first period for which instrumental records of many environmental parameters have become available and for which detailed statistical records of many human activities have also been collected.

The most remarkable phenomenon on Earth in the 20th century was the "Great Acceleration," the sharp increase in human population, economic activity, resource use, transport, communication and knowledge–science–technology that was triggered in many parts of the world (North America, Western Europe, Japan, and Australia/New Zealand) following World War II and which has continued into this century. Other parts of the world, especially the monsoon Asia region, are now also in the midst of the Great Acceleration. The tension between the modern nation-state and the emergence of multinational corporations and international political institutions is a strong feature of the changing human-environmental relationship. The "engine" of the Great Acceleration is an interlinked system consisting of population increase, rising consumption, abundant cheap energy, and liberalizing political economies.

Globalization, especially an exploding knowledge base and rapidly expanding connectivity and information flow, thus acts as a strong accelerator of the system. The environmental effects of the Great Acceleration are clearly visible at the global scale – changing atmospheric chemistry and climate, degradation of many ecosystem services (e.g., provision of freshwater, biological diversity, etc.), and homogenization of the biotic fabric of the planet. The Great Acceleration is arguably the most profound and rapid shift in the human–environment relationship that the Earth has experienced.

Towards the end of the 20th century, there were signs that the Great Acceleration could not continue in its present form without increasing the risk of crossing major thresholds and triggering abrupt changes worldwide. Transitions to new energy systems will be required. There is a growing disparity between the wealthy and the poor, and, through modern communication, a growing awareness by the poor of this gap, leading to heightened material aspirations globally – a potentially explosive situation. Many of the ecosystem services upon which human well-being depends are depleted or degrading, with possible rapid changes when thresholds are crossed. The climate may be more sensitive to increases in carbon dioxide and may have more inertia than earlier thought, raising concerns of abrupt and irreversible changes in the planetary environment as a whole.

From the past, we know there are circumstances in which a society is resilient to perturbations (e.g., climate change) and there are circumstances in which a society is so vulnerable to perturbations that it will be unable to cope. The evolutionary biologist and biogeographer Jared Diamond identifies what he considered to be the 12 most serious environmental problems facing past and future societies – problems that often have led to the collapse of historical societies:

1. Loss of habitat and ecosystem services;
2. Overfishing;
3. Loss of biodiversity;
4. Soil erosion and degradation;
5. Energy limits;
6. Freshwater limits;
7. Photosynthetic capacity limits;
8. Toxic chemicals;
9. Alien species introductions;
10. Climate change;
11. Population growth; and
12. Human consumption levels.

More importantly, Diamond, and several others before him, have emphasized that the interplay of multiple factors is almost always more critical than any single factor. Societies on the edge become brittle and lose resilience (including the ability to adapt social values to new circumstances) making them more susceptible to the impacts of potential perturbations of several kinds, including climate change, political corruption, war, and terrorism. In addition, what happens to any society is an emergent phenomenon, the result of individual decisions and conflicts in combination with environmental factors.

To make further progress, we need to construct a framework to help us understand the full range of human-environment interactions and how they affect societal development and resilience. We now have the capacity to develop this framework in the form of more comprehensive integrated models, combining approaches from geophysical, systems dynamics and agent-based models to implement approaches including simulation games and scenario analysis. Insights from modeling and analysis of the rich array of well-documented integrated historic events can be used to structure, test and further develop these models. A few examples of integrated dynamic historical simulation models now exist, including Turchin's work on historical dynamics with several case studies on everything from the rise and fall of religions to imperial expansion and dynastic cycles, and agent-based simulation models of the growth and decline of the Anasazi in the Southwestern U.S.

The fundamental question we need to ask is: *how does the history of human-environment systems generate useful insights about the future?* In trying to gain insights from the past, tests of alternate models must play a central role. While in the natural sciences, alternate models can be tested against numerical data sets, in testing models (conceptual and computational) of the human-environment system, we need to use the full range of data from numerical time series to historical narratives. We also need to develop new skills and techniques for integrating these disparate data sources of fundamentally different characters. The extent to which we can (or cannot) reproduce historical behavior in socio-ecological systems determines the confidence we can place in future projections. An array of different modeling approaches, some focused strongly on the biophysical aspects of the Earth System (e.g., General Circulation Models of climate) and others centered on socio-economic aspects (e.g., models of the global economy) have been developed for projecting Earth System behavior into the future. Integrated models at multiple spatial and temporal scales have also been developed. Recognizing that no single approach has intrinsic advantages, a strategy of comparing, synthesizing and integrating the results from different modeling approaches is probably more productive, paralleling the use of multiple working hypotheses. Developing an integrated historical narrative and database will allow testing of alternate models, more rapid evolution of paradigms, and better answers to IHOPE related questions.

Q4. Discuss the significance of preservation in tourism development.

Ans. Development does not mean only moving ahead. It should also include the need to preserve the achievements made till date. Since future is imagined on the basis of our past experiences, it is necessary to preserve the art, culture, etc. Culture heritage and the arts have long contributed to the appeal of tourist destinations.

Tourism can be a major stimulus for preservation of important elements of the cultural heritage of an area. Their preservation can be justified for enhancing tourist attractions and it includes:

- preservation of archaeological and historic sites and interesting architectural styles,
- preservation and sometimes revitalization of traditional arts, heritage, dance, music, drama, customs and ceremonies, costumes and certain aspects of traditional life styles,
- revitalizing traditional arts and crafts, including development of new forms utilizing local skills and materials,
- financial assistance for the maintenance of museums, theatres and other cultural facilities and activities used for supporting the

organization of special cultural festivals because they are important attractions for tourists as well as being used by residents. For example, theatre tickets purchased by tourists at important urban centres help support those facilities; Admission fees paid by tourists at some major museums in the world provides substantial revenues to maintain those institutions.

A sense of pride by residents in their culture can be reinforced and even renewed when they observe a tourist appreciating it. This is especially true of some traditional cultures that are undergoing change as a result of general economic development and are leaving their sense of cultural self-confidence.

At the same time there are problems with this kind of tourism development. Over commercialisation and loss of authenticity of traditional arts and crafts, customs and ceremonies can be a result if these are "over modified to suit tourist demands." For example, important traditional dances and music performances, some of which may have religious significance, are being greatly shortened and changed to fit tourists' tastes and schedules. Similarly, traditional high quality handicrafts are being mass produced to provide tourist souvenirs. This situation often results from the desire to maximise the profit by tourism.

Further, overuse or misuse of environmentally fragile archaeological and historic sites can damage these features through excessive wear, increased humidity, vandalism, graffiti writing, etc. For example, the cave paintings of Ajanta and Ellora are being damaged by over crowding of tourists.

Q5. Discuss the importance of conservation in tourism development. [Dec 2008, Q5]

Ans. Another form that is widely used in connection with tourism is conservation. It refers to the planned management of specific sites and places and natural resources in general and not necessarily categorical preservation which is used to mean no change of the site, place or resources. Sometimes, it includes restoration to its original condition. Conservation implies that some use and controlled change can take place if the basic integrity of the site, place or resource is maintained.

The protection, enhancement and improvement of the various components of man's environment are among the fundamental conditions for the harmonious development of tourism. Similarly, orderly management of tourism can contribute to a large extent for protecting and developing the physical environment, as well as improving the quality of life. Major categories of natural environmental attractions for tourism include following types:

(i) Climate: A warm, sunny, dry climate is typically considered desirable by most tourists from cold winter areas. To this are added certain other attractions such as seasonal festivals or added physical attractions that provide opportunities for recreation activities. Conservation of a desirable climate through control of air pollution or retaining the architectural styles suitable to the climate is, therefore essential for tourism. Climatic seasonality must be considered in promoting or evaluating climate as an attraction. A long climatically desirable season is obviously an advantage for development of tourism so that the investment made in facilities, services and infrastructure is maximised. For example, generally the tourist season for a destination like Goa used to be September-March. However, now it is being promoted for June-August also as "monsoon on golden beaches."

(ii) Scenic Beauty: The overall natural scenic beauty of an area may be a major motivation to visit the area, especially if conservation measures have been applied to maintain the cleanliness and natural character of the environment. Remote scenic areas may offer opportunities for nature or adventure oriented tourists engaging in such activities as river rafting, rock climbing and long distance trekking.

(iii) Beaches and Marine areas: Beaches and associated marine areas for sunbathing, swimming, boating, wind and board surfing, water skiing, parasailing, snorkeling and scubadiving, sport – fishing and other water recreation activities are major attractions in many places in the world. Beach and marine areas should also have conservation measures application in the form of banks, reserves and development controls.

(iv) Flora and Fauna: Unusual and interesting flora and fauna can be very important attractions, especially when combined with scenic landscapes. Game parks of East Africa and the Redwood parks of California fall under this category. Zoos, aquariums and botanical gardens are also specialised attractions as far as the features of flora and fauna are concerned. Adequate conservation measures are thus an absolute necessity for the promotion of tourism in such areas.

Evidently the attraction features of a country or region provide the basis for developing tourism. They form the most essential element of the tourism product. Conversely the development of tourism can be one of the techniques used to accomplish environmental and cultural conservation and maintain an area's unique sense of place. However, there are situations where development of special types of features, such as theme parks or gambling casinos, not already related to the character of the local areas, is justified because of profitability. This type of tourism should be developed in the manner that the country believes to be the most appropriate for its own environment and socio-cultural benefits. In the long run, socially and environmentally, the casino variety of tourism has proved to be disruptive. Profit generation from the kind of tourism should never become the prime concern, as excessive exploitation of natural attraction will destroy the natural beauty and in turn will reduce profit in the long run.

Animal and plant life conservation is a major issue in many parts of the world because of various problems, especially reduction of wild-life habitat by encroachment of agricultural and urban uses and poaching of protected animals. Because wild life constitutes an attraction feature, tourism can often be used as the rationale for wild-life conservation. As is the case in several East African countries, there is much concern about the diminishing numbers of several species of animals and major conservation efforts are underway. For example, in South East Asia, **Project Tiger,** in part sponsored by **World Wildlife Fund**, has been so far successful in regenerating the tiger population in that region. Sunderban has been able to conserve the Bengal tiger population which is a major tourist attraction.

Q6. Explain the importance of participatory tourism in development. [June 2008, Q4]

Ans. International tourism is promoted as a factor which brings people together and helps peace and understanding. Tourists should not become only guests and locals only the hosts. There should be participation by both sides in this industry. We are aware that the present tourism is based on inequalities and the reality is that it totally precludes a sensitive relationship between hosts and tourists. Tourism is a 'space' specific and labour intensive activity. This means every tourist site has its own district character which is often governed either by a natural attraction, historic significance or local culture. All these attractions can generate tourism which by its very nature codifies human relationship, tourists being the paying guests and locals as hosts.

The search for information about host population attitudes to tourism is hampered by one difficulty. Opinions about and expectations from tourism can be very different depending on which population or occupation groups are considered. The first category includes people who are in **continuous and direct contact with tourism** personnel in the catering trade in transport, shops, travel agencies, etc. Because they depend on tourism and would perhaps be unemployed without it, they welcome visitors. Their attitude is not determined by inborn hospitality but rather by a simple desire to earn money.

The second group of locals is of those **proprietors of business who have no regular contact with tourists**, for instance the building industry. For them tourism is purely a commercial matter as it brings more construction and building contracts. It should bring as high a turnover and profit as possible. The manner in which this happens is of little consequence; the end justifying the means. The third category consists of those population groups **who are in direct and frequent contact with tourists but who desire only a part of their income from tourist**. Members of this group do see the advantages resulting from tourism, but they also feel more critical about it and point out its disadvantages such as interference with their private lives and environmental damages.

The fourth category comprises the **large group of locals who have no contact with tourists**. Here a variety of attitudes is possible, approval, rejection, interest or indifference, the latter being the most common. **Politicians and political lobbyists** represent the fifth group. They would like to raise their fellow countrymen's living standard. There are hardly any politicians who do not either openly advocate or quietly support tourism both for economic reasons and for reasons of development. However, nobody will dispute the fact that tourism has a considerable impact on local development in the form of employment and economic earnings. At least ten million people work in tourism in the world over and many more live off tourism indirectly. But some of the social costs weigh particularly heavily where there is a big development gap and lack of mutual participation. In most of the cases development is imposed from outside with little or no consideration of the opinions of the local residents. The outsiders are often not sensitive about local customs, ecology or environment. Besides the use of local resources is also denied to locals residents.

Q7. What is sustainable development?

Ans. Sustainable development is defined as a pattern of social and structured economic transformations (i.e. development) which optimizes the economic and societal benefits available in the present, without jeopardizing the likely potential for similar benefits in the future. A primary goal of sustainable development is to achieve a reasonable and equitably distributed level of economic well-being that can be perpetuated continually for many human generations.

Sustainable development implies using renewable natural resources in a manner which does not eliminate or degrade them, or otherwise diminish their usefulness for future generations. It further implies using non-renewable (exhaustible) mineral resources in a manner which does not unnecessarily preclude easy access to them by future generations. Sustainable development also requires depleting non-renewable energy resources at a slow enough rate so as to ensure the high probability of an orderly society transition to renewable energy sources.

Based on similar arguments, sustainable development has been alternatively defined in various manners also, some of them are as follows:

"Development that meets the needs of the present without compromising the ability of future generations to meet their own needs".

—The World Commission on Environment and Development, Brundtland Commission 1987.

"Sustainable development ensures that the maximum rate of resource consumption and waste discharge for a selected development portfolio would be sustained indefinitely, in a defined planning region, without progressively impairing its bio-productivity and ecological integrity. Environmental conservation, therefore, contrary to general belief, accelerates rather than hinders economic development.

Therefore, the Development plans have to ensure:

- Sustainable and equitable use of resources for meeting the needs of the present and future generations without causing damage to environment.
- To prevent further damage to our life-support systems;
- To conserve and nurture the biological diversity, gene pool and other resources for long term food security".

– State Of The Environment Report - 1999, Ministry of Environment and Forests, Government of India.

"The primary objective of the Sustainable Development is to reduce the absolute poverty of the world's poor through providing lasting and secure livelihoods that minimize resource depletion, environmental degradation, cultural disruption and social instability".

– E. Barbier, "The Concept of Sustainable Economic Development", Environmental Conservation, 1987.

Tourism is becoming one of the most important social and economic activities of today's world. However, the socio-economic impacts of tourism have made this field a rather controversial one in recent years, especially where tourism development has been rapid and largely unplanned and uncontrolled. The result is that there have been adverse socio-economic impacts. Appropriate relationships between tourism and the socio-cultural environments which places responsibilities on both the tourist receiving countries and the tourists themselves, were further specified by the **WTO** in 1985 during its sixth General Assembly through its adoption of the **Tourism Bill of Rights** and **Tourist Code**. This statement contained the following provisions :

- In the interest of present and future generations (states should) protect the tourism environment which, being at once human, natural, social, cultural and economic is the legacy of all mankind.
- The populations constituting the host communities in place of transit and stay are entitled to free access of their own tourism resources.
- They are also entitled to expect from tourists an understanding of and respect for their customs, religious and other elements of their cultures which are part of human heritage. Resilient environments and fragile environments can be given the most rigid protection measures. In

this manner, nature conservation interests can be accorded their appropriate priority where it is the prime land use designation.

- To facilitate such understanding and respect the dissemination of appropriate information should be encouraged on:

(1) the customs of host communities, their traditional and religious practices, local taboos and sacred sites and shrines which must be respected,

(2) their artistic, archaeological and cultural treasures, which must be preserved, and

(3) wild life and other natural resources, which must be protected. Tourists should, by their behaviour, foster understanding and friendly relations among peoples, etc.

The concept of planning for sustainable development, as well as for sustainable development in general for all types of human activities is being given increasing emphasis internationally. However, it must be noted that discussing or talking about sustainable development is one thing, implementing another. While the former is easy to do, the latter difficult. Today every politician and tourism promoter claims to be an environmentalist and one has to be cautious in differentiating between the **real** and **pseudo** environmentalists.

Q8. 'Alternative tourism provides an alternative answer to the problem of tourism'. Comment.

Ans. Alternative tourism emerged from the Third World as a reaction to the negative effects tourism heaped on its countries.

Alternative tourism came in different names and various models. All tried to stop the onslaught and improve the situation. Backyard tourism, for instance, sought 'to preserve the original rural appeal' of the tourist destination. It also relied on the services of small local enterprises while rejecting the development of modern resorts.

Endemic tourism, on the other hand, used the 'special characteristics of individual communities which attracted tourists' and the 'great value of the cultural characteristics of communities' as tourism assets.

Increasing global concerns for the environment, meanwhile, produced eco-tourism which tried to 'shy away from commercial destinations and focused on environmental themes.' Sustainable tourism is yet another new form of alternative tourism that is led by an 'empowered and gender-sensitive community' that 'protects and enhance ecological resources.'

Alternative tourism is a kind of tourism which, while safeguarding the experience of travel, would also further mutual understanding between people, prevent environmental and cultural degradation and most of all, exploitation and dehumanization of the local population. Because of these features it is also termed as responsible tourism. While alternative tourism may also provide the visitor 'authentic' experiences, this is not its principle concern. Indeed it is critical of romantic 'experience seeking' and counter-cultural tourists, who may have a negative impact on the host setting.

Alternative tourism is thus a synonym of responsible tourism. It is argued that with the help of alternative tourism we can overcome the problems raised by tourism industry. Responsible tourism can be interpreted as an umbrella term embracing supposedly more caring and aware form of tourism. Its prefixes include alternative, appropriate, sustainable, soft, green, etc. In responsible tourism the host community plays a very crucial role in the decision-making on tourism and tourism development. The hosts also control the pace of development which is vital. Raising the awareness of the traveler prior to the arrival at the destination and sensitizing him to the local environment is very important. Hence, education plays the key role in this form of tourism.

The idea of alternative tourism has its source in two contemporary ideological pre-occupations :

- one is the counter cultural rejection of modern mass consumerism, and the other
- a concern for the impact of the modern industrial development on the Third World societies.

Each of these pre-occupations raises the problems of conventional tourism and criticizes it, though from different angles. It therefore proposes different conceptions of alternative tourism.

(1) Counter Cultural Alternative Tourism : Counter cultural alternative tourism inverts the values, motives, attitudes and practices of conventional mass tourism. The image of counter cultural alternative tourist is that of one who would not go for mere entertainment, recreation or 'relaxation'. S/he is an 'adventurer' or who rejects his/her home society and culture and seeks the strangeness of the world of others and tries to experience the authentic life. S/he travels by himself/herself or in small groups, in an unhurried manner, spontaneously changing his/her plans according to his/her interests, disposition and opportunities. The ideal 'traveler' is self-reliant and enterprising, accepting the hospitality of humble peasants and tribal people, eating their food and drinking their water, without concern for comfort or health. S/he also participates in the conservation efforts and contributes in environmental protection.

(2) Concerned Alternative Tourism : Concerned alternative tourism has been defined as a just form of travel between members of different communities. It seeks to achieve mutual understanding, solidarity and equality among participants. It is an alternative to both mass and 'rucksack' tourism. Its protagonists emphasize the tourists attitudes and relationships with the locals and the resulting socio-economic and cultural impacts. 'Just' tourism is intended to mean that both parties should equally benefit, personally and economically from the encounter. The principle means of promotion of this type of tourism are various small-scale projects in developing countries, established with local consultation and participation. They typically bring small group of visitors to a locality where they are given the opportunity for direct interaction with the locals as equals and for a comprehension of their 'real' life and problems unadulterated by embellishments. The visitors are understood to pay for their stay and there is no exploitation involved.

Q9. Point out the problems of responsible tourism.

Ans. The definition of responsible tourism ,according to the Ecotourism Society, is "responsible travel to natural areas which conserves the environment and improves the welfare of the local people". What it means is that a mere visit to a ecologically rich geographical location does not constitute ecotourism. It involves much more on the part of the visitor. For instance a walk through the rainforest is not eco-tourism unless that particular walk somehow benefits that particular environment and the people who live there. To put it in simple words your trip should help conserve and also improve the ecological condition of the place you visit.

The validity of Alternative tourism, though seen as a solution by many, is being questioned also. **B. Wheeller** in his paper on **Egotourism, sustainable tourism and the environment – a symbiotic, symbolic or shambolic relationship** (1994) has observed:

Currently ecotourism seems to be neatly and conveniently, side stepping the critical issues of volume of mass. As projections for increased participation in tourism, including ecotourism, are realized then the futility of eco/sustainable tourism will, I believe, become painfully apparent.

The number of tourists is to go up and up and Wheeller maintains that **"Eco tourism is not immune from this explosion"**. This means that as the volume of eco-tourists goes up all the problems related to mass tourism will effect this area also. Many in the tourism industry are already using it as a market ploy.

Another point raised by Wheeller is in relation to tourist behaviour. There is no guarantee that the eco-tourist or alternative tourist will behave differently from the mass tourist i.e. wanting the maximum at the least cost. He believes that **"tourism will always include an element of exploitation" as it is "a human activity"**:

- the commercial provider is motivated by profit,
- the tourist is motivated by self interest i.e., what is in it for me type of an attitude, and
- the host community likes to extract something from the tourist.

These traits will be present in any form of tourism leave aside alternative tourism.

Similarly the emphasis on interaction and direct experience among the visitor and the host does not take away the possibilities of negative cultural impacts. The indigenous people of local community welcome the visitors in the spirit of hospitability and substantially adopt western ways in the process. In this way they are increasingly adversely affected by the massive scale and intrusive character of tourism.

For a caring tourism the watchword is slow steady development at a small scale. But there are fundamental economic dilemmas in converting this ideal into reality. If tourism is to generate income and significant number of jobs in relation to the economy of the area, then how can one limit the size of development? The result is that **"tourism developments have frequently operated ahead of the regions ability to provide infrastructure and sound management"**. Citing the example of Khumbu Robinson mentions that **"the regions must pressing environmental problems that have been associated with tourism include forest degradation, competing land uses on fragile land surfaces and waste disposal"**. The economic multiplier impact has enriched the locals and they themselves are exploiting the natural resources like cutting forests for constructing new forest lodges or bigger homes for wealthy families. Litter along the trekking routes, indiscriminate disposal of human waste etc. poses serious threat to the destination. And all this environmental degradation is taking place at a destination which is promoted as and known for alternative tourism.

Developing countries have weak economy and are in greater need for foreign exchange. They, therefore, prove sometimes, weaker in terms of controls on tourism development. Thus, notions of community-based approaches to tourism decision making seem fine to those communities where there is a cohesive, established network based on economic viability. They can afford to be selective. But at the micro-level this will not stop 'unsuitable' development. It will merely transfer it specially to another area, another community, less able to have a constructive say in its own destiny. 'Community approach' appears to be that the strongest remain strong.

Responsible tourism is increasingly being adopted more as a marketing tool than as a sensitive planning mechanism. Tourism on a micro-level can perhaps be sensitively planned, but at the macro-level because of the enormity and complexity of the task, it becomes cumbersome, uncontrollable and not plannable.

The ideology of alternative tourism rejects conventional tourism in toto. It strives to be a full-fledged alternative to it. This precludes it from seeking a chance to reform the tourist establishment and mass tourism from within. For years tourism industry and pro-tourism lobby have welcomed planning policies. But the irony is that responsible tourism's very ineffectiveness is likely to see its overt acceptance as global tourism strategy by an industry eager to foster a better image and keen to be seen to be green. Even more than other industries, the tourism industry can now see profit in ostensibly becoming green. Responsible tourism appeases the guilt of the 'thinking tourist' while providing the holiday experience. The industry is happy because the more discerning range of market can be catered for by 'legitimately' opening up new areas to tourism and the overall demand and growth of tourism, on a global basis, continues unabated. This makes the idea of responsible tourism superficial in practice. In spite of these problematic issues opinions have been expressed that **"every step, no matter how small, adds to the sum of the over all responsible effect"**. The idea here is that doing something is better than doing nothing.

Q10. The government can play a positive role in the development of alternative tourism. Analysis.

Ans. Their lies a heavy responsibility on the governments as regards making the idea of responsible tourism a success. It must be noted that environmental issues cannot be tackled merely by passing laws. Very often there is no coordination among the various government departments. This not only leads to confusion but provides loopholes for flouting laws and regulations.

Well drafted laws, with a minimum number of loopholes, can make a difference, particularly in ensuring that those deliberately destroying the environment through acts of omission or commission are deterred. Such laws also provide public-spirited citizens and environmental groups an opportunity to fight for their implementation. However, bad laws, particularly those which are loosely framed, can do more harm than good, for they provide a legal basis for flouting environmental standards. They also create an illusion of legal remedies being provided when, in fact, they are of little use. Often public debate on a draft Bill can ensure that some of the more obvious loopholes are plugged.

In the end, regardless of whether the law is adequate or not, its effectiveness is entirely dependent on the **political will** of the authorities who implement it. Many good laws have been wasted because they have not been backed by political will. The performance of the **Ministry of Environment and Forests** at the Centre, which has been instrumental in introducing several environmental laws has been mixed. While in some cases it has allowed time for public consultation in others it has not. It has also not been entirely consistent in demonstrating its determination to implement the laws.

Thus, the government policies have a crucial role to play in decreasing the problems of tourism industry, as well as of environmental degradation. Without the government concern, one will not be able to save the environment as government has the power of making things run. A positive support from Government would result in a positive development of responsible tourism.

Certain measures must be initiated and implemented by the Government. For example :

- **Carrying capacity** of each destination must be defined and there should be specific guidelines in this regard.
- It must be ensured that tourism is considered integral to land use planning at the destination and environment friendly construction guidelines are there.
- **Offenders should be punished** and there should be no political pressures used for flouting the laws or regulations. Rather, the law enforcing agencies should be so empowered that they carry out their duties meaningfully.
- All types of media should be used extensively for creating environment awareness.

In tourism the world travels very fast. Once the message is clear to the industry as well as tourists that the government or the local authorities mean business as far as environmental protection is concerned and the laws or regulations are not just for the sake of having them but for reality, the results are bound to come.

Environment, Community and Tourism

Q1. What are the main infrastructural qualities of a tourist destination?

Ans. If tourism is to effectively function as an integral component of the development package for any region, development of tourist related physical infrastructure becomes imperative. Infrastructure should also be conceived on an integrated basis considering the overall needs of the area and the host population. Imparting an adequate measure of attractiveness to a resort is a vital aspect for development of tourist spot. Broadly speaking, the three main components which collectively impart this quality to the tourist centre should be identified as :

(i) Accessibility

(ii) Accommodation Facilities and Services, and

(iii) Recreation

(i) Accessibility : Accessibility in the context of a tourist spot or a tourist destination area consists of:

(a) Local accessibility to the specific place of tourist interest within the town from the nearest transportation inter-change point namely an airport, a railway station or a roadways terminal or from the entry point to the town as the case may be. It also means connecting roads from one spot to the other to facilitate easy movement of tourists within the town and its vicinity including adequate parking, servicing and garage facilities.

(b) Regional accessibility to the tourist centre and tourist destination area by the three conventional modes of transport namely roads, rail and air from the nearest tourist embarkation point in the country and transport linkages to other important centres of tourist interest within the region.

(ii) Accommodation Facilities and Services: Provision of adequate accommodation at the tourist centres and destination area satisfying quantitatively as well as qualitatively, the needs of tourists, is an important factor. Accommodation can sometimes provide the incentives to the tourist for a longer stay. In the present context of India, lack of this basic amenity has even been a greater deterrent to tourist influx compared to "lack of accessibility." The quantum and type of accommodation to be provided at individual centres would again depend on an assessment of needs in each case, but by and large, accommodation for tourists should be comfortable, complete with all utilities and services and built-in infrastructure facilities required for residential development as per the location and of varying range and choice from economic as well as physical points of view.

Uninterrupted power and safe water supply, sewerage, drainage and sanitation are essential elements of basic utilities and services to be ensured in order to make a tourist complex attractive. Besides, civic services like health clinic, telecommunication, post-telegraph and banking facilities are also considered essential part of tourist infrastructure. However, these aspects vary as per the form of tourism and the location of the destination.

(iii) Recreational Aspects: If availability of accommodation is largely influential in prolonging a tourist's stay, adequate provision of recreational elements at a tourist centre can lengthen the tourist season as a whole. This aspect of development is vitally important for relaxation and diversion. Recreation, in the context of tourism, has many manifestations and includes, apart from organized outdoor active and passive recreation, all forms of commercial recreation as well. The problem in the context of metropolitan and major cities is simplified to some extent as the tourists can draw upon such recreational facilities, both indoors and outdoors, which form legitimate requirements of the local population. However, in case of smaller palaces, which may be of even larger tourist interest and attraction, exclusive recreational amenities are to be provided for the tourists. But this has to be done keeping in view the socio-cultural milleu and environment at the destination.

In addition to the primary elements of tourist infrastructure, "ancillary infrastructure facilities and services" are considered vital for comprehensive development of a tourist centre. These largely consist of facilities for growth of traditional and indigenous arts and crafts and cottage industries of tourist interest along with ancillary facilities namely housing for artisans and craftsmen engaged in such activities with land earmarked for such uses. Facilities for housing and ancillary requirements of the "service population" needed to man the service and tourist facilities and amenities is a vital factor. Ignoring this aspect can result in the creation of slums with inhuman living conditions.

Q2. Write down the essential factors of a tourism master plan.

Ans. Tourism planning in India started quite late with the first tourism policy being announced by the Government of India in November, 1982 after tourism was recognized as an industry by the Planning Commission of India in June, 1982. In July, 1986 the Planning Commission of India set up the National Committee on Tourism in order to formulate plans for this sector. The government's initiatives of incorporating a planned tourism sector in India went a long way in boosting Indian tourism.

In all countries of the world where a systematic approach to tourism development has been a part of the national policy, emphasis has been given on formulation of Tourism Master Plan for development of tourist infrastructure. This has been conditioned by several factors. Some of these are as following :

(a) Positive and negative factors which have influenced or may influence proper exploitation of the particular tourist resource.

(b) Carrying capacity of particular resource for tourism development in relation to environmental and ecological impacts as well as socio-cultural impacts of tourism development programme at macro and micro levels.

(c) Problems relating to financing and management of access and infrastructure provision.

In Corsica, designation of favourable zones for tourist infrastructure, identification of important natural and man-made resource areas and their designation for protection and provision of Access and Land Control Policy for development in and around the designated area, are important components of an overall Tourism Master Plan. Such a policy plan at a macro level shall guide programme planning at micro levels.

In regard to coastal tourism development in France, the Master Plan lays emphasis on :

(a) Tourism development organized generally perpendicular to the coast in the hinterland of existing resorts, and

(b) Creation of extended sectors of environmental protection which are designated as protected forests, natural reserves, agriculture and forestry land to provide ecological conservation.

In all these exercises, environmental protection and conservation of tourism resource and natural endowments have been the key factors.

In any case, the importance of Physical Development Plan as the key component of the overall Tourism Master Plan at both macro and micro levels can hardly be over-emphasised.

At macro level a comprehensive Master Plan for tourism development should consist of :

(a) Recommended policies and priorities for tourism and recreation,

(b) Programme of infrastructural development,

(c) Physical plan detailing location of areas to be developed, conserved and protected and in what manner,

(d) Strategy for implementation, coordination and financing,

(e) Evaluation of resulting ecological as well as socio-economic impacts and their resolutions,

(f) Action programmes and mechanism of monitoring the changes and their effects.

For regulating, reducing or restricting the pressure on a resource of a finite capacity like a popular tourist centre, hill resort or a beach complex which are exposed to incompatible uses, the basic development policy should consist of :

(a) restricting access,
(b) limiting facilities,
(c) zoning the various activities spatially,
(d) scheduling activities, and
(e) developing alternative destinations.

As a first step towards formulation of a Master Plan, it would be necessary to conduct surveys of the tourist resource characteristics and potential. These should be analysed in relation to physical, social, economic and environmental attributes of the destination area. The basic framework for developing the Tourism Master Plan for planning, development and management of tourism destination areas is established through:

- a synthesis of the resources and their optimal exploitation for tourism purposes, and
- an analysis of projected tourist flow.

The physical component of the Master Plan would establish a framework for spatial organisation of tourist facilities and infrastructure, accessibility and linkages, both internal and external, of various parts of the tourism activity areas and zonation of major recreational and open spaces as an integrated open space system. Measures and programmes for environmental protection, landscaping, site development are important components of such a Master Plan. Besides, linkages of the complex with the surrounding hinterland as well as measures to control development along the periphery of the complex should also be spelt out. It is also imperative to consider appropriate planning measures to integrate the tourism complex development with the surrounding smaller settlements whose socio-economic development is linked with the tourism activities concentrated in the complex. These policies and programmes are to be detailed out and concretised through an integrated Physical Development Plan for phased development of the complex and provision for tourism infrastructure.

Q3. What are the main problems involved in providing accessibility to tourist destination in a hill area?

Ans. Accessibility to hill towns, resorts and places of tourist as well as movement within the area are important considerations in any kind of planning for hill tourism. The question of accessibility poses special problems due to:

Difficult terrain,

Inevitable restrictions to movement by automobiles,

Heavy investments involved in road building and improvement,

Limitations of railway to connect all the hill-resorts with the nearest railway center in the plains, and

General difficulty in providing adequate terminal and parking facilities within the local area of tourist attraction.

In the Himalayan foot-hills of northern, north-western and north-eastern India, there are over 60 major and minor tourist centers and hill resorts. Of these hardly nine are located on the railway. It is apparent that accessibility factor in respect of hill resorts is heavily dependent on road transport. It is imperative that despite the heavy cost of road-building and improvement in hilly terrain, and integrated Road Development Programme should be formulated region-wise and implemented in suitable stages to promote tourism. Such a road network should comprise of a minimum two-lane black-topped carriageway with maneuverable gradient and curvature limitations and an alignment merging with the landscape. There should be appropriate traffic signs and signals, pull-out bays and protective fencing wherever necessary. Simultaneously, air-network should be extended to all major hill-resorts. At terminal points and destination areas, parking spaces should be provided for tourist cars, coaches and taxis in sufficient manner. A road-cum-ropeway transportation network should form an important element of any physical development programme for hill towns and hill resorts to improve accessibility.

Q4. Write in brief on developing coastal settlement as a tourist resort.

Ans. The global trend in the development and use of coastal areas is towards :

- large scale urbanization,
- attendant concentration of trade and industries around major port cities,
- intensive extractive activities for marine resources, and
- catering to increasing international tourism as well as domestic demand for recreation and leisure.

The rapid growth of such large-scale economic and recreational activities in a relatively narrow and shrinking coastal strip always leads to competitive claims of industrial, residential and recreational uses for coastal locations. But more recently several environmental issues affecting both coastal resources and human habitations are also being raised. This calls for proper management and regulation of the multifarious coastal developments.

The Indian coasts vary widely in their structural and surface characteristics. This has a bearing on the relative levels of resource potentials, sectoral developments, settlements pattern, structure and linkages of the respective coastal zones. Peninsular India is straddled with 55 coastal districts having 104 higher order urban centres of which 6 are metropolitan centres and 49 class I cities. Out of these all the 6 metros, Bombay, Calcutta, Madras, Kochi, Vishakapatanam and Surat and 27 class I cities have coastal locations. While both the east and west coasts are dotted with tourist spots of varying interests, major coastal tourism destination areas functioning as sea-resorts are only few and far between, namely, Digha in West Bengal; Puri-Konark, Chilka Gopalpur in Orissa, Rameshwaram – Kanyakumari – Kovalam in Tamil Nadu and Kerala and several beach resorts of Goa which attract most of the sea-faring domestic and international tourists.

The major coastal settlements, like port cities tend to attract not only the location-specific port and maritime activities, but also allied activities and uses. These include industry, trade and commerce, as well as institutional uses, which have a tendency to proliferate, through a suction phenomenon, rendering other off-coast settlements impoverished. As a result of this the coastal tourist resources like beach, etc. get depleted owing to urban and industrial expansion or pushed out to more outlying locations. An integrated policy approach, therefore becomes essential for overall development of a coastal settlement to cater to both tourism and non-tourism functions effectively.

Development of a coastal settlement as a tourist resort requires a scientific approach to planning interventions. The planning interventions have been identified as follows :

(i) Sea resorts and beach tourism complexes should be ideally conceived as separate entities. They should be physically separated from the main urban mode to avoid functional conflicts in tourism and non-tourism activities.

(ii) Tourism infrastructure should also be planned in a dispersed manner along vantage stretches of the coast-line appropriate for tourism activities. It should not be unduly concentrated at one or two locations only. This would extend benefits from the tourism activity over a wider area, particularly to the smaller rural settlements of the coastal hinterland.

(iii) A comprehensive scheme for extensive water-front development incorporating various recreational elements should be formulated for optimal utilisation as also protection of the tourist-resource.

(iv) It is also imperative to discourage proliferation of tourist infrastructure along the coast, by organising its development perpendicular to the coast, generally in the hinterland of existing resorts. At an area level, the main network should be planned to run along but a distance away from the coast, connecting various urban centres in the hinterland region and having link roads leading down to select points of tourist infrastructure on the coast. This concept widely advocated in coastal resorts development in several European countries like France, Yugoslavia, Cyprus, Corsica, Turkey, Greece and others, is directed at regulating, reducing and restricting the development pressure on a resource of finite capacity like a coastal zone, exposed to incompatible uses. Its salient points are restricting access, limiting facilities, zoning the various activities, scheduling the activities and developing alternative destinations.

Q5. What do you know about the formation of community in pre-colonial India?

Ans. In pre-colonial India, village communities were in many ways self-sufficient and dealt with the machinery of the state as a group. In the plains, taxes were paid in the form of surplus production of grain to the state by the village community as a whole and not by any individual householder. Village Councils regulated most of their socio-economic affairs themselves. Any recourse to an outside authority was a rare occurrence. Though each members of the community had a piece of land to be cultivated the peasant did not have the exclusive right to sell or dispose it off. Ownership of the land was collective, more so in the case of common lands. The caste based village society had developed a variety of institutions to regulate the use of resources. The pre-colonial rulers only claimed the taxes on the produce and not the right on the land itself from the village community. There were various ways in which the traditional communities adapted to their existing habitat. They organised themselves to live in harmony with their surroundings. For instance in pre-British Maharashtra, village community assigned village guards to prevent any unauthorised wood cutting in village common land. In addition, they had to harvest and deliver all the wood needed by village householder. Harvests from village common lands were governed by a variety of regulations, notably quotas on the amount harvested by different families and in different seasons.

Here, it is appropriate to talk of the different ecological stratum of the various caste groups in terms of the habitat they occupied and the relationship with other caste groups with whom they interacted. We can take the example of Masui Lukheri village situated on an island in the estuary from the river Aghanashine close to the town of Kumta in the state of Karnataka. Spurs of the hill ranges of Western Ghats ran along this region right upto the sea, giving the region a rich mosaic of territorial, repairers and coastal habitats, supporting a great diversity of natural resources. One can find as many as 13 different endogamous groups co-existing in the same region. Resource use was diversified among different castes, fishing community (Ambigas), agriculturists (Malakkis, Palgars and Naiks), horticulturists (the Haviks), entertainers (Bhandaris and Deshbhandaris), service castes (Kooleyas-barbers and Madwals – washerman), artisans (Slets, Achari and Muhkri) and traders (Gowd Saraswats). These different caste groups had their characteristic modes of subsistence and often occupied their distinct habitat much like the species within a biological community. Within this institutional set up of caste system, different social groups were regularised in harmony with each other and their habitat.

Q6. What is cultural environment?

Ans. Cultural environment is composed of people and their culture: folklore, dress, handicrafts, religious handicrafts, work and lifestyle. It also includes the built environment from individual buildings, historic monuments and archaeological sites.

Indigenous tribes form an important part of the cultural environment. In the context of the hill tribes, their lifestyle and customs form an important part of the habitat. Continuance of the traditional form of customs, rituals and folklore forms an attraction in the world constantly undergoing fast changes. In the records of the travellers to the hills of Darjeeling and other hillstations, there exist numerous references to the customs and practices of the hill tribes. Practices and lifestyle of the tribes are a part of the cultural environment of the hill resorts. They hold an appeal for the travellers from different cultures. It is a cultural encounter of the 'advanced' occident and the traditional, 'exotic Orient' in the most direct manner. Many European writers have written in detail about the tribal settlements, customs, daily life, rituals, festivities and mode of expressing sorrows and joys as peculiarities. Habits and attitudes of various hillmen were broadly generalised by the British writers of the nineteenth century. This general impression has carried forth in more recent times. For example, Edward J. Buck, an early twentieth century author of a book on Simla, characterised Tibetans as "simple shepherds of Tibet. Wild and unkempt looking fellows with their long hair falling down - a mass of rags and dirt." Their small squat noses, sallow faces and upturned eyes were unfavourably compared to the "delicate Aryan features of the Punjab hillmen." However, Buck found Tibetans to be eminently truthful, honest and chaste, easily amused, easily satisfied and very sociable.

The Bhutias include Sikkimese, Sherpas, Dhrukpa and Tibetan Bhutia. These people are a cross-breed between the Tibetans, who settled in Sikkim and the aborigines of that land, the Lepchas.

Lepchas are original inhabitants of the Darjeeling hill tracts. Their number and their customs and lifestyle have been gradually diminishing since the onset of British empire into Darjeeling. Sikkim gazetteer of 1891 describes them as: the "rongpa." They are, above all things, woodmen of the woods, knowing the ways of birds and beasts and possessing an extensive zoological and botanical nomenclature of their own. They have been rightly considered by scholars as "born naturalists." A characteristic trait of the Lepchas was that they had separate names for nearly every bird, plant, orchid and butterfly to be found in their region. Sir Joseph Hooker, a renowned 19th century naturalist, was full of praises for these born naturalists in his Himalayan journal. He wrote in 1848:

"A more interesting and attractive companion than the Lepchas I never lived with: cheerful, kind and patient with the master to whom he is attached, rude but not savage, ignorant and yet intelligent; with a simple resource of a plain knife he makes his house and furnishes yours with a speed, alacity and ingenuity that wile away the well known long hour."

Lady Dufferin, during late 1880s, described 'Tendook,' a Lepcha chief and the usual costume of the Lepcha men. They dress in "a selves petticoat," wrote Lady Dufferin, "red jackets, a hat like flower pot turned upside down, with a peacock feather struck in the front of it. These men all beat big drums." This somewhat amusing description her and the analogies she drew up provide a highly touristic impression of the tribes. A travelogue of the 19th century also observed this distinct costume of the Lepchas:

"Their dress is quite unique and graceful. It consists of thick blue and white or red and white cotton cloth. This is crossed over the breast and back, leaving the arms bare and free and descends to the calf of the leg, it is then gathered in round the waist by a leather or ornamental girdle, ..., the women's dress is a slight modification of the men's, but with a loose kind of bed-gown over it. They wear heavy silver earrings, a profusion of imitation coral and coloured bead necklaces. They take great pride in their hair plaits."

The fondness of hillmen and in particular hillwomen for jewellery is also drawn out in case of hill tribes around Simla. Edward J. Buck observed the hillwomen to be fond of gay attire and bangles and nose-rings. He also drew up a colourful picture of a Simla hill chieftain: **"He is a mountain chieftain, whose home is lonely castle on hillside overlooking a great rich valley which is his own. One cannot help observing how gallantly he is dressed in gay but well matched colours and cloth of richest coloured material."** Such descriptions indicate the extent of curiosity that existed among the European visitors **vis-a-vis** the native hill tribes. Such colourful narratives about their dress, food, habits, fairs and festivals intrigued and enchanted the tourists.

This enchantment for the tourists was further stimulated by the colourful festivities of the hills. Edward Buck vividly described the famous **Sipi** fair held annually at Tara Hill, Simla. It gives an insight into the traditional form of gaiety of the hill people. He wrote :

"On the one side, ... picture dozens of swings and roundabouts

crammed with hill people in a blissful state of happiness, on the other a long line of stalls, crammed with glass beads, necklaces and cheap finery of every description and surrounded by a merry, excited throng of wrangling purchases. Add to the above the dozens of sweet shops with their overpowering scent of ghee and frizzling sweet meats, the crash of tom-toms, the chorus of dancing jampanies,' ... and you have a fair idea of the fun bustle and noise of Sipi fair."

Like the Sipi fair of Shimla hills, the Tibetan new year, celebrated in Darjeeling hill tract, has also attracted writers and tourists. 'Devil dance,' in which the participants dance wearing animal masks, is an important part of the festivities. Thus it is clear that the cultural environment of the traditional hill community is exceedingly light hearted, generous to a fault, fond of pleasure in any form, excitable and aggressive to a degree. Besides the culture of the hill tribes developed over the centuries, the Raj created its own cultural milieu in the form of the institution of hillstations and its trappings. 'Raj nostalgia' is in evidence in a number of residents of the hills. Many tourists also seek the 'Raj' culture in the country clubs, the English type cottages and hotels with typical English furnishings and tastes. Grand public Buildings erected for the Imperial rulers are the everlasting monument, opened for public viewing. Viceregal lodge at Shimla, 'Shrubbery, the Lieutenant Governor's residence at Darjeeling, various clubs and other public buildings, theatres and townhalls are the contribution of the British community to the hill environment along with the mall roads. In fact, cultural environment is a major tourist attraction.

Q7. What do you understand by sustainable tourism?

Ans. Employing 260 million people and generating 10.7% of world's GDP, Tourism is the largest as well as the fastest industry of the world. Bigger planning and management is in dire need to control the tourism industry, and more important, to protect and conserve the biodiversity of tourist places. Dealing predominantly with such serious issues, sustainable tourism comes in great handy, as it is all about conserving the resources, valuing the local culture and tradition and, contributing largely in economy.

Sustainable tourism is a kind of approach to tourism meant to make the development of tourism ecologically supportable in the long term. The very importance of sustainable tourism lies in its motives to conserve the resources and increase the value of local culture and tradition. Sustainable tourism is a responsible tourism intending to generate employment and income along with alleviating any deeper impact on environment and local culture.

Characteristics of Sustainable Tourism

- Sustainable Tourism tries its utmost to maintain the importance of local culture and tradition.

- Sustainable Tourism is informatory, as it doesn't only let tourist know about the destinations but also it helps locals knowing about the culture and civilisation of tourists.
- This kind of tourism is aimed to conserve the resources of destinations where one is visiting to
- Sustainable Tourism seeks deeper involvement of locals, which provide local people an opportunity and make their living. Above all, Sustainable Tourism stresses pointedly upon integrity of the tourist places.
- With the increased footfalls of tourists, the deep need today is that tourism like other sector be planned and managed suitably. Sustainable development of tourism is possible only if its follows some of its guidelines and principles. Tourism ought to be initiated at any location with the help of local community. The involvement of local community helps maintaining the appropriate tourism development.
- The local community has to meet the direct benefit of flourishing tourism in their area. Link between local business and tourism enable local people gain economically as well.
- To cause large growth in sustainable development, there is need that codes, ethics and some fair guidelines be appointed.
- In order to heighten the importance of heritage and natural resources, and manage them better, training and education programme should be instituted.

Q8. Write in brief about the nature of the traditional society in the hills of Uttrakhand.

Ans. Uttarakhand became the 27th state of the Republic of India on the 9th of November 2000. The State is carved out of Uttar Pradesh. It occupies 17.3% of India's total land area with 51,125 sq. km. It has a population of about 6.0 million at 94.4 per sq. km. It borders Tibet, Nepal, Himachal Pradesh. 13 Districts Comprise

Pithoragarh **Almora**
Nainital **Bageshwar** **Champawat**

Uttarkashi **Udham Singh Nagar**
Chamoli **Dehradun**

Pauri **Tehri Garhwal**
Rudraprayag **Haridwar**

Nestled in the mountain ranges of the Himalaya, Dehradun is the Capital of Uttarakhand. It is one of the most beautiful resort in the submountain tracts of India, known for its scenic surroundings. The town lies in the Dun Valley, on the watershed of the Ganga and Yamuna rivers. The name Dehradun is a collection of two word "dera" meaning Camp and " dun" meaning valley. Some of the best public schools and convents are housed here. The Indian Military Academy, The Forest Research Institute, ONGC and many more offices of Central and State Govt. are also situated here. In Uttarakhand, negation of community ownership led to a sense of alienation with their habitat. These hill dwellers, who had nurtured the forest growth by preserving sacred groves, etc. now grew indifferent to the forest. Goaded by the loss of their habitat by the 'reserve' forests and scientific management brought about by the colonial rulers, these forest inhabitants quickly exhausted the resources left to them, out of fear that their conservation would lead to state appropriation.

While farming systems in the Himalayas continued to be subsistence oriented, cumulative demographic, social and environmental changes undermined the hill society's capacity to feed itself. Moreover, the rapid developments of the commercial and industrial society degraded the hill ecosystem leading to further reduction in productivity. It led to the fragmentation of the family and community structure. While the diversification of resource use between different castes moderated or removed intercaste competition, the fragmentation of the community structure and lack of livelihood intensified the competition during the colonial times. Once the linkage between the agriculture and forests was broken, there emerged intense competition for the different source of livelihood. All this meant disaster for the traditional economic structure.

Ramachandra Guha thus sums up in his book, **The Unquiet Woods :**

"Moreover, by exposing their subjects to the seduction of the industrial economy and consumer society, the British ensured that the process of ecological change they initiated would continue and indeed intensity, after they left Indian shores."

These economic changes have had their political ramifications. The forest communities have often resisted these changes being brought about in their region against their will. In Tehri region in Uttarakhand, for example, localised resistance movements against commercial management were organised in 1904, 1906, 1930, 1944-48 to claim a full and exclusive control over forests and pastures.

Q9. What is multiplier effect?

Ans. Tourism not only creates jobs in the tertiary sector, it also encourages growth in the primary and secondary sectors of industry. This is known as the multiplier effect which in its simplest form is how many times money spent by a tourist circulates through a country's economy.

Money spent in a hotel helps to create jobs directly in the hotel, but it also creates jobs indirectly elsewhere in the economy. The hotel, for example, has to buy food from local farmers, who may spend some of this money on fertiliser or clothes. The demand for local products increases as tourists often buy souvenirs, which increases secondary employment. The multiplier effect continues until the money eventually 'leaks' from the economy through imports - the purchase of goods from other countries.

A study of tourism 'leakage' in Thailand estimated that 70% of all money spent by tourists ended up leaving Thailand (via foreign-owned tour operators, airlines, hotels, imported drinks and food, etc.). Estimates for other Third World countries range from 80% in the Caribbean to 40% in India. Source : **Sustainable Living**

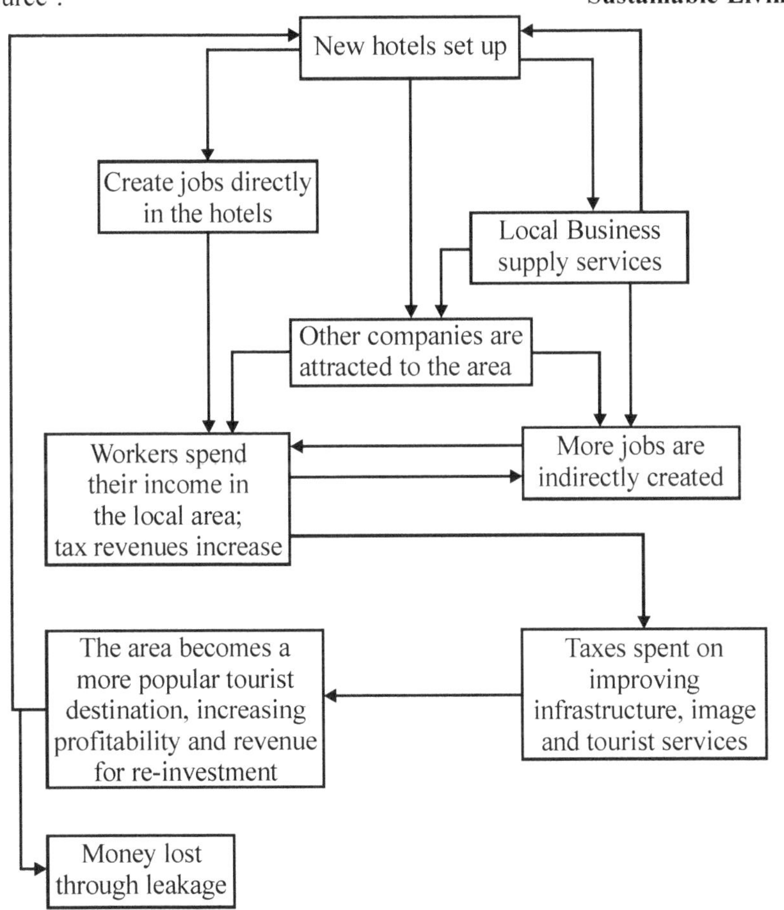

Tourism Multiplier Effect

Q10. Explain the relationship between tourism and employment.

Ans. Tourism is an important sector which not only provides employment opportunities but helps to earn valuable foreign exchange. The tourism development also helps to achieve balanced and sustainable regional growth by providing employment opportunities for unskilled workers specifically from the rural areas and also developing interior and remote areas. However, the development of tourism has been constrained by poor accessibility to various places of tourist interest, due to bottlenecks in infrastructure and other facilities. There is an urgent need to remove all these constraints for development of tourism. The number of foreign tourist arrivals and foreign exchange earnings during the period 1995-2001 is given in table below:

There has been a decline of about 20 per cent in the foreign tourist arrivals and 16 per cent in the foreign exchange earnings through tourism in the two months of September and October 2001. In the aftermath of the terrorist attacks in USA on September 2001, a programme to meet the adverse conditions arising out of this incident has been drawn up and is being implemented.

Performance of the Tourism Sector				
Year	**Foreign Tourist Arrivals (in Lakh)**	**Percent increase**	**Estimated foreign exchange earnings (in million US$)**	**Increase**
1995-96	21.9	-	2,714	-
1996-97	23.3	6.6	2,878	6.1
1997-98	23.7	1.6	2,914	1.2
1998-99	24.0	1.1	2,993	2.7
1999-00	25.2	5.0	3,055	2.1
2001-01	26.8	6.0	3,168	4.8
2001-02				
(Apr-Oct)	12.3	-6.3	1,636	-1.3

Being a very wide field, the scope of employment in tourism sector is very bright and the potential is still largely untapped. Career opportunities exist both in the public and private sector. In the public sector, there are opportunities in the Directorates and Departments of Tourism of the center and the state as Officers, information assistants, Tourist guides etc. Another good prospectus for qualified tourism professionals are in the private sector with travel agencies, tour operators, airlines, hotels, transport and cargo companies etc. The opening up of the skies to private airlines and their emerging tie-ups with foreign airlines has removed bottlenecks in the transport and communication network resulting in easy flow of domestic and foreign tourists in the country. Since this is a new area of employment, not many qualified and experienced people are available and the promotion prospectus are also very bright and rapid. After a few years of experience, One can also start their own business by handling all travel requirements of a client and gradually building up business, taking on additional employees. Career Options are in:-Tourism Department, Airlines, Tour Operators, Travel Agencies, Hotels, Transport etc.

Q11. Write down the positive socio-economic benefits of tourism.

Ans. Tourism can and does bring about socio-economic changes and is usually deliberately developed to generate economic benefits and through them social betterment. Therefore, it is important to understand the specific types of impacts whether positive or negative, that tourism generates in a society. Because of their close relationship, socio-cultural and economic impacts are examined together.

The socio-economic impacts of tourism have made this field a rather controversial one in recent years, especially where tourism development has been rapid and largely unplanned and uncontrolled, with the results that there have been adverse socio-cultural as well as environmental impacts.

Economic Benefits: Direct economic benefits include provision of employment, income and foreign exchange, which lead to improve living standards of the local community and overall national and regional economic development. In economically depressed areas, the employment and income provided by tourism especially to young people, may help stem out migration from those areas. Increased government revenues, through various types of taxation on tourism that can be used to develop community and infrastructural facilities and services to assist in general economic development are also a direct economic benefit. These direct and indirect economic benefits are usually the primary positive impact of multiplier effect of tourism.

An indirect economic benefit of tourism is that it serves as a catalyst for the development or expansion of other economic sectors, such as agriculture, fisheries, construction, certain types of manufacturing and handicrafts through their supply of the goods and services used in tourism. Another indirect socio-economic benefit is the improvement brought about in transportation and other infrastructural facilities and services for tourism that also serve general national, regional and community needs. Although dependent very much on local economic and cultural development policy, tourism may be seen by the host country or region as being advantageous in trading technical and managerial skills for segments of its population, some of which can be transferred to other sectors which would generally encourage people to adopt regular employment habits and work for things they want. Tourism in large traditional societies, can also provide an opportunity for emancipation of women through training and employment.

Conservation of Cultural Heritage: Tourism can be a major stimulus for conservation of important elements of the cultural heritage of an area because their conservation can be justified, in part of whole, by tourism as tourist attractions. In other words, the conservation of the cultural heritage acquires a certain economic incentive through the instrumentality of tourism. These are as follows:

(1) Tourism provides the incentive and helps pay for the conservation of archaeological and historic sites and as attractions for tourist that might otherwise be allowed to deteriorate or disappear, thus resulting in the loss of the cultural heritage of an area. In South and South-East Asia, most of the archaeological and historic preservation taking place can be economically justified in such lower income countries because they provide attractions for tourists. In some cases such as Sri Lanka, admission fees paid by tourists is used directly for archaeological research and conservation.

(2) Conservation and revitalisation of traditional arts, handicrafts, dance, music, drama, customs and ceremonies and certain aspects of traditional life styles directly feed into tourism.

(3) Conservation of important natural areas also acquires an impetus. Without tourism, those natural areas might be developed for other uses or allowed to ecologically deteriorate, with consequent loss of environmental heritage. This factor can be of especially important benefits in countries with limited resources for nature conservation. For example, marine conservation especially of reef areas, is receiving much attention in some places because there are important attractions for tourism.

(4) Financial assistance for the maintenance of museums, theatres and other cultural facilities and activities and for supporting the organisation of special cultural festivals and events because they are important attractions for tourists as well as for residents. Admission fees paid by tourist at some major museums in the world, for example, provide substantial revenues to maintain those institutions. Similarly, tickets purchased by tourists at important urban theatres help to support their maintenance and other facilities.

Renewal of Cultural Pride: A sense of pride by residents in their culture can be reinforced or even renewed when they observe tourists appreciating it. A kind of cultural awareness emerges. In multi-cultural countries, regional tourism can help in maintaining the cultural identity of minority cultural groups that otherwise might be submerged into nation's dominant culture. The preservation of regional or local culture is very important in modern societies where economic compulsions have tended to discourage and inhibit the growth of local cultures.

Q12. Discuss the impact of tourism on environment.

Ans. Tourism has been a major source of revenue for countries, specifically in the Third world, in the past few decades. It is predicted that by 2010, one billion tourists would have traveled abroad and by 2020, this would have increased to 1.6 billion. In terms of revenue, it is predicted that by 2020, $1.5 trillion would be earned. Tourism is touted as a major source of employment worldwide.

The rise in global tourist arrivals in various countries demands an increased effective preservation. With globalization have increased deforestation, pollution, and disruption in the ecological balance. Pollution caused by littering and improper waste disposal has now become a major problem for the community. Hotels and inns mushroomed, changing the town's landscape and straining its water resources. Commercial production of wood carvings has also affected nearby forests. Trees have been cut down to support commercial wood carving activities that cater to foreign as well as domestic tourist demand.

(1) Water Pollution: If a proper sewage disposal system has not been installed for hotels, resorts and other tourist facilities, there may be pollution of ground water from the sewage or if a sewage outfall has been construed into a nearby river, lake or coastal sea water and the sewage has not been adequately treated, the effluent will pollute that water area. This situation is common in beach resort areas where the hotels construct an outfall into the adjacent water area which can also be used for swimming by tourists or for fishing by locals. Recreational and tourist transportation motor boats in surfaces water result in pollution in river, lakes and sea water due to spilling oil and gas and cleaning their bilge in water. This is usually common in enclosed harbour and places where natural water circulation is slow.

(2) Air Pollution: Tourism is generally considered a "smokeless industry." But it can also result in air pollution by tourist vehicles in a particular area, especially at major attraction sites, that are accessible only by road. This is due to improperly maintained exhaust systems of the vehicles. Also, pollution in the form of dust and dirt in the air may be generated from open, devegetated area if the tourism development is not properly planned, developed and landscaped or is in an interim state of construction.

(3) Noise Pollution: Noise generated by a concentration of tourists road and certain types of tourist attractions such as amusement parks or car/motorcycle race tracks may reach uncomfortable and irritating levels for nearby residents and other tourists. Such loud noise can often result in ear damage and also a phychological stress.

(4) Visual Pollution: It may result from several sources. These can be due to poorly-designed hotels and other facility buildings which are not compatible with local architectural style or not well integrated into the natural environment. Other reasons can be poor maintenance of buildings and landscaping obstruction of scenic views by development use of large and ugly advertising signs. Littering of landscape also results in visual pollution.

(5) Waste Disposal Problems: The most common problem in tourism areas is the littering of debris on the landscape. This is due to large number of people using the area of picnicking. Improper disposal of solid waste from hotel restaurants and resorts generate both litter and environmental health problems from vermin, disease and pollution. It can also lead to the degradation of tourist sites.

Q13. Explain the economic and employment distortion because of tourism?

Ans. Economic distortions can take place geographically, if tourism is concentrated in only one area or a few areas of a country or region, without corresponding development in other places. Resentment by residents in the under developed areas may ensue from this situation. Even within tourism areas, there may be resentment against persons earning relatively good income in tourism by those who are unemployed or have lower income jobs. Employment distortions may be created if tourism attracts employees from other economic sectors such as agriculture and fisheries, because of its higher wages and perhaps more desirable working conditions, if there is not an overall surplus of workers available. There may be resentment by residents if migrant workers are brought into works in tourism, especially if they stay on after they are no longer needed. It also leads to loss of potential economic benefits. If expatriate managers and technical staff are employed in tourism, at much higher wages than local scale, there may be resentment by local, less skilled workers, in addition to the loss of potential economic benefits.

Considering that the tourism industry is seasonal it inevitably results in underemployment, unemployment and social unrest. Employment in the hotel industry has its own patterns. According to the hotel industry's own calculations every hotel room built at an average estimated cost of Rs. 3.5 lakhs provides direct employment to three persons and indirectly for an additional six only. Even if we take both categories together the cost works out to Rs. 30,000 per job as against an estimated Rs. 12,000 in the small scale sector. The present day growth of tourism therefore transfers a country's resources from weaker sectors of the economy to the tourism sector which also displaces people from their traditional occupations. As is evident from the pattern in Goa and Orissa, instead of providing a boost to employment, increasing tourism has actually led to a loss of employment. Some recent researchers have informed that the percentage of fisheries displaced into urban sources of livelihood in Goa stood at a staggering 75%. The luxury oriented tourism industry world wide also features control by outsiders and the marginalisation of the locals. Since resort tourism demands huge tracts of land for sports, golf-courses, car-parks and gardens, lands are bought by outsiders who can afford to buy sites at high prices. In Goa when the locals were unwilling to sell their land, the government acquired it for tourism development. Another problem here is that in many cases these outsiders are not sensitive to the local ecology, environment and community sentiments.

Q14. What is Cost Benefit Analysis?

Ans. A cost benefit analysis finds, quantifies, and adds all the positive factors. These are the benefits. Then it identifies, quantifies, and subtracts all the negatives, the costs. The difference between the two indicates whether the planned action is advisable. The real trick to doing a cost benefit analysis well is making sure you include all the costs and all the benefits and properly quantify them. Should we hire an additional sales person or assign overtime? Is it a good idea to purchase the new stamping machine? Will we be better off putting our free cash flow into securities rather than investing in additional capital equipment? Each of these questions can be answered by doing a proper cost benefit analysis.

Tourism as a Tool for Conservation

Q1. How and why should tourism conserve and preserve the followings :

(1) Physical feature

(2) Historical sites

(3) Wildlife, and **[Dec 2006, Q10(iii)]**

(4) Culture of a land

Ans. (1) Physical Feature: Physical features of a country – land forms (mountains, cliffs, etc.), terrain, water bodies (lakes, rivers, waterfalls, seas, beaches and all other scenic attractions that nature bestows – have captivated and lured human beings since time immemorial. They have always had a more universal appeal and are the most 'visible' of the tourist attractions and hence the most vulnerable to 'irresponsible tourism.' While the physical features have suffered the most at the hands of tourists, they also have the maximum potential to be 'preserved' by tourism for a physically degraded land is virtually impossible to 'reclaim' and is lost forever to tourism. The role of tourism for conservation of physical features of a land is essentially secondary to their economic usefulness. The physical features have not generally been protected for their own sake but owing to their potential for tourism and thus economy. Authorities, together with tour operators have been working towards conserving the physical features of significance to tourism for primarily economic purposes. Throughout the world, there are many instances of tourism serving as a tool for conservation of the physical features of a land.

It is because of the potential for tourism that the beautiful beaches of Southern Europe have been preserved; the Alps mountains (especially in Switzerland and Austria) have not been plundered; the Geysers of Iceland and Giant Causeways of Northern Ireland have remained conserved. The waterfalls and the huge five lake complex that lie between Canada have retained their natural beauty almost entirely due to their attractiveness to tourists. This island of Bermuda is a particularly glorious example of conservation for tourism. In Bermuda, where tourism's contribution to Gross National Product is almost 50%, no family may own more than one car and the speed limit remains at 20 miles an hour – much to the benefit of environment and tourists.

In India, the role of tourism in conservation of physical features, though realized, has been negligible. The only instances of such exercise pertain to the Himalayas and the beaches of the country – where some efforts have been made to preserve their natural grandeur, keeping in mind their tourism potential.

(2) Historical Sites: Together with physical features, historical sites form the most important of the "tourist assets" of a country. Tourism has the potential to provide for their preservation too. In fact, tourism has been instrumental in inspiring and assisting the conservation of historical heritage in many ways. As in the case of physical features, tourism has helped preservation of historical sites for their broader economic usefulness. Famous monuments form the backbone of local economy for their attractiveness to tourism and hence the authorities are forced to protect them for fear of losing important source of revenue and employment. Moreover, the locals too, who reap the economic benefits of tourism, are motivated to work for the preservation of these historical sites.

Further, while preservation efforts for a historical site involves expensive technologies, the governments, generally, tend to keep conservation of these low down in their order of priority. To say that the money earned from tourists is the most important source of finance for conservation of historical sites, would not be an exaggeration. To quote some actual instances, the great pyramids of Egypt remain preserved for eternity by the best 'preserving' techniques entirely due to the money provided by tourism and essentially to retain the inflow of tourists who come to see them. The same, more or less, is true of the vast archaeological complexes of the Graeco-Roman world and the ancient sites of America which are extremely well preserved almost entirely due to their attractiveness to tourists.

In India too, the large number of historical sites that exist throughout the country are being protected for their tourism potential and by the money provided by tourists. More specifically, Taj Mahal, which is one of the best preserved monuments in the world, could never have been so well-preserved but for its 'attractiveness' to world tourists and the money thus earned from them. Again, Khajuraho, which was just another sleepy village with ancient monuments in a state of utter neglect, is now one of the best known of Indian historical sites and a 'world-heritage', thanks to tourism which promoted the place to the international tourists. In India, yet another example of tourism being a 'tool for conservation' comes from the increasingly popular and fast developing concept of 'heritage-resort' – whereby, old and ruined havelis and mahals are being renovated in strictly traditional styles to woo tourists to lodge in.

(3) Wildlife: Those animals living in a natural state, unimpeded and undomesticated by humans. The term is sometimes used to include plant life as well. Tourism has been immensely helpful in wildlife protection through the creation, development and operations of national parks, nature reserves and sanctuaries. These parks, which operate under strict laws, not only maintain natural environmental conditions for birds and animals, but enable tourists to enjoy nature's bounty as well. Amongst tour operators specialising in animal shoots, safaris or shikars, greater consideration is now paid to the protection and preservation of animal life and photographic safaris, tours of national parks and game-reserves and ecological trips are gaining interest. The idea is to promote 'conservation exercises' for tourism – thereby benefiting both. Tourism has further helped these reserves and thus the environment, by providing alternative employment opportunities to the local population, who would otherwise burden the forest land for their livelihood. Also, the money earned, from tour operators, has been of tremendous help in maintaining them.

The increasing popularity of 'national parks' is a testimony of tourism's potential as a tool for conservation. In fact, there are specific instances where tourism has helped conservation in a big way. In East Africa, the Serengeti grasslands in Kenya and Tanzania were being laid waste by large scale poaching and irresponsible, primitive cultivation methods. In the late 70s, the governments of Tanzania and Kenya in a joint conservation programme, converted the entire Serengeti region into a mammoth wildlife reserve of tremendous tourist attraction. This has been one of the very successful examples of conservation programmes combining with tourism potential to enrich a whole geographical region both ecologically and economically. In Central Africa, the opening up to visitors of the Saint-floris Nature Park, permitted the effective protection of the wildlife, in that the income from tourism allowed the proper maintenance of the trails and ranger's camps and the very presence and movement of tourists kept poachers effectively at bay. In Benin to, it has been found that the non-availability of the Pendjari Park for tourism would risk destruction of the future possibility of its development.

In India too, the idea of formation of National Parks and Nature Reserves and their opening to tourists, has gained tremendous acceptability with the authorities and environmentalists. The large number of such 'reserves' that have come and to be established are maintained to an extent, by the money provided by tourists and tour operators. For example, Bharatpur Bird Sanctuary in Rajasthan, the Project Tiger Reserves throughout the country and many other protected forests are being financed, solely or mainly, by the money provided by tourism.

(4) Culture of a Land - Culture (from the Latin *cultura* stemming from *colere*, meaning "to cultivate,") generally refers to patterns of human activity and the symbolic structures that give such activities significance and importance. Cultures can be "understood as systems of symbols and meanings that even their creators contest, that lack fixed boundaries, that are constantly in flux, and that interact and compete with one another"

Culture can be defined as all the ways of life including arts, beliefs and institutions of a population those are passed down from generation to generation. Culture has been called "the way of life for an entire society." As such, it includes codes of manners, dress, language, religion, rituals, norms of behavior such as law and morality, and systems of belief as well as the art. Culture, which forms an inseparable part of a country's environment, too has been regarded, more recently, as an inexhaustible source of wealth and hence 'to be protected.' Here too, tourism has immensely motivated authorities and people to 'preserve' their culture by promoting 'cultural heritage' to touring outsiders for its uniqueness under the concept of 'cultural tourism.' This is done by organising dance and other performances, handicrafts and souvenir trade for tourists. Once brought into the economic circuit, culture of a country can and has also become self-sustaining rather than depending solely on authorities for preservation.

In many countries tourism has not only economically exploited the local cultural traditions but has provided a tremendous motivation for the preservation and revival of cultural traditions, arts and crafts. But for its contribution, many art and craft forms would have become extinct and many more would have followed the path of doom. Actual examples of tourism being the guiding factor for cultural preservation are too numerous to be discussed here. Some examples may, however, be taken to illustrate this point. The stories of the revival of the dance forms and traditional silk industry in Thailand, the folk culture of Eastern Europe, the recreation of ancient arts and crafts through designers' and artists' competition in Sweden, the 'Port Royal' series in Jamaica and the rich musical traditions of the entire Caribbean region, the rich cultural heritage of Africa in its various manifestations, the revival and promotion of South Eastern Asian dance and handicrafts, are good examples of how tourism has benefited cultural heritage in these countries and assisted in retaining their traditional authenticity.

India, with its rich cultural heritage and extreme diversity is a remarkable example of cultural tourism and its role as a tool for conservation. In India, each year a large number of cultural festivals are organised by the government and private tour agencies to attract and entertain tourists. The Festival of Laddakh, the Desert Festival and the Khajuraho Dance Festival are the most noted examples of such festivals. During these 'tourist festivals,' Indian culture is presented in its colourful best to the visiting outsiders and mainly involves music and dance forms, both classical and folk, the arts and handicrafts, dress and food, etc. The sheer size of tourists coming to these 'festivals' to experience India's enormously unique and enchanting cultural diversity has motivated both the authorities and people to preserve their 'cultural assets' inspite of pressures of modernisation and westernisation.

Q2. What are the techniques for regulating and controlling tourism?

Ans. The key to balance is to control tourism, as unchecked mass tourism can never be beneficial to environment. The prime initiative for these controlling efforts must rest with the governments, which are in the best position to appreciate the needs, interests and resources of their countries and to ensure that tourism is kept in harmony with them. To depend on private initiative and expect tourism to be controlled is foolhardy as private operators' prime concern is profit and not environmental conservation. Each country must set its objectives, evaluate its resources and the alternative options for using those resources and adopt its tourism development strategies to meet those objectives. The essential implementation of such plans require legislative, administrative and financial arrangements followed by suitable operational mechanisms and these inputs have to function interdependently in a coordinated and integrated manner.

A key principal advocated by those who seek a balance between tourism and environment is that the type and scale of tourist development and activity should be related to the carrying capacity of tourist resources. This includes not just the facilities and infrastructures, but also the bio-physical and the socio-cultural capacity of the region. The excess in flow of tourists would lead to a deterioration of facilities and infrastructures and straining of socio-cultural system – much to the detriment of overall environment. Assessment of carrying capacity and the balancing of levels of tourist development and activity with the capacity, are thus crucial means of preventing environmental damage, protecting resources and securing the continuance of tourism itself on a 'sustained yield' basis.

Lastly, we may quote an extract from the Manila Declaration on World Tourism, 1980, for its relevance for our discussion.

"Tourism resources available in the various countries consist at the same time of space, facilities and values. These are resources whose use cannot be left uncontrolled without running the risk of their deterioration or even their destruction. The satisfaction of tourism requirements must not be prejudicial to the social and economic-interests of the population in tourist areas, to the environment or above all, to natural resources, which are the fundamental attraction of tourism and historical and cultural sites. All tourism resources are part of the heritage of mankind. National communities and the entire international community must take the necessary steps to ensure their preservation. The conservation of historical, cultural and regional sites represent at all times and notably in times of conflict, one of the fundamental responsibilities of States.

Q3. What is the importance of tourism planning?

Ans. Tourism planning in India started quite late with the first tourism policy announced by the Government of India in November, 1982 after tourism was recognized as an industry by the Planning Commission of India in June, 1982.

In July, 1986 the Planning Commission of India set up the National Committee on Tourism in order to formulate plans for this sector. The government's initiatives of incorporating a planned tourism sector in India went a long way in boosting Indian tourism.

In May, 1992 the National Action Plan for tourism was announced. The objectives of this landmark plan for **tourism planning in India** were :

- To improve the economy category domestic tourism
- To develop the tourist areas socially and economically
- To preserve the environment and the national heritage
- To encourage international tourism
- To improve in world tourism India's share
- To increase opportunities for employment in this sector

India tourism planning increased with the seventh five year plan India (1985-1989). The various polices advocated by the seventh plan for **tourism planning in India** are:

- To promote aggressively domestic tourism
- It laid stress on creating more beach resorts
- To conduct conferences, trekking, conventions, and winter sports so that various options are available to the foreign tourists

These polices of the seventh five year plan gave a boost to the tourism planning and further encourage **tourism planning in India**, the eighth five year plan (1992- 1997) mentioned that the private sector should increase its participation in the sector. The various polices advocated by the eighth plan for tourism planning in India are:

- To develop the tourists places
- To develop winter sports, beach resort, and wildlife tourism
- To restore the projects of national heritage
- To provide in tourists centers economy class accommodation

Tourism planning in India has increased by leaps and bounds in the last few years and the government and Department of Tourism needs to make continuous efforts to ensure that **tourism planning in India** takes the tourism sector of the country to greater heights on a sustainable basis.

Q4. What should be tourism planning be based on in particular tourist site?

Ans. The uncontrolled and uncoordinated endeavours of the societies all over the world to harvest the profit potential of growing magnitude and changing structure of tourist traffic have, on the one hand, enhanced the magnificance of some selected tourist spots and areas. But, on the other, they have also stimulated the ugly growth of hutments, slums etc. The unkindled use of resources to commercialization taking precedence over the protection of landscape and environment has resulted in insufficient infrastructure and inappropriate superstructure. It is ironic that profit maximising approach to tourism development has by causing concentration of tourist beyond the "absorption capacity" of the area, converted many of the world's finest resorts into over crowded abhorring areas. In the name of tourism, this development has triggered off the process of destruction of these very attractions which had excited the tourists to visit them.

The destruction caused by tardy and haphazard development has awakened the societies to the paramount need for planning of tourism development based on scientific research of requirements of the travel market and absorptive capacities of the tourist's destination spots. The process of planning inevitably involves identifying certain areas or locations with a long term tourist potential. Mass tourism demands environmental resources in a big way and with the problem of mass tourism arises the issue of protecting and conserving the ecological system which the tourists erode unintentionally. It is, therefore, necessary that while planning the construction of new hotels, buildings, roads, etc. due consideration should be paid to the fragile beauty and unique natural setting. Every new construction in that area should be environment oriented and adequate facility for garbage and dirt disposal should be made. The ecology of any site, no matter how small, is an integral part of the environment. Simple adjustments to a modern landscape such as planting of flowers and trees re-establish the ecological integrity. There should be, thus, a close co-ordination amongst the planners, ecologists and technocrats to develop new spots for tourism.

Before demarcating a tourist spot, a proper site study should be undertaken. At the outset, an identification of the various pollutants that would go with the tourists should be done and steps be taken to monitor their disposal effectively. Secondly, the allied industries of the tourism industry that suffocat the environment should be identified and sidelined. In such spots where automobiles may cause disruption, vehicular movement should be banned or at least restricted. At another level, the Hotel Licensing Methodology must include certain surrounding green areas as a precondition. Furthermore, at the site itself, there should be mass participation. Once the public is made aware of the benefits of a sound ecology and environment then there would be an overall change in the attitude of the tourists. It should be highlighted that tourism be considered an ally and not an adversary in conserving ecology. Finally, there should be the introduction of planning procedures and controls to ensure good management of the environment. Once the site becomes a tourist spot, the popularity of its attractions demand management controls which might not have seemed necessary without tourism.

Q5. Tourism need not to be banned from environmentally fragile areas. Comment.

Ans. Despite pressing demographic and economic needs, India is still left with some of the wildest landscapes of the world and some of the relatively better preserved areas are found in Uttar Pradesh. This is because of two reasons. Firstly, Uttar Pradesh took the lead in the modern conservation movement in India. The submountain tract of the U.P. Himalayas had been constituted into a reserved forest, as early as 1879. Moreover, the establishment of India's first National Parks, in 1935 saved wildlife from destruction and extinction in this part of the Himalayas. The concept of National Parks is important both for conservation and tourism. It feeds into both. Actually, National Parks are a part of a large tourism and conservation system and are interdependent. Unquestionably, one of the greatest lures India has for the foreign tourists is its unique image as the home of the tiger, the panther and the cobra.

There are numerous adventure tourism options in India which provide outlets for an experience in the mountains, rivers, forests or on the beaches. But, by their very nature such destinations are environmentally fragile, their attractiveness being endangered by visitors well above the viable carrying capacity. Moreover, successful conservation of natural areas can no longer be defined by simply making the area off-limit to human population, it is here that conservations seek to make tourism a genuine conservation tool.

Conservationists believe that it is only through exposure of tourists and visitors of all ages and background to the beauty and bounty of nature in its unspoilt splendours that people can be near the nature and be educated and motivated to maintain ecological balance and be environmentally friendly. Tourism can act as a watchdog over the environment. The Valley of Flowers for example is a Valley of Flowers because of tourist boom. If there would be a ban on tourism there, it would just decay and become a pasture land for grazing.

Institutional planning, primarily at the site scale in imperative for promoting tourism. Tourism depends on the identification and protection of natural and cultural resources as it does upon the building of facilities. A rare and exemplary case is that of a resort complex business organization that operates in South Carolina, Puerto Rico and Florida. It not only is an integral part of tourism but includes conservation. A major division deals only with "environmental systems development".

If tourism is well planned, developed and managed, it can generate important positive environmental impacts. These include the following :

• Helps justify and pay for conservation of important natural areas and wildlife, including marine environments and development of national and regional parks and reserves, because these are major attractions for tourists. This is an especially significant benefit in countries with limited resources for undertaking environmental conservation.

• Helps justify and pay for the conservation of archaeological and historic sites as attractions for tourists. Otherwise many of these sites would be allowed to deteriorate or disappear. Even entire historic districts in towns and cities are being conserved and developed for tourism.

• Helps improve the environmental quality of areas because tourists like to visit places that are attractive, clean and not polluted. Tourism provides the incentive to clean up environments through controlling air, water, noise and visual pollution, reducing congestion and upgrading overall appearance with suitable landscaping and building design. Also, well sited and designed tourist facilities themselves can contribute to the attractive appearance of both urban and rural environments. Improvement of infrastructure, especially of water supply and sewage and solid waste disposal, also contributes to improve environmental quality.

• Increases local environmental awareness when residents and especially young people, observe tourists' interests in conservation. They then begin to realize the importance of conservation in their areas.

Q6. What do you mean by regional imbalance? What are the main causes of regional imbalance?

Ans. The concept of regional development may be described in the following words: a systematic and planned effort to bring about equality between various geographical segments in such a way that the indicators listed below don't reveal wide variations :

- income per capita,
- availability of wage and goods,
- agricultural and industrial output,
- employment opportunities, and
- general standard of living (including infrastructure facilities).

Such type of equalisation effort has its own built-in limitation. Some regions, because of historical and locational factors, would always enjoy certain advantages vis-a-vis other regions. What we are supposed to do, however, is to provide the necessary external support so that the potential for growth in other regions may also be fully realised? The biggest hurdle in the development of backward areas as tourist centres, is the lack of infrastructural support viz., roads, railways, airways, telephone, telex, facilities etc.

It is now a real perception that underdeveloped regions can be greatly upgraded through planned programme and policies. We may cite for example, the case of Khajuraho. About forty years ago, Khajuraho was a remote and unknown village. Today it finds a place on the world tourism map and attracts each year thousands of tourists. The tourists visit this place by air, rail and road transport throughout the year to see and appreciate the architectural marvel that temples are and erotic sculptures belonging to Chandela kings between 9th to 13th centuries A.D. As a result the place has provided employment to hundreds of local people and thus helped in redressing somewhat regional imbalances.

In this way many such areas of varied tourist interest where industrial development is out of question due to lack of raw material or other resources can be developed through proper planning. Such development would provide lot of jobs for unskilled workers and thus increase the prosperity of the region.

In the following sections we have taken a stock of regional disparities in this regard, primarily from a national perspective. We have suggested some of the growth possibilities too from the point of view of tourism planning.

(1) Natural Imbalances: Different regions of a potential tourist area are endowed with uneven distribution of resources – natural, human and other location advantages. Even regions having similar land resources may differ in landscape, topography, climatic conditions etc. Regions placed in more advantageous position attract development or progress on a preferential scale. Thus the process of development starts first in regions endowed with natural attractions or advantages. As the development process advances, the investment opportunities and mobility of tourists increase due to availability of infrastructural facilities, markets, skilled labour etc. This gives rise to a curious phenomenon whereby the resources from the regions less developed or not developed of all begin to flow of those sectors where such development has started. The backward regions thereby get their resources drained gradually and the developed regions prosper at the cost of former. The gap between advantaged and unfavourably placed regions gets widened with every stage of development. One of the possibilities, however, is that the advanced regions create stimulus for development in their hinterland. But the gap we are talking about between the two would even then remain.

(2) Created Imbalances: Created imbalances emerge from a wilful or otherwise ignorance on the part of policy makers who pay little attention to regional resources while formulating and executing developmental plans. Generally an argument generally put forward by people in support of lopsided policies reads: in view of limited resources and their uneven distribution over space it is not possible to develop every region at the same time on the same line or scale. They further argue that in a developing economy it would be proper to invest limited resources in a limited number of developmental centres, which have got better facilities for development. Such investment would create adequate surplus for the development of surrounding backward regions. It would help to maintain the economic efficiency on the one hand and maximum utilisation of resources on the other hand. Under this system of development strategy some regions are favoured while the development of other regions is put in abeyance for a long time. No serious attempt is made to develop the surrounding backward regions even after complete development of the first selected region. As a result the gap between regions widens giving impetus to regional imbalances.

(3) Historical Factors: Regional imbalances may be created due to historical factors attributed to either the initial advantages enjoyed by some regions or to the ill-conceived public investment programmes effected under colonial rule. The regions which attracted the attention of various rulers and administrators grew at a faster rate and thus became developed regions. The development of metropolitan cities like Bombay, Calcutta, Delhi and Madras can largely be attributed to historical factors. As a matter of fact we know that before 1912 Bengal, Bihar and Orissa were collectively known as Bengal province. Bengal attracted the attention of British Government due to some historical reasons but Bihar having rich natural and human resources never got their proper attention. As a result pace of development was much rapid in Bengal in comparison to Bihar and Orissa. This is one of the important factors that has still kept Bihar as a backward province of India and so it is one of the least developed tourist centering the country despite an extremely rich heritage of natural and historical attraction features.

Q7. How tourism can help in the minimisation of regional disparities?

Ans. The balanced socio-economic development of a region requires proper planning. It should be based on maximum utilisation of resources in a rational way to lure more and more tourists but without jeopardizing the interest of surrounding regions. We are aware of the fact that tourism industry has enough potential to generate employment and economic growth even in backward regions. If we are able to channelise this potential, it shall help to mitigate regional imbalances. Apart from direct employment created in hotels, restaurants, tourists shop, travel agencies and transportation, the industry also generates **Employment Multiplier Effect** by providing employment opportunities in the ancillary sectors such as handlooms, handicrafts, art and crafts, crockery, furnishings and many others.

Once a tourist centre is established firmly it generates a continuous movement of population, goods and money. The excess of inner movement makes the expansion and enlargement of the region imperative in turn stimulating the formation of new sub-areas of tourist interest. These areas further act as a centre of attraction around which different residential and goods supply zones are formed. The local population may, from this, derive considerable benefits due to new and improved infrastructure. It is thus important for the tourism planning to adopt a systematic and holistic approach to development. Decision makers need to assess the character of their current local environment in order to establish and carry out the kinds of change which they feel would be beneficial socially, culturally and economically. The end result would be better environment and a stronger tourist industry.

Need for a Policy: We have seen in the above discussion as to how tourism can be helpful in redressing regional imbalances in an effective way. At the same time though the necessity of a proper perspective on policy has been strongly felt for the desired result. The basic thrust of such strategy should be aimed at increasing the rate of growth ensuring simultaneously that the highest and lowest pockets of development come closer rather than the gap between them enlarging. The plan should aim at taking a region to that stage of development, where it becomes self-sufficient, can generate savings, attract capital from outside and thus starts growing automatically.

Since the number of backward regions will be very large, it may not be worthwhile to distribute limited resources in all regions. A thin distribution of resources is not likely to have a marked impact on the development of these regions. For an intensive development a limited number of regions have to be selected. This will require survey of the region by a team of experts consisting of conservationists, bio-scientists, environmental geologists, anthropologists, tourism planners etc. who should in the first instance prepare an inventory of natural areas. A variety of natural areas should be selected, ranging from those that should be maintained unperturbed, forever wild, where public access should be limited and areas which should be preserved for intensive recreational use with varied facilities. If such policies are at work there will be fewer problems in realising the objective of rapid tourism growth and balanced regional development. Since rapid growth will generate large surplus, the capacity of the economy to divert more resources to the backward areas will also increase. In order to reduce the widening gap between the levels of living in different regions, a phased programme of development shall have to be formulated.

Q8. Give some tips for balanced development.

Ans. On the basis of the discussion held in the preceding **sections** it is clear that for an overall tourism growth different regions in the country need to be developed equitably. Here we shall give you some important tips in this regard. While we do not propose to be prescriptive, a tourism development programme, in general, may include the following measures:

- Regions with tourism potential but lacking in agricultural and industrial resources should be selected first and then economic benefits of tourism development in such areas be evaluated. On the basis of such evaluations priority relation and input for these undeveloped areas in the tourism master plan may be fixed.
- The most backward cluster need not necessarily be taken up first for an intensive development. Selection should be based on their development potential. Such potentialities can be determined in terms of supply of water, power, transport and communication and the location of tourist attractions e.g. historical sites and natural attractions, etc.
- Planning should be made in an integrated way to avoid, as far as possible, disparities in the standard of amenities for visitors and that of the local population.
- Tourism planning should not be exclusively left to private enterprises in search of profit. Government must actively participate in it.
- Emphasis should be laid on the maintenance and encouragement of social and cultural basis of life of local people including the preservation and best use of a region's natural resources.
- Regional Tourist Boards or any other body on similar lines should be organised to coordinate, within the regions, all activities of a tourist nature and to maintain relations with other regional centres engaged in the same nature of work.

Q9. What are the alternative measures of conservation?

Ans. The task of conservation and creation of desirable environment has become a difficult objective. Highrise buildings, pollution, depletion of resources, congestion, etc. have made tourism a bad name. It is therefore necessary to discuss in detail the factors that should be taken into consideration before formulating the plan and policy of any tourism development activity. Following guidelines are suggestive of such considerations:

(i) Allocation of land use according to its potential is a must. Areas with tourism potential but lacking in agricultural and industrial resources should be selected and economic benefits of such areas should be evaluated periodically. On the basis of this evaluation relative priority and inputs for these underdeveloped areas should be given.

(ii) Tourism development should be based on rational utilisation of resources. Excessive utilisation which leads to exhaustion or destruction of resources must not be allowed under in any circumstances. This inter-relationship between growth of tourism and ecology as a whole should be emphasised. Preservation of wildlife, forests, mountains and sea beaches should be given priority. Emphasis should be given on the use of renewable source of energy. Rare or non-renewable sources should not be used. Scientific but environment friendly technology, should be used for utilisation of resources.

(iii) Proper planning of tourism and a coordination with other related branches is the essence of a property managed tourist development. Constant monitoring and periodic assessment of the situation should be carried out which could alert us to the forthcoming danger. The accepted policies of conservation should be promoted to maintain the saturation capacity of the area concerned. Through a careful planning the man-made and natural endowments can be blended together to satisfy even the most stringent demands.

(iv) Top priority must be given to meet the basic human needs. In doing so local residents must be involved because they know better how to manage their resources efficiently. Such involvement can help us in minimizing the impact on resources to ensure environment's sustained productivity.

(v) To make tourism more viable it is necessary to promote professionalism and management skill in this industry. Establishment of training programme centres at different levels can be set up. In doing so, the conservation of resources as well as growth of tourism can be better achieved.

(vi) Selection and classification of natural resources areas should be made on their potentiality and sustainable capacity. We may follows the pattern given below:

First category: Such areas should be maintained unpertubed forever. They should not be used under any circumstances.

Second category: Public access to such areas should be limited one. They should be known as semi reserved areas.

Third category: Intensive recreation can be made in such areas but they should not be used in a haphazard or irrational way.

Such categorisation helps not only in preservation of resources but it also increases the beauty of places along with their sustainable capacity.

(vii) For conservation it is necessary to promote:

- biological and cultural diversity,
- decentralised planning,

- utilisation of multiple value systems,
- simple technology, and
- use of indigenous management.

Application of such strategies would result in radical changes in social, economic and environmental aspects of life.

(viii) There is an urgent need for a change in our attitude and approach towards utilisation of resources. Recreation resources should be regarded as precious patrimony of nature and conservernism should not be the guiding philosophy of its utilisation. Resources should be projected as the most valuable asset for our common future.

Policy and Infrastructure

Q1. What were the objectives of national tourism policy 1982?

Ans. The first ever Tourism Policy was announced by the Government of India in November 1982. It took ten long years for the Government to feel the need to come up with a possible improvement over this. Thus the National Action Plan for Tourism was announced in May 1992. Between these two policy statements, various legislative and executive measures were brought about. In particular, the report of the National Committee on Tourism, submitted in 1988 needs special mention. In addition, two five-year plans - the Seventh and the Eighth - provided the basic perspective framework for operational initiatives.

The Seventh Plan advocated a two-pronged thrust in the area of development of tourism, viz., to vigorously promote domestic tourism and to diversify overseas tourism in India. While laying stress on creation of beach resorts, conducting of conventions, conferences, winter sports and trekking, the overall intention was to diversify options available for foreign tourists. The Tourism Policy, 1982 was more an aggressive statement in marketing than a perspective plan for development. Its main thrust was aimed at presenting India to the foreigners as the ultimate holiday resort. With a view to reach this destination, the following measures were suggested by the Policy :

1. To take full advantage of the national heritage in arriving at a popular campaign for attracting tourists;

2. To promote tourist resorts and make India a destination of holiday resorts;

3. To grant the status of an export industry to tourism;

4. To adopt a selective approach to develop few tourist circuits; and,

5. To invite private sector participation into the sector.

The Planning Commission recognised tourism as an industry by June 1982. However, it took ten years to make most of the States to fall in line and accord the same status within their legislative framework. At the beginning of the Eighth Plan (1992-97), 15 States and 3 Union Territories had declared tourism as an industry. Four States had declared hotels as an industry. The National Committee on Tourism was set up in July 1986 by the Planning Commission to prepare a perspective plan for the sector. Within the broad framework of the Seventh Plan, the Committee had to evolve a perspective plan for the coming years.

The Committee, headed by Mr. Mohammed Yunus, submitted its recommendations in November 1987. The list of Members was as impressive Mr. S.K. Mishra (Secretary, Department of Tourism), Mrs. Kapila Vatsayan, Mr. K.L. Thapar, Mr. Rajan Jaitley, Mr. A.B. Kerker, Mr. R.K. Puri and Mr Pran Seth. The Committee in its Report recommended that the existing Department of Tourism be replaced by a National Tourism Board. It suggested that there be a separate cadre of Indian Tourism Service to look after the functioning of the Board. It also submitted proposals for partial privatisation of the two airlines owned by the Union Government.

By September, 1987, the Central Government declared more concessions for the sector: these included tax exemption on foreign exchange earnings from tourism (a 50% reduction on rupee earnings and a 100% reduction on earnings in dollars), a drastic reduction in tariff on import of capital goods, and concessional finance at the rate of 1 to 5% per annum.

The Tourism Development Finance Corporation was set up in 1987 with a corpus fund of Rs. 100 crores. Until then, the sector was financed on commercial lines by the Industrial Development Bank of India, Industrial Credit and Investment Corporation of India and other commercial banks. The National Action Plan for Tourism, published in May 1992, and tabled in the Lok Sabha on 5 May 1992, charts 7 objectives as central concerns of the Ministry:

- socio-economic development of areas;
- increasing employment opportunities;
- developing domestic tourism for the budget category;
- preserving national heritage and environment;
- development of international tourism;
- diversification of the tourism product.,
- and, increase in India's share in world tourism (from the present 0.4% to 1% during next 5 years)

As per the Action Plan, foreign exchange earnings are estimated to increase from Rs.10,000 crores in 1992 to Rs.24,000 crores by 2000 AD. Simultaneously, the Plan aims at increasing employment in tourism to 28 million from the present 14 million. Hotel accommodation is to be increased from 44,400 rooms to 1,20,000 by 3 years. Other provisions in the Action Plan include a discontinuance of subsidies to star hotels, encouraging foreign investment in tourism and the setting up of a convention city for developing convention tourism.

The Action Plan envisages the development of Special Tourism Areas on lines of export processing zones. Special Central assistance is to be provided for the States to improve the infrastructural facilities at pilgrimage places. It proposes to set up a National Culinary Institute, and projects a liberalised framework for recognition of travel agents and tour operators.

The Eighth Plan document makes a special mention that the future expansion of tourism should be achieved mainly by private sector participation. The thrust areas as enumerated in the Plan include development of selected tourist places, diversification from cultural related tourism to holiday and leisure tourism, development of trekking, winter sports, wildlife and beach resort tourism, exploring new source markets, restoration of national heritage projects, launching of national image building, providing inexpensive accommodation in different tourist centres, improving service efficiency in public sector corporations and streamlining of facilitation procedures at airports. The Eighth Plan aims at luring the high spending tourists from Europe and USA. It also envisages a 'master plan' to integrate area plans with development of tourism. This is envisaged to ensure employment opportunities for the local population.

In April 1993, the Government announced further measures aimed at export promotion. The existing Export Promotion of Capital Goods Scheme (EPCG) was extended to tourism and related services. Against the existing 35%, the tourism sector would now pay an excise duty of 15% only on capital goods import, subject to an export obligation of 4 times the cargo, insurance and freight (CIF) value of imports. With an obligation period of five years, this came as a boon to the hotel industry. The cost of construction had also come down by 20%. In addition to the above policy pronouncements by the Union Government, our planners had envisaged the possibilities of developing specific regions on a zonal plank. Special area programmes like the Hill Area Development Programme and the Western Ghats Development Programme form part of the overall national plan.

The Eighth Plan document stipulates that the strategy in such designated special areas is to devise suitable location-specific solutions, so as to reverse the process of degradation of natural resources and ensure sustainable development. This approach perhaps needs to be integrated into the project of special tourism areas, now being made popular by the Government. Administrative Control and Developmental Compromises The federal principles enshrined in the Indian Constitution require that the tourism sector be treated as a State subject. As such, the Department of Tourism (under the Ministry of Civil Aviation and Tourism at the Centre) undertakes certain promotional and developmental activities with a view to enhance the sectoral potential.

The Department has certain regulatory functions to perform involving the hotel industry, travel agencies and tourist operators. Over the years, there has been considerable erosion of powers so far as State Governments are concerned. The sustained campaign for privatisation in all the policy documents has left limited space of operation for the States. The public sector is increasingly being perceived as an agent of inertia than of change and hence the pressure for a hands-off policy. On the other hand, the Union Government has been usurping the powers of the State with some pretext or the other.

Promotion schemes, designed at the Centre, are transferred for implementation at the State level. The special Central Assistance, for example, granted for the development of infrastructure at the pilgrim centres, carries with it a pre-defined scheme and mode of execution. Furthermore, there are occasions when the Centre forces the State Governments to extend certain subsidies and concessions to the sector. The terms of such concessions would have been fixed by the Centre and the States would have no choice but to fall in line.

For example, during the State tourism minister's conference in December 1991, the States were urged to freeze water and electricity rates for 10 years. They were also asked to exempt certain hotels from local and state taxes for 10 years. Seventeen circuits and destinations were identified under the National Action Plan for development through Central assistance and investment by the States and the private sector. The centres were identified by the Centre and the States were asked to do the needful. There were also times when the federal division of power resulted in operational contradictions. For instance, by 1989, many foreign hotel chains like Hilton, Hyatt, Penta and Kempinski had applied for licenses for investing in India. However, the revenue departments of the respective States failed to locate and allocate land for the construction of hotels.

The scheme, thus, fell flat. Curiously, the Union Government was not hesitant to make use of Constitutional provisions when it suited its interests. As has been stated earlier, the Yunus Committee had suggested the creation of the Tourism Board on lines of the existing Railway Board. (Perhaps, it was the brainchild of Mr. K.L. Thapar, then adviser to the Planning Commission, in charge of Transport and Tourism Sector. Being from the Railway Service, it is not surprising that Thapar thought about a 'Tourism Board'). To begin with, the empowered committee of secretaries challenged the idea of creation of a Board. It was said that the Railway Board as an independent entity was created for historical reasons. It would be difficult for tourism to be looked after by a Board, because legally the sector would come under the Industrial (Development) Act. It was also found that such a Board would not be viable financially. In 1991, the think-tank on tourism created by Minister Madhavarao Scindia rejected the idea of a Board in toto. It was emphasised that the Board cannot be in charge of a sector that is basically under the jurisdiction of the States! Scope for Federal Interventions

The previous section highlights the dubious ways by which the Centre attempts to hijack initiatives at the State-level. This is achieved essentially by threatening to curtail Central assistance or by cajoling through promises of more financial aid. It is common knowledge that the resource-base of the States is very narrow, making them vulnerable at the negotiating table. However, States have the freedom to resist the Centre's strong- arm tactics, provided State assemblies stand-by the interests of the States. For instance, State legislatures may refuse to freeze water and electricity rates on grounds of revenue generation. In that event, the concerned Chief Minister or the Minister of Tourism may convey the intensity of resistance that he is confronted with, and thus refuse to comply with the Centre's diktats. It is heartening to realise that the States have often exercised their power of self-determination and consequently refused to toe the line drawn by the Centre. This offers enough scope for possible interventions at the federal strata of our political system in matters of policy formulation. Privatisation and its Implications According to the Approach Paper to the Seventh Plan, " there is a vast potential for development of tourism in the country.

Tourism should be accorded the status of an industry. Private sector investment will have to be encouraged in developing tourism and public sector investments should be focused only on development of support infrastructure". Thus the seeds of private initiatives were sown during the Seventh Plan. The Government took the matter of privatising the tourism sector seriously by 1988. It was during the tenure of Mr. S.K. Mishra as Tourism Secretary that the talk of inviting private investment into the sector began. The Government permitted foreign equity participation up to 5 1 %in tourism projects. Foreign charters were allowed to operate in the country for the first time. Foreign companies were allowed to repatriate their profits to the extent of 3%. The structural adjustment programme, initiated in June, 1992, paved the way for privatisation in almost all sectors of the economy.

The Annual Plan (1992-93) document emphatically enunciated the Government's position vis-a-vis tourism: "The future growth of tourism will have to be achieved mainly through private initiative. The State will contribute to tourism by planning broad strategy of development, provision of monetary and fiscal incentives to catalyse private sector investment." The process of privatisation brought in its wake big investments and private involvement at various levels. As an offshoot, environmental considerations were thrown to the winds and there were instances of large scale human rights violation. The self-correcting nature of policy made provisions for stricter controls in this regard. More seriously, privatisation meant alienation of the majority of our population and their deprivation. Employment generated in tourism is generally seasonal and ill paid.

The private sector- induced pockets of tourism had the potential of turning into centres of pollution, drug trafficking and prostitution. Industry status granted to Tourism the Seventh Plan proposed that tourism be declared an industry. However, it took time for the States to implement this, even though they agreed in principle. The smokeless industry had the advantage of generating maximum value-added, because of low-cost inputs. The Tourism Policy Statement carried certain provisions in favour of the hotel industry. It stated that there should be provision for depreciation in the balance sheets of hotels. Being an export industry, hotels were to be given excise concessions. The provisions of the Monopolies and Restrictive Trade Practices (MRTP) Act were relaxed for hotels, because any hotel with 300 or more rooms would have incurred an investment of Rs. 25 crores.

The document also hinted at lower tariffs for power and water and regulations for easy import of equipment. As a follow-up, hotel and shipping were added to the list of 27 industries exempted from Section 22 A of the MRTP Act. The consequences of declaring tourism as an industry need to be studied in detail. It is not possible to capture its implications in an exploratory work like this. However, it is obvious that the private sector has primarily benefited to a great extent by this measure. Importing Modifications to Policies We have earlier stated that the arena of policy formulation should be self-evaluating and self-correcting. In the case of Tourism Policy, this has proved to be the plus point. As an illustration, the Policy statement of 1982 made no mention of infrastructure development.

The successive governments at the Centre failed to create proper tourism infrastructure, thus resulting in loss of traffic. This lacuna was corrected in the National Action Plan. However, much of this change was due to intensive lobbying by such agencies like the Indian Association of Tour Operators (IATO), the Travel Agents Association of India (TAAI) and the Indian Hotels and Restaurants Association (IHRA). It is for the voluntary agencies and pro-people forces to exploit the avenue of lobbying at various levels. The environmental implications of tourism development did not form part of the 1982 Policy. The consequences are too obvious to be written about. However, the NAP, 1992 did carry specific provisions for environmental protection and harnessing. From Policy to Cartooning Policy statements may also lead to justifiable flights of fantasy. Two examples would illustrate how policies were used to justify stands taken by the politicians: a. Shri Devi Lal, the then Deputy Prime Minister wanted a 50% discount for farmers at Five Star Hotels run by India Tourism Development Corporation. The scheme had teething problems since it was not easy to distinguish a farmer from amongst the clients who visit such hotels. However, on his insistence, the so-called CHAUPALs recreated a village ambience to the amazement of foreign tourists, who took a liking for them. b. Pursuing the objective of the Seventh Plan to diversify overseas tourism to its logical conclusion was what prompted Jagdish Tytler to float the idea of casinos. It was an attempt to provide some entertainment for foreigners during the evenings. It was said that Indian classical music would not provide much needed entertainment for foreign guests because the artists spend a lot of time tuning their instruments! Folk dances get over in an hour. So much for our much touted cultural diversity.

It is embarrassing to believe that the consultative committee attached to the Ministry of Civil Aviation and Tourism had endorsed the idea. Conclusion broadly, our successive policy pronouncements in the realm of tourism falls within the "liberalising" framework of the macro-economic policy environment. The Finance Bill, 1988, had assured 50% tax exemption on foreign exchange earnings in the sector, and a further 50% exemption if re-invested. In effect, it amounts to 100% tax concession. Luxury hotels enjoy exemptions of all kinds with a view to encourage tourism earnings. These tax exemptions coupled with provision of soft loans to the sector led to a boom in the tourism related private investment. The Economic Survey 1991-92 aptly summarises the ultimate aim of such incentives for private sector participation :

"The Government has tried to expand the economic space in which the people can exercise their initiative and ingenuity. It hopes to do more to expand their opportunities, to enhance their potential. But what shape the economy takes ultimately depends on what the people make of it. In that sense, the future is in their hands." We should not forget that tourism is an industry which emerges in the context of unresolved socio-economic structural issues, such as land distribution patterns or the take over of traditional occupations by modem mechanised capital. Tourism happens to be a source of livelihood for millions in India and aggressive privatisation does not ensure social and economic safety nets. In the face of the unhindered entry of international capital and successive alienation, perhaps, it is difficult to agree that "the future is in our hands"

Q2. Did the perspective plan for tourism in 1988 recommend complete takeover of tourism industry by state?

Ans. In 1988 Government (Planning Commission) appointed a National Committee on Tourism under the chairmanship of Shri Mohammed Yunus, Chairman, Trade Fair Authority of India, to prepare a perspective plan for development of tourism in India. The committee submitted its recommendations in May 1988, after a detailed analysis of

- the role of tourism in the socio-economic development, dynamics of tourism industry and strategic path,
- profile of international tourism in India,
- international tourism and its prospects,

- tourist accommodation and lodging,
- travel trade, marketing and export services, tourism transport linkages,
- upgradation for development of human resource for the tourism sector and
- the ecological aspects of tourism.

Accommodations:

(a) A need for reappraisal of the future role of the state in tourism development and the extent of its participation. It is neither necessary for feasible for the State to continue with larger investments in the tourism sector. The development of this industry should best be left to the initiative of the private sector.

(b) The State should concentrate on building growth strategies of tourism development, provision of fiscal and monitoring incentives to channelise private sector investments and devising an effective regulatory and supervisory mechanism to protect the interest of the industry and the consumer.

(c) The development strategy for tourism sector should be based on the principle of low cost economy, higher levels of productivity, improvement in efficiency and competition.

(d) An estimated one lakh hotel rooms will be required by the end of the century.

(e) The Tourism Finance Corporation should be set up with an initial equity of Rs. 100.00 crores.

(f) Regulation of tariffs in hotel sector should be removed.

(g) Suitable incentives should be given to revive and maintain national heritages like old Havelies, Palaces etc.

As a result, it was estimated that the tourist arrivals will increase to 2.75-3 million by the year 2000 A.D. Foreign exchange worth Rs. 4,000 crores – 5,000 crores can be earned by the year 2000 A.D. on 1986-87 prices.

Q3. What are the main objectives and recommendations of national action plan-1992?

Ans. National Action Plan for Tourism was presented to the Parliament in May, 1992. It outlined the importance of the industry in the global context and in the national context, its effect on employment generation, foreign exchange earnings etc. It recognised the great potential which existed in the country for the development of tourism and the tremendous scope for accelerated growth.

Following were some of the main objectives of the National Action Plan of 1992 :

- Socio-economic development of the area.
- Increase in the employment opportunities.

- Preservation of national heritage and environment.
- Optimisation of foreign exchange earnings through international tourism.
- Increase in India's share of world tourism.

After examining the state of infrastructure, other resources and the potential for growth, the Action Plan summarised following recommendations:

(i) Creation of Special Tourism Areas as notified zones for intensive investment and development.

(ii) Starting the Scheme for giving Assistance for Special Tourism Areas (ASTA) for providing finances for tourism and tourism related industry in specified areas/circuits.

(iii) Special category of Heritage Hotels/Health Resorts to be created and provided.

- technical/consultancy help
- loans for financial institutions
- interest subsidy
- marketing and operational expertise.

(iv) Tourist trains to be started on important tourist routes based on the success of Palace-on-Wheels.

(v) River cruises to be operated in specified circuits.

(vi) Revamping of foreign offices to make them more accountable in terms of specified targets.

(vii) Information revolution; information system to be revamped to provide positive projection of India in all leading markets.

(viii) Special airline/hotel packages for selected tourist destinations.

(ix) Provision of information counter for airlines, trains, hotels, tourist information at major international airports.

Q4. Examine the economic and fiscal impact of tourism policies.

Ans. Travel & Tourism's Economic Impact

Travel & Tourism – encompassing transport, accommodation, catering, recreation and services for visitors – is one of the world's highest priority industries and employers.

In India, Travel & Tourism's economic impact includes :

Total Demand : India Travel & Tourism is expected to generate INR1,846.3 bn (US$38.8 bn) of economic activity (Total Demand) in 2004, growing (nominal terms) to INR7,027.7 bn (US$90.4 bn) by 2014. Travel & Tourism Demand is expected to grow by 8.8% per annum, in real terms, between 2004 and 2014.

Employment : India T&T Economy employment is estimated at 24,456,600 jobs in 2004, 5.6% of total employment, or 1 in every 17.8 jobs.

By 2014, this should total 27,790,000 jobs, 5.7% of total employment or 1 in every 17.5 jobs. The 11,404,000 T&T Industry jobs account for 2.6% of total employment in 2004 and are forecast at 12,441,200 jobs or 2.6% of the total by 2014.

Gross Domestic Product : India's T&T Industry is expected to contribute 2.0 per cent to Gross Domestic Product (GDP) in 2004 (INR618.4 bn or US$13.0 bn), rising in nominal terms to INR2,002.3 bn or US$25.8 bn (2.1 per cent of total) by 2014. The T&T Economy contribution (percent of total) should rise from 4.9 per cent (INR1,477.4 bn or US$31.1 bn) to 5.2 per cent (INR4,972.5 bn or US$64.0 bn) in this same period.

Capital Investment : India Travel & Tourism capital investment is estimated at INR485.3 bn, US$10.2 bn or 7.2 per cent of total investment in year 2004. By 2014, this should reach INR1,663.9 bn, US$21.4 bn or 7.8 per cent of total.

Personal And Business Travel & Tourism : India Personal Travel & Tourism is estimated at INR927.3 bn, US$19.5 bn or 5.0 per cent of total personal consumption in year 2004. By 2014, this should reach INR3,612.9 bn, US$46.5 bn or 6.1 per cent of total consumption. India Business Travel is estimated at INR114.5 bn, US$2.4 bn in year 2004. By 2014, this should reach INR387.4 bn or US$5.0 bn.

Exports : Visitor Exports play an important development role for the resident Travel & Tourism Economy. India Travel & Tourism is expected to generate 6.7 per cent of total exports (INR283.2 bn or US$6.0 bn) in 2004, growing (nominal terms) to INR1,267.3 bn or US$16.3 bn (5.4 per cent of total) in 2014.

Fiscal and Financial Incentives: The Tourism Finance Corporation of India has been set up specifically to provide loan assistance to entrepreneurs.

The approved hotels upto 3 star category set-up in places other than the four metropolitan cities are eligible for 3% interest subsidy on loans taken from specified financial institutions and an enhanced subsidy of 5% is available for such hotels constructed in the travel circuits and destination identified for intensive development in the NAPT (National Action Plan for Tourism and for heritage hotels).

In addition to interest subsidy, a new scheme of capital subsidy has been recently introduced for 'heritage hotel'. Under this scheme, a capital subsidy of Rs. 5 lakhs or 10% of the capital cost, whichever is less, is available for development of any monument/structure over 75 years old into a heritage hotel. A major fiscal incentive available to tourism industries is the exemption of profits derived from foreign exchange earnings from income tax – the first 50% is also exempt if re-invested in tourism.

Q5. Discuss the impact of tourism policies on accommodation and transport.

Ans. Accommodation : Accommodation of quality is basic infrastructure for the development of Tourism. The Ministry of Tourism approves hotels from the point of view of their suitability for international tourists. Various incentives and benefits are linked to such approvals. As on September, 1999 there were 1229 hotels with 68032 rooms and on the approved list of Ministry of Tourism. Break up of these hotels category wise is as below:

Star Category	No. of Hotels	No. of Rooms
5-Star Deluxe	55	12948
5-Star	50	6654
4-Star	79	6131
Heritage Hotels	62	1916
3-Star	316	15590
2-Star	324	11391
1-Star	146	5059
To be classified	197	8307

Transport: Deregulation and Privatisation: It is important to note that the domestic airlines have been de-regulated by amending the Air Corporation Act. As many as 17 Private Airlines are competing for the domestic Indian travellers and foreign travellers within India. However, not much progress has been made regarding privatisation of Air India.

India Tourism Development Corporation (ITDC) has been partially privatised by dis-investing 10% equity to the public. Some of the State Tourism Development Corporations have also started privatisation on these lines. Some State Tourism Development Corporation hotels/resorts are leased out to private sector and some State Tourism Development Corporations have entered into joint venture agreements with private sector.

5 more tourist trains like Palace on Wheels are being introduced by Indian Railways with private participation. Highways are being privatised on **BOT** basis. Even Airports are being built with private sector participation in places like Cochin and Bangalore.

Q6. Discuss the impact on tourist and tourism?

Ans. The remarkable increase in the number of tourist has been achieved as a result of a policy framework.

Tourist Arrivals in India (1997 to 2001)									
				Jan. to Dec.		% Change			
Country of Nationality	1997	1998	1999	2000	2001	1998/97	1999/98	2000/99	2001/00
Australia	50,647	57,807	73,041	53,995	52,691	14.1	26.4	23.8	-2.4
American Somoa	312	3,651	4,188	2,992	-	1,070.20	14.7	-28.6	-
New Zealand	11,409	14,720	18,324	11,551	11,700	29	24.5	-22.4	1.3
Fiji	1,379	1,917	3,000	1,541	1,422	39	56.5	-11.2	-7.7
Others	1,640	2,117	2,684	480	291	29.1	26.8	47.2	-
Total	65,387	80,212	1,01,237	70,559	66,104	22.7	26.2	12.9	-2.2
Grand Total	19,73,647	19,74,815	20,25,031	21,52,926	25,37,282	0.1	2.5	6.3	-4.2

Classification of Tourists According to Purpose of Visit -2001					
Country of Nationality	Arrivals (In Number)	Proportion to the Total (%)			
		Business (In Number)	Conference	Education & Employment	Tourism & Others
South-East Asia					
Indonesia	7767	5	0.5	0.2	94.3
Malaysia	57869	2.1	0.1	0.1	97.7
Philippines	7199	5.5	0.5	0.3	93.7
Singapore	42824	5.8	0.2	0.1	93.9
Thailand	18623	2.1	0.2	0.4	97.3
Total	139975	3.5	0.2	0.2	96.1
Australasia					
Australia	52691	4.7	0.3	0.1	94.9
NewZeland	11700	4.1	0.4	0.1	95.4
Others	90	2.2	1.1	0	96.7
Total	64481	4.6	0.3	0.1	95
Grand Total	2537282	2.8	0.1	0.2	96.9

Indian visitors to Australia 1992 - 2002

	Visitors '000	% Change
1992	9.6	-
1993	9.7	10.4
1994	12.1	24.7
1995	17.1	41.3
1996	21.3	24.6
1997	26.1	22.5
1998	29.4	12.6
1999	33.6	14.3
2000	41.5	23.5
2001	48.2	16.1
2002	45	-6.6

Indian visitors to Australia have been growing regularly except for the dip in 2002. Visitors could have been less due to the outbreak of SARS in 2002, which affected the whole tourism industry.

Domestic Tourism : For the development of domestic tourism, both the State Governments and Central Government are giving special incentives and concessions under plan assistance. Budget accommodation such as Yatri Niwases, Tourist Lodges etc. have been built all over India. Similarly for the promotion of pilgrim tourist Yatrikas, Dharamshalas etc. have been built in various pilgrim centres.

Youth and Adventure Tourism : Various schemes have been drawn up for promotion of Youth and Adventure tourism. Construction of Youth Hostel is part of the scheme to increase accommodation available to budget tourists and youth tourists. Various adventure tourist activities such as water sports, winter sports, aero sports, trekking and mountaineering etc. have been introduced in various States through the active cooperation of the State Tourism Development Corporations, State Tourism Departments and the Central Department of Tourism. In many cases the private sector is also actively involved in these activities.

In environmentally sensitive areas where permanent structures are not desirable, tented and temporary accommodation have been provided as part of the overall efforts to boost adventure tourism. Under Central assistance State Governments and Tourism Development Corporations have been given financial assistance for the purchase of tents, swiss cottages, etc. to be used for trekking, mountaineering, wild life activities, safari treks, river rafting etc.

Q7. Write a short note on tourism infrastructure.

Ans. Tourism involves activities of persons traveling to and staying in places outside their usual environment for leisure, business and other purposes. **Tourism Infrastructure** demands for goods and services, and the establishments which provide such services are considered as part of the **tourism industry**. Further, the **Tourism Infrastructure** also includes establishments whose products are mainly sold to visitors, though they do not form a major share of **tourist** consumption. Several infrastructure sectors like **power, telecommunication, water supply, roads** and some production sectors like travel items, sports equipment, photographic materials, medicines and cosmetics are included in this category along with **Tourism Infrastructure**. The **infrastructure for tourism** thus includes basic infrastructure components like **airports, railways, roads, waterways, electricity, water supply, drainage, sewerage, solid waste disposal systems** and **services**. Moreover, **facilities like accommodation, restaurants, recreational facilities** and **shopping facilities** also comes under the ambit of **Tourism Infrastructure**. Planning for sustainable development of **Tourism Infrastructure**, therefore, involves the integrated development of **basic infrastructure** and amenities along with all the **tourism facilities** in a balanced manner.

The basic requirements for the development of **Tourism Infrastructure** are :

Accommodation :

- Forest lodges
- Tented accommodation
- Tourist complexes/tourist lodges
- Wayside amenities
- Restaurants
- Tourist reception centers
- Pilgrim sheds/dormitories, etc. at pilgrimage centers

Tourist transport :

- Mini-buses, jeeps, elephants, etc. for wild life viewing.
- Cruise boats, ferry launchers, etc. for water transport.
- Tourist coaches in selected circuits.
- Special tourist trains.

The **Central Department of Tourism** meets almost the entire expenditure, except the cost of land and interior decoration in the case of construction projects. The **Central Government** provides 28% cost of the project and 12% is provided by the **State Governments**. The remaining 60% has to be raised as a loan from financial institutions or banks. It is expected that the **State Governments** would be able to mobilize more resources from financial institutions for investment in **Tourism Infrastructure.**

Q8. What are the special tourism product?

Ans. Having identified accommodation and transport as the significant entry points into the tourist infrastructure, it is now time to look at some other tourism product.

(1) Convention Tourism : Conventions and conferences have become important in all countries as multi-national companies spread their activities to the remotest locations of the world. India envisages the setting up of convention -cum-conference complexes and the first such destination is being developed in Bombay and Delhi is to follow. Bangalore in the South is also a destination to be developed for convention tourism. On a smaller scale country clubs and hotels are to strengthen their conference and convention facilities by creating telecom and other communication facilities to attract such business.

(2) Circuits/Destinations for concentrated development : 15 circuits/ destinations have been identified for concentrated development. These are :

- Kullu-Manali-Leh
- Gwalior-Shivpuri-Orcha-Khajuraho
- Bagdogra-Sikkim-Darjeeling-Kalimpong
- Bhubaneshwar-Puri-Konark
- Hyderabad-Nagarjunasagar-Tirupathi
- Madras-Masmallapuram-Pondicherry
- Rishikesh-Gangotri-Badrinath
- Indore-Ujjain-Mandu
- Jaisalmer-Jodhpur-Bikaner-Barmer
- Lakshadweep Islands
- Andaman Islands
- Manali
- Bekal Beach
- Muttukadu Beach
- Kangra

Facilities and infrastructure are to be developed in these circuits/destinations with central assistance and investment by State/private resources.

(3) Special Tourism Areas : The Government in collaboration with State Governments had notified a few Special Tourism Areas for intensive development of state of the art facilities for international tourists. These areas are to play the same role as export processing zones. The State Transport Authorities (S.T.A.'s) would have notified boundaries where land is to be allotted for hotels and tourism related industries at concessional rates to investors, according to a Master Plan. An area development authority set up by the State will administer the area with full delegation of powers, so that the preparation of the Master Plan and single window clearance facilities to investors can be provided. The state government will invest in basic infrastructure like roads, transport, terminals, wayside amenities, electricity, water, law and order and municipal services. The central government will provide support infrastructure like airports and airline links, communication and postal links, banking services and railway stations. Taxes and rates will be frozen for ten years by both Centre and States, in order to attract investment. The aim will be to attract foreign investment.

Island Tourism: It has been decided to selectively open islands to tourism, particularly Andamans and Lakshadweep. The carrying capacity and environment are however to be kept in mind. These destinations would be developed for high value and low volume tourism. A Tourism Development Fund is to be set up for equity support to investors and a coordinating body is to be set up to include State governments, Travel Trade and the Centre to coordinate all matters relating to tourism development.

Golf Tourism : This form of tourism is another popular development for the tourism planners, since golf courses are being opposed all over the world by resident populations on environmental grounds. The cost of golf is so high that its relocation has now become imperative and new destinations are transforming plantation and agricultural land into golf courses. The Tourism Ministry has also set aside 50 crores for upgrading existing golf courses in Bombay, Delhi, Jaipur and other locations. Historical golf courses developed by the British were located in areas that did not interfere with the livelihood of people. Modern international level courses are not only land intensive but the turf and the obstacles that are constructed destroy the natural verges and food chains in the area that is being transformed. Such courses are also developed with international expertise, which adds to the infrastructural cost. The above indicators of infrastructure for tourism are clearly defined in terms of the private market-dominated model that is now being pushed in the less and least developed economies.

Q9. How can an alternative model of development emerge?

Ans. People centered development is based on low cost and low intensity input planning and implementation in the hands of panchayats and municipalities who determine the carrying capacity and expansion of the activity. Investment is also to be determined at the local level with inputs in kind. The cost of tourism is therefore to be determined by the local population and not by the travel trade, which looks at costing from the international perspective and does not consider the unique or special quality of a new destination. The activity and the infrastructure on which it should be based is also to be determined at the local level, so that it is carried on at the sustainable level.

Tourism should be considered a people's developmental issue and it is the people who should evaluate its costs and benefits so that real transfer of income and exchange of culture can take place without the negative consequences of infrastructure being developed and controlled by national and international capitalist agencies. Appropriate and sustainable technologies and skills should be developed to ensure the minimum of displacement and alienation of communities and regions that have historical and traditional rights. Above all, decision making, planning and implementation must be transparent and involve all beneficiaries in as equal a manner as possible. If this is not done, there will be a feeling that development is being carried in the interests of those who consider the local population dispensable. As a result, tourism which depends on inter-personal subjectivities will face hostility.

Q10. What is the problem with negotiation as a system of dispute resolution?

Ans. There has been uncertainty and debate over the consequences of recreational use of natural resources and natural habitats. The debate reflects the break down in trust between people of the locality and Government planners. People feel powerless to influence policies and have begun to oppose the very policies they had once supported. It is a truism to state that without public support conservation policies are impossible to implement because conservation is often seen to be in contradiction with survival.

It is important therefore to develop methodologies that can help to resolve conflicts, gain public support and find a balance between the needs of the approached in several ways. The most popular method is to impose regulations, which are then strictly imposed. However, more interactive systems try to develop a consensus that helps the public to adapt its behaviour so that the negative impact of any developmental intervention can be reduced or corrected.

As society faces a growing complexity of environmental issues, an assessment of the way in which disputes can be resolved is useful :

- use negotiation to reconcile the disputants' underlying interests
- determine who is right and whose rights are being infringed
- determine which interests are more powerful and how they influence decision making.

The nature of a negotiated settlement of disputes, although time consuming, is more lasting in the long term. This is due to the following factors :

- it is a voluntary, face-to-face process
- its procedures are more informal and therefore make for better communication
- it protects the existing relationships between people and their resources and therefore their group and individual interests
- there is greater flexibility in designing a solution
- the outcomes are more predictable

- negotiations, being collaborative, are better than simple compromises, which are often repudiated.

Change as	Decision by	Decision by Authority	Decision by Force
arbitrator of decision making	negotiation		
avoidance mediation	cooperation	litigation	unilateral power play

The problem with any dispute resolution system will, however, depend on the willingness of the interested parties to enter negotiations, to get to the table and their perception of their relative strength and weakness in determining the outcome of the negotiations.

Q11. Can you throw light on disputes over the tiger show?

Ans. Environmentalists and the trade have come into conflict over the tiger show at Kanha and Bandhavagarh, which were prime attractions for international tourists. Mahouts used to track the tiger on their elephants, sending the information to the gate, so that tourists could be rushed to the location and taken off the road if the tiger was located in the grass. In this way the tourist was assured a view of the tiger, which was privileged over all other species, in a close to nature setting. The tour operator and the mahout were the beneficiaries of the system, because they could promote their services and ensure that the tourist did not go away disappointed. Environmentalists opposed this kind of viewing as contrived and invasive of the privacy of the animal. Poachers were also assisted in locating the tiger, which has now become an important trade item in the international market. Since than ban there is no guarantee for sighting the tiger and this promotes the theory that they are an endangered species. This is a fairly complex debate and the position of various groups is determined by their interests. Thus sighting of the tiger has now become a unique privilege. This issue has shown how conservation of the tiger has been given priority over the tourist business and to reorient the forest administration towards their primary purposes, the conservation of the species.

Q12. List the areas in which the Indian state has intervened to promote environmental impact control.

Ans. In India too the state has intervened significantly to protect its environment in wake of tourism. Regulation concerning the Tiger show or protection of animals are cases in point. The Indian Wildlife Protection Act of 1972 provides protection to much of the Indian fauna. As a consequence India has 66 national parks, 333 wild life sanctuaries and 35 zoological gardens. Under the Act severe penalties are imposed upon violators.

There are also specific acts regarding conservation and preservation which relate to both environment and heritage. These establish various environmental and heritage zones, offer special facilities to visitors and regulate visitor behavior.

The need to develop environmental impact control measures also means taking other developmental measures into account. Consequently these include:

(i) Installation of water supply, sewage treatment systems in tourism areas.

(ii) development of proper sanitary disposal of solid waste generated by hotels and other tourist facilities

(iii) careful management of visitor flows where necessary, application of visitor use controls at natural and cultural tourist destinations to avoid congestion and environmental deterioration of these places

(iv) Provision for Open spaces and parks and generous provision for suitable landscaping programmes in resorts and at tourist facilities.

(v) development and application of suitable land zoning regulations and site planning standards in tourism development areas, such as adequate setting back of buildings from beaches and roads, etc.

(vi) maintenance of environmental health and safety standards for both residents and tourists, especially to control environmentally – derived diseases and high accident rates resulting from traffic congestion, badly maintained vehicles, unsurveyed boats, fire and other hazards.

(vii) incorporation of energy conservation techniques in to the design of tourist facilities including solar energy.

(viii) formulation of an environmental impact assessment procedure to assess the impact of proposed development projects.

Apart from environment and health the State in India also intervenes through regulation concerning passport and visa requirements, special permits for restricted areas, custom regulations. Similarly law and order problems which could arise in the context of visitor – host interface are handled by the state.

Q13. Why did the colonial state pass environment regulations?

Ans. In India industry developed under the restrictions imposed on free trade by British colonial government. Therefore protective regulation was its foundation stone. The debate on the new liberalized, free – trading economy today needs to be understood in this context. There are both pulls and pushes to create a free trading private enterprise and also the counterpull of the foundation of protection under which the Indian industry itself came up.

The rules and laws regarding private sector therefore reflect these contrary pulls. Licensing laws were set up by the Indian state to direct the industry towards the concerns of the state. However these came in the way of entrepreneurship needs of the industry. Hence we see the dismantling of these laws today. Economists like Jagdish Bhagvati have recently argued that the concerns of free trade and environment can go together. Industry in today's liberalized regime is attempting a move towards such a direction.

Q14. What are the major impact of tourism legislation?

Ans. Tourism industry itself has undergone the fluctuation of such a change. From the stage of curious traders and oriental onlookers under colonialism the inflow from abroad has increased to diversity of cultural, heritage and eco tourists. This diversification has sustained under the larger debate of liberalization versus control which the rest of the industry has undergone.

Thus the foreign exchange regulations work within strict currency laws. Import and export of Indian currency is subject to strict controls. Similarly the license system has ensured that the small operators and entrepreneurs found it difficult to work their way up in a monopoly environment.

By and large the demands of the monopoly tourism industry led to legislations which protected its domestic trade from international competition. These prevailed mostly in hotel and catering sector. Hence the result was high priced accommodations on the one hand and accommodations without any quality of service on the other. Similar situation has prevailed in the catering industry. With the liberalization of the economy some competition was offered to established monopolies but we are yet to see any quality growth of small entrepreneurship. Existing legislations like ones on quality control, lodging rights, privacy of guests, fire security etc., therefore remain mostly on paper.

Concerns voiced by groups fighting for social and environmental justice : This is an important and a major source of legislation. Over the years social and environmental issues have interlocked. Governments and political parties have had to sit up and listen to these concerns. Often the issues come up in the wake of developmental strategies pursued by different nations. For example in India setting up of big dams like at Narmada led to protests against displacement of people living in the area and demand for reducing the height of the dam. Similarly the **Chipko** movement in India led by Sunderlal Bhauguna created the need for environmentally sensitive legislation.

On the international scene we see today a debate over the beef crisis. Consumption of breef of certain diseased cows have led European Union to ban the consumption of British beef. Britain on the other hand is disputing the ban and arguing for a scientifically sensitive procedure to assess the nature of what is called the 'mad-cow' disease. Involved here is also the issue of 'animal-rights' with Maneka Gandhi, a prominent environmentalist, advocating that the diseased cattle should not be slaughtered but be sent to India!

These issues demand both instant and long term legislations which impact tourism as well. For example in Britain the tourism operator would be faced with the question of offering British beef to the tourists etc.

However the impact of environmental legislation has a deeper implication for tourism. The questions of displacement of people or degradation of environment leads planners to rethink their strategies for tourism. Therefore acts and laws on hotels, catering industry or construction of resorts etc. – reflect this. Thus we see in Goa that there is a legal limit placed on the construction of hotels on the beaches. More importantly acts and laws designated to protect wildlife or vulnerable eco-zones e.g. wildlife Act of 1972 actually decide the direction in which tourism in a country can move. Wildlife protection acts ensure that there is no killing of animals for hunting or pleasure, therefore curbing this unsavoury aspect of tourism. Similarly laws on protection of displaced people create a sensitivity to ethnic cultures. And this has even created a new kind of tourism called Ethnic Tourism where the tourist interacts with local community with full respect to their local culture and tradition.

Q15. Do local, regional and national concern overlap in framing tourist legislation?

Ans. The major sources of acts and laws in tourism are (a) Customs and convention (b) Legal-judicial power of the State (c) Concerns of the functions of the private sector of Trade and Industry and (d) Concerns voiced by groups fighting for social and environmental justice. These sources provide the base on which various law making bodies in our country draw upon. In India, law-making is the function of the (a) national parliament (b) state legislature and (c) local or municipal bodies. The jurisdiction of these bodies is defined by the Indian constitution. However in an area like tourism there can be many overlaps. For example tourism education would be a subject for legislation by the state legislature while regulation of foreign and Indian currency would be in the hand of the central parliament. Similarly the laws regarding pollution, waste disposal etc. could be specific and different for local bodies like municipalities and panchayats. Clearly then a tourism person in India would have to be sensitive to both the local and national context of any legislation on tourism. Similarly it would be more important for him to know the dynamics of law making processes rather than learn all the laws and acts passed by various bodies. Of course for working in his particular context he would have to know the acts and laws of his area of operation.

Q16. Discuss on the issues that were taken up by the representatives of the national environmental groups with the American president.

Ans. Environmentalists advocate the sustainable management of resources and stewardship of the environment through changes in public policy and individual behavior. In its recognition of humanity as a participant in (not enemy of) ecosystems, the movement is centered on ecology, health, and human rights. Globally speaking, there have been two phases of environmental concern and politics. The initiative in this direction has been taken by the developed countries, mainly the United States of America. The first phase, starting roughly in the 1970s, was more localized in nature. The environmental issues of local importance only were highlighted with little concern for their larger implications. The environmental politics, in its first organized phase, did not succeed in leaving an impact and was dismissed as trendy and transient.

The second phase of coordinated concern for the environment was a lot more successful and attempted to integrate the local issues with the global context. The universality of the environmental issues was also emphasized. In November 1988, the leaders of 30 national environmental groups met the American president and presented more than 700 recommendations for his consideration on environmental issues like :

- global warming,
- destruction of the planet's ozone layer,
- loss of tropical rain forests,
- acid rains, and
- ocean land and atmospheric pollution.

Unlike the first era of environmental awakening, the politics of the second phase displayed a more global conception of environmental degradation. It was now emphasized that the ecological ills may have local roots but they create an intricate chain of effects which link different ecosystems and natural orders. For example, gases created by the smoke clouds from the burning of rain forests in Brazil can be carried to the Antarctic region where they can deplete the tropospheric ozone layer. In short, the difference between the environmental concern of the 1970s and the 1980s was that whereas the former tended to have local concerns, the latter was more universal in its perspective and placed the environmental concern on the global agenda for the first time. As was mentioned earlier, the spectrum of the politics of environment represents a combination of consensus and divergence. The global debate on environmental concern encompasses both these dimensions.

Q17. What are the different positions on the question of environment?

Ans. Broadly speaking, at the global level, one can discern three different positions and accompanying concerns.

(a) This position can be said to have originated in the third world or the developing countries and it represents some of the apprehensions of these countries on the environmental initiatives of the west. This position looks upon the general environmental concern as the conspiracy of the developed countries of trying to prevent the third world countries from developing their economies, by raising the bogey of environment. Briefly, the argument is as follows: the western countries have developed their economies by going through a process of rapid industrialization. They did it by intervening in the environment in a big way and by exploiting the natural resources of the earth to the maximum with the help of advanced technology. Having achieved general prosperity for their population, their priority now is to generate a clean environment, which they can enjoy. Therefore, the question of environment should be taken up only after the developing countries have achieved the same level of production and consumption.

(b) The second position is quite close to the first in that it also has its roots in the developing countries. It tends to dismiss all talk of environment as a luxury of the rich, wherever they are. According to this position, the preserving of the tiger and the aesthetic beauty of the nature is a prerogative of the moneyed people and societies which have nothing more than a touristic interest in the environment. The obsession with environment diverts the attention from the problems of the poor. The environment is seen as a non-issue as far as give a better deal to the poor is concerned since their problems can only be solved by creating employment. The environmental concern should not, therefore, stand in the way of societies trying to solve their basic problems of hunger and employment.

(c) The third position, taking roots mainly in the developed countries, attempts to turn the first and the second upside down by considering the poor countries as mainly responsible for the degradation of the environment. This perspective considers the ever growing population responsible for environmental crisis. According to this position, the scarce natural resources are put to a severe strain by the growing population in the poor countries. The industrialized west has taken measures to minimise its environmental problems, mainly those of air and water pollution, by the application of advance pollution control technology. But these problems continue to grow in the third world countries of Asia, Africa and Latin America. The advance countries have succeeded in providing a cleaner atmosphere to their people. At a meeting of the United Nations in 1982, the minister for environment in the British government declared that all environmental problems in the west had been solved and they remained only in the third world.

Q18. Describe the objectives of chipko and apikko movements. [Dec 2008, Q6]

Ans. Chipko Movement- The forests of India are a critical resource for the subsistence of rural peoples throughout the country, but especially in hill and mountain areas, both because of their direct provision of food, fuel and fodder and because of their role in stabilising soil and water resources. As these forests have been increasingly felled for commerce and industry, Indian villagers have sought to protect their livelihoods through the Gandhian method of satyagraha non-violent resistance. In the 1970s and 1980s this resistance to the destruction of forests spread throughout India and became organised and known as the Chipko Movement.

The first Chipko action took place spontaneously in April 1973 and over the next five years spread to many districts of the Himalaya in Uttar Pradesh. The name of the movement comes from a word meaning 'embrace': the villagers hug the trees, saving them by interposing their bodies between them and the contractors' axes. The Chipko protests in Uttar Pradesh achieved a major victory in 1980 with a 15-year ban on green felling in the Himalayan forests of that state by order of India's then Prime Minister, Indira Gandhi. Since then the movement has spread to Himachal Pradesh in the North, Kamataka in the South, Rajasthan in the West, Bihar in the East and to the Vindhyas in Central India. In addition to the 15-year ban in Uttar Pradesh, the movement has stopped clear felling in the Western Ghats and the Vindhyas and generated pressure for a natural resource policy which is more sensitive to people's needs and ecological requirements.

The Chipko Movement is the result of hundreds of decentralised and locally autonomous initiatives. Its leaders and activists are primarily village women, acting to save their means of subsistence and their communities. Men are involved too, however, and some of these have given wider leadership to the movement. Prominent Chipko figures include: Sunderlal Bahuguna, a Gandhian activist and philosopher, whose appeal to Mrs. Gandhi results in the green-felling ban and whose 5,000 kilometre trans-Himalaya footmarch in 1981-83 was crucial in spreading the Chipko message. Bahuguna coined the Chipko slogan: 'ecology is permanent economy'.

Chandi Prasad Bhatt, one of the earliest Chipko activists, who fostered locally-based industries based on the conservation and sustainable use of forest wealth for local benefit. Dhoom Singh Negi, who, with Bachni Devi and many village women, first saved trees by hugging them in the 'Chipko embrace'. They coined the slogan: 'What do the forests bear? soil, water and pure air'.

Ghanasyam Raturi, the Chipko poet, whose songs echo throughout the Himalaya of Uttar Pradesh. Indu Tikekar, a doctor of philosophy, whose spiritual discourses throughout India on the ancient Sanskrit scriptures and on comparative religion have stressed the unity and oneness of life and put the Chipko Movement in this context.

A feature published by the United Nations Environment Programme reported the Chipko Movement thus: 'In effect the Chipko people are working a socio-economic revolution by winning control of their forest resources from the hands of a distant bureaucracy which is concerned with selling the forest for making urban-oriented products.'

"The solution of present-day problems lie in the re-establishment of a harmonious relationship between man and nature. To keep this relationship permanent we will have to digest the definition of real development: development is synonymous with culture. When we sublimate nature in a way that we achieve peace, happiness, prosperity and, ultimately, fulfilment along with satisfying our basic needs, we march towards culture." Sunderlal Bahuguna.

Appiko movement : The **Appiko movement** was a revolutionary movement based on environmental conservation in India. The "Chipko Andolan" (Hug the Trees Movement) in Uttarakhand in the Himalayas inspired the villagers of the Uttara Kannada district of Karnataka Province in southern India to launch a similar movement to save their forests. In September 1983, men, women and children of Salkani "hugged the trees" in Kalase forest. (The local term for "hugging" in Kannada is appiko.) Appiko Andolan gave birth to a new awareness all over southern India.

In 1950, Uttara Kannada district forest covered more than 81 percent of its geographical area. The government, declaring this forest district a "backward" area, then initiated the process of "development". There major industries - a pulp and paper mill, a plywood factory and a chain of hydroelectric dams constructed to harness the rivers - sprouted in the are. These industries have overexploited the forest resource, and the dams have submerged huge-forest and agricultural areas. The forest had shrunk to nearly 25 percent of the district's area by 1980. The local population, especially the poorest groups, were displaced by the dams. The conversion of the natural mixed forests into teak and eucalyptus plantations dried up the water sources, directly affecting forest dwellers. In a nutshell, the three major p's - paper, plywood and power - which were intended for the development of the people, have resulted in a fourth p: poverty.

The Appiko Movement uses various techniques to raise awareness: foot marches in the interior forests, slide shows, folk dances, street plays and so on. The movement has achieved a fair amount of success: the state government has banned felling of green trees in some forest areas; only dead, dying and dry trees are felled to meet local requirements. The movement has spread to the four hill districts of Karnataka Province, and has the potential to spread to the Eastern Ghats in Tamil Nadu Province and to Goa Province.

The second area of the Appiko Movement's work is to promote afforestation on denuded lands. In the villagers to grow saplings. Individual families as well as village youth clubs have taken an active interest in growing decentralized nurseries. An all-time record of 1.2 million saplings were grown by people in the Sirsi area in 1984-1985. No doubt this was possible due to the cooperation of the forest department, which supplied the plastic bags for growing saplings. In the process of developing the decentralized nursery, the activists realized that forest department makes extra money in raising a nursery. The cost paid for one sapling grown by a villager was 20 paise (US 2c), whereas the cost of a single sapling raised by the forest department amounted to a minimum of Rs 2 (US 15c). In addition, the forest department used fertilizers and gave tablets to saplings. The Appiko Movement's experience has brought an overuse of chemical fertilizers into the forest nursery, making it a capital-intensive, money-making program. The nursery program propagated by the forest department is really a means for utilizing village labor at cheap rates. Appiko activists have learned lessons from this experience, and they are now growing saplings only to meet their own needs, not to give to the forest department.

The villagers have initiated a process of regeneration in barren common land. The Youth Club has taken the responsibility for the project and the whole village has united to protect this land from grazing, lopping and fire. The experience shows that in those areas where soil is present, natural regeneration is the most efficient and least expensive method of bringing barren area under free cover. In the areas in which topsoil is washed off, tree planting - especially of indigenous, fast-growing species - is done. The irony is that the forest department is resorting to the mechanized planting of exotic species, and also uses huge amounts of fertilizers on these exotic, monoculture plantations. This work will definitely harm the soil, and eventually the tree cover, in the area. Two obvious techniques of greening are being performed: one the forest department's method, is capital intensive, and the other, the people's technique of growing through regeneration, is a natural process for sustainable development of the soil.

The third major area of activity in the Appiko Movement is related to rational use of the ecosphere through introducing alternative energy sources to reduce the pressure on the forest. The activists have constructed 2,000 fuel-efficient chulhas ("hearths") in the area, which save fuelwood consumption by almost 40 percent. The activists do not wait for government subsidies or assistance, since there is spontaneous demand from the people. Even in Sizsi town and in other urban areas, these chulhas are installed in hotels, reducing firewood consumption. The other way to reduce pressure on the forest is through building gobar gas plants. An increasing number of people are building bio-gas plants. However, the Appiko activists are more interested in those people who are from poorer sections - who cannot afford gas plants - so they emphasize chulhas. Some people deter the regeneration process in the forest area through incorrect lopping practices. The Appiko Movement is trying to change people's attitudes so that they realize their mistake and stop this practice. The thrust of the Appiko Movement in carrying out its work reveals the constructive phase of the people's movement. Through this constructive phase, depleted natural resources can be rebuilt. This process promotes sharing of resources in an egalitarian way, helping the forest dwellers. The movement's aim is to establish a harmonious relationship between people and nature, to redefine the term development so that ecological movements today form a basis for a sustainable, permanent economy in the future.

Q19. What are the arguments of the environmentalists against the building of a big dams? [Dec 2008, Q6]

Ans. Building dams has figured very prominently in independent India's schemes of economic development. A total of 1554 large dams have either been built or are being constructed at an estimated cost of Rs. 10,556 crores, nearly 14% of India's planned expenditure. As was mentioned earlier, opinion on the viability of dams has been sharply polarized between the advocates of development and the environmentalists. In fact, different positions on the building of dams represent fairly the spectrum of conflicting perspectives on the question of environment. The proponents of dams have demonstrated the significant achievements not only in irrigation, generating hydroelectric power and effecting flood control but also in taking water to remote areas. In 25 years, from 1954 to 1979, India's hydroelectric generating capacity has gone up 12 times and the irrigation potentials increased from 9.7 million hectares to 26.6 million hectares. This has been responsible in India achieving self sufficiency in food production, to a large extent.

As against this, the environmentalists point to grave long term ecological and other disasters, involved in these large projects. Following are some of the reservations expressed by the environmentalists :

- The projected benefits of some of the dams have been found to be exaggerated.
- There were strong imbalances in the distribution of these benefits. It

were mainly the outsiders who benefited at the expense of those who were adversely affected by these projects. In other words the displaced people seldom got the benefits.

- Only very few dams were designed for flood control. Sometimes, dams have also led to flood situations as a result of having to release excess water. The floods in Punjab in 1978, rendering 65,000 people homeless, were a result of the inability of the reservoirs to absorb extra water caused by unexpected rains.

- The big dams contained the risk of a high rate of situation and the degradation of the soil.
- They inevitably involved the destruction of the habitat, submergence of the area including wildlife, plants and forests resulting in a loss of valuable biodiversity and genepools.
- Large reservoirs could also trigger the possibilities of earthquakes.
- Small rivers have tended to become even smaller and lifeless, therefore unable to withstand pollution load.
- Inadequate compensation to the displaced people has led to their pauperization. Tribal, peasants and the hill people have been the main victims of the dam projects. Benefits have gone to the urban population.

The sum of their argument is that the environmental and human cost of these dams far outweighs the possible advantages. Also, the designing of the dams has been generally viewed from a civil engineering perspective with little regard for its consequences on the ecosystem. The long term consequences have generally not been taken into account. Moreover, the dam construction rests on a certain notion of development which is oblivious to the large sections of rural and tribal population and caters only to the urban people.

Pressure and Thresholds

Q1. Explain the pressures on wildlife as a result of increased tourism.

Ans. The World Tourism Organization (UNWTO) forecasts that international tourism will continue growing at the average annual rate of 4 %. By 2020 Europe will remain the most popular destination, but its share will drop from 60% in 1995 to 46%. Long-haul will grow slightly faster than intraregional travel and by 2020 its share will increase from 18% in 1995 to 24%. With the advent of e-commerce, tourism products have become one of the most traded items on the Internet. Tourism products and services have been made available through intermediaries, although tourism providers (hotels, airlines, etc.) can sell their services directly. This has put pressure on intermediaries from both on-line and traditional shops.

Tourism and Wildlife – Nature has always helped in flourishing the mankind. But this isn't about what nature gives to you, its what you, as a human being give back in return. Fuelled by media coverage and inclusion of conservation education in early school curriculum, Wildlife tourism & Ecotourism has fast become a popular industry generating substantial income for developing nations with rich wildlife specially , Africa and India. This ever growing and ever becoming more popular form of tourism is providing the much needed incentive for poor nations to conserve their rich wildlife heritage and its habitat.

National parks for wildlife and conservation increase the levels of tourism and recreation. The regulating authorities of tourism sector believe that with proper regulations a delicate balance can be retained between nature and tourism. But the facts suggest otherwise. The increase in tourism has decreased the number of birds in Kashmir. This has sacred away the birds to higher altitudes. Entertaining the tourists has also affected the arrival of the 'Whiskered tern' and the 'Indian Great seed warbler' around Dal Lake. The same is the situation due to tourist pressure in the national parks near Delhi – Corbett, Sariska and Ranthambhore.

Even forest resorts have caused a lot of damage. Cottages for the tourists have resulted into forest clearance – Mollem – 'Mahavir Wildlife' sanctuary is a case in sight. The same is the case with Pitchanaram mangrove forests at the mouth of Vella river in Tamil Nadu. This can result into take over by the common forest plants & the death of the mangrove. The mangrove which acts as resistant to coastal erosion, tidal erosion and cyclones, has already disappeared on the eastern coast which is rich in different species of flowers and fishes. All this bring villages closer to water front due to commercialisation. Close to water they might lead to dumping of waste in the water in turn affecting the trees. Lack of planning and management is a crucial factor.

Q2. Describe the thresholds to environment. [June 2007, Q6]

Ans. While the last decades have seen increasing environmental damage around the globe, for the most part this change has progressed incrementally rather than abruptly. Several factors explain the sudden attention recently given the issue. First, with the waning of the ideological and military confrontation between the superpowers, a space for other issues has opened in public discourse in Western societies. Second, public and media awareness of global environmental change was catalyzed in North America by the particularly hot and dry summer of 1988. These two factors are principally circumstantial. But there is a third factor at work: during the last decade there has been a genuine shift in the scientific community's perception of global environmental problems. The environmental system, in particular the earth's climate, used to be regarded as relatively resilient and stable in the face of human insults. But now it is widely believed to have multiple local equilibria that are not highly stable. In 1987, for example, geochemist Wallace Broecker reflected on recent polar ice-core and ocean-sediment data: "What these records indicate is that Earth's climate does not respond to forcing in a smooth and gradual way. Rather, it responds in sharp jumps which involve large-scale reorganization of Earth's system. . . . We must consider the possibility that the main responses of the system to our provocation of the atmosphere will come in jumps whose timing and magnitude are unpredictable."

Q3. Suggest some solutions to increase the environmental awareness among general public. [Dec 2007, Q8]

Ans. It is very necessary to check the pressures on our environment. The various pressures and points of a thresholds are questioning the very feasibility of our attitude towards environment. It is also argued that tourism, though a smokeless industry, contributes in the destruction of "natural equilibrium" of Environment. It is therefore suggested that the problem should be tackled in a very wide perspective. It should not conform only to the environment friendly tourism management. School curriculum should include environmental education as an intrinsic part of other subject so that conservation attitude can influence all activities. As a separate subject so that ecology can be taught more formally and its concepts more readily grasped environmental studies are an absolute must. Study materials such as text books, audio-visual aids, posters, pamphlets etc. should be prepared with a view on the aforesaid problem. The materials should explain ecological concepts. The objectives of conservation and environmental education should also be an important part of the school activities of children. Wildlife clubs should be encouraged and environmental education included in the activities of youth groups.

Advantage should be taken of those occasions when the tourist/general public comes into contact with plants and animals – in National Parks, Zoos etc. – to explain conservation objectives and their contribution to human survival and well being. Such conservation education besides serving their essential education function, could also help take pressure off reserves protecting particularly fragile or unique ecosystems. Public concern for popular animals, such as deers, should be used to foster the better understanding of the ecosystems of which those animals are part. To evoke and retain as much of this attention as possible, it is essential for conservation to be seen as central to human interests and aspirations.

Q4. Discuss the level of participation of the host population in tourism. [Dec 2008, Q7]

Ans. In the 21st century the global economy will be driven by three major service industries – Technology, Telecommunications and Tourism. Travel and tourism will be one of the world's highest growth sectors in the current century. Tourism, according to experts is expected to capture the global market and become the largest industry in the world.

Tourism involves the host population in diverse ways.

Thus the **first category** includes people who are in continuous and direct contact with tourists: the personnel in the catering trade, in transport, in shops, travel agencies etc. They support tourism because they depend on it and perhaps they would be unemployed without it, hence they welcome visitors. Their attitude is not determined by an inborn hospitality or the joy of being of service as is often claimed, but rather by a simple desire to earn money.

The **second category** consists of those population groups who are in direct and frequent contact with tourists but who derive only a part of their income from tourism. They live in or near tourist centres and engage in various activities such as farming, selling of handicrafts and participating in performing arts. Their link with tourism and consequent knowledge about its negative impact through personal experience, often makes their attitude towards tourism somewhat critical. Thus we find that members of this group do see the advantages resulting from tourism, for instance extra income to farmers, but they also feel more critical about its disadvantages such as interference with their private lives and environmental damage.

The **third category** comprises of well-to-do local elites, who derive maximum benefit from tourism promotion, because they are financially sound and are able to invest money in tourist activities. This group supports tourism vehemently.

The **fourth group** is the large group of locals who have no contact with the tourists or see them only in passing. Here a variety of attitudes are possible – approval, rejection, interest or indifference, the last being the most common. Another group comprises of citizens, who oppose tourism, often in an organized manner. This group attempts to point out the ill-effects of tourism through pamphlets, positions to the authorities concerned and also through protest demonstrations.

Q5. What kind of protection does tourism does provide to the host population and can it be justified on economic grounds? What are the social costs of this protection?

Ans. There is no doubt that tourism can and does provide some amount of economic protection to local community through employment and income. According to a rough estimate atleast 10 million people work in tourism industry the world over and many more million live on tourism indirectly. Tourism has yet another dimension. It may provide possibilities of bridging the economic gap between industrialized urban area and agricultural rural ones. Thus it is often regarded as an economic panacea for slowing down the exodus from the countryside and develop those areas which have nothing to sell except their natural assets.

In the above sense tourism does provide some economic protection to the host population. But there is a reverse side to the coin, seldom mentioned in political discussions. Jobs in tourism are mostly unattractive. Working conditions are hard, the hours are irregular, there is seasonal overload, overtime is more or less compulsory and one is at the mercy of the guest. Earning on the other hand is below average. Many jobs are unskilled and considered as socially inferior, e.g. the work behind the scene, such as in kitchen or cleaning. Tourism also leads to resentment and frustration, since money in the tourist business come from the big business houses in the city and most of the surplus flows back there only.

Further, economic analysis claim that a "multiplier-effect" follows investment in tourism. This operation of economic multiplier leads to rise in Gross Domestic Product. But, it has been proved beyond doubt, that, a simple rise in GDP, does not necessarily mean development. Therefore the tourist destination might witness lopsided economic growth, but not development. It is also well documented that, tourism results in the rise of prices of the essential commodity, real estate and transportation which in turn have an adverse effect on the host population.

Social Cost of Tourism: Tourism does provide an opportunity to learn and understand different cultures. It also makes available occasions for an appreciation of the host culture by the tourists thereby renewing the locals' pride in their culture. But, along with this there are immense social costs resulting from tourist promotion, which do not appear on any balance sheet. Tourism leads to profound changes in the society of the host community. It builds up the desire to imitate habits and behaviour of the tourists. This brings in dis-satisfaction about one's own lot or even resignation because, the living standard of the tourists are generally much higher then that of the hosts. This may lead to an inferiority complex and servility etc.

Furthermore, an extensive literature covering all the main tourist regions indicates that tourism is closely related to increase in the sale of sex child prostitution, crime of various kinds and organized gambling. The prime example of this in India are some coastal regions where the degeneration of societal behaviour due to tourist influx may go beyond redemption. Not only this, there also exists at a several other places a positive relationship between tourism and increase in crime. Tourism also acts as vehicle to spread some very dangerous diseases. Given the positive relationship between tourist influx and rise in prostitution, the threat of AIDS is always looming large over the host communities. Tourism also tends to distort local customs, traditions and norms resulting in the disruption of family and social life. This sometimes leads to a corruption of language and cultural standardization etc.

Thus, we see that tourism does provide some economic protection, but at a very high social cost. Moreover attempts are generally made to hide or embellish such costs or present them as the unavoidable reverse side of the tourism coin. If you want to enjoy the advantage you must also put up with the disadvantages is the kind of argument extended in support of the adverse features.

Q6. What kind of impact has tourism on environment?

Ans. In most of the tourist destinations we find the following:

Water Pollution: resulting from bad sewage disposal management in hotels and resorts, because it is normally connected to nearby river, lake or sea.

Air Pollution: resulting from excessive use of internal combustion vehicles used by and for tourists in particular area, especially at tourist attraction sites that are accessible only by road.

Waste Disposal Problems: Cutting of debris, improper disposal of solid waste from hotels, restaurants and resorts can generate both litter and environmental health problems from vermin, disease and pollution as well as being unattractive.

Ecological Disruption: It is generally observed that an overuse of fragile environment by tourists leads to an ecological damage. For instance the local paths of the community get damaged from the trampling of horses used for re-creational riding in certain coastal and mountain areas. Deforestation of ski-slopes may lead to erosions, landslide and avalanches. Animal behaviour pattern gets disturbed by uncontrolled photography and regular feeding of the animals. Their habitats can be disrupted or reduced by excessive encroachment of tourism development into them. The coastal and mountain environment is particularly vulnerable to overuse and unsuitable development. Excessive collection or an urge for endangered species, collection of the sea shells, coral, turtle shells and other such items by tourists or by local persons for sale to tourists as souvenirs, can deplete those species. Breaking of coral by boats and ship anchors has become a major problem, as in Andaman and Nicobar Islands. Such environmental damage makes the host area/region, apprehensive to any tourist development, though they still invite tourists for limited economic benefit. The discussion above amply reflects the fact that in the name of limited economic protection and benefit, the hosts go on to bear the immense social and environmental cost.

Q7. Discuss about the impact of tourism on culture.

Ans. Local Customs: Tourism reduces every asset of the country/region i.e. cultural asset or natural asset to a commodity, which can be sold in the tourist market place. To an extent, this process allows some funds to flow into local cultural activity. Among this, is the support for local musicians or an investment in making a cultural artifact etc., which might otherwise disappear under the onslaught of globalisation. But, with the advent of tourist gaze and its attendant market impact, the material form and content of much indigenous art have become adapted to meeting external tourist demand. Thus overseas as well as domestic tourists are allured to experience and listen to traditional music and see ritual dances of some ethnic/tribal community. The colourful brochures promise the tourists to take them to the past of the host societies by assuring the visitor of the same setting in which these items were originally held, as if history can be re-created. This commercialisation of their culture, means performance for money and not for personal faith and satisfaction. The ritual dances performed by a particular community were because of their unflinching faith in the deity concerned.

Physical Culture : One of the most obvious signs of cultural reawakening or deterioration is to be found in the state of traditional art forms in the third world societies. The growth of tourist handicrafts market has stimulated local production in both positive and negative direction.

One of the positive influences no doubt is that many types of decaying traditional art get a boost due to the inflow of tourist money. On the other hand, the sheer pressure caused by a ready market for handicrafts has also led to a fall in the quality of workmanship and the manufacture of cheap imitations known as 'airport art'. Some observers claim that in this cultural oversell the real thing is prettified and deodorized to such an extent, that for instance craftsmen in Goa and Rajasthan have forgotten traditional patterns, shapes and designs.

Moral Behaviour: An extensive literature with regards to the effects of tourism on hosts points out to the emergence of a positive relationship between increase in tourist inflow and increase in the sale of sex (prostitution), crime of various kinds and organized gambling.

The 'demonstration effect' of tourists from different cultural background on residents, especially on young people, may completely or partially alter their value system and beliefs. It may also drive a wedge and create friction between different generations in a community. It may also result in loss of cultural character, self respect and an overall social identity because of submergence of local society by outside cultural patterns brought by affluent and seemingly successful tourists. It must have become fairly evident to you by now that social costs outweight the little economic benefits that are derived from a growth of tourism unmindful of the host cultures.

Q8. Define Visitor.

Ans. In the context of tourism, a visitor is to be identified with tourist itself. Hence for all practical purposes, visitors are taken to mean tourists. In this Unit also the words visitors and tourists are thus used interchangeably. It is the tourist who is the principal character in the phenomenon called tourism. Without 'his/her' being around, the tourism phenomenon in meaningless. The origin of the word 'tourist' is traced to thirteenth century. It comes from the word 'tour' a derivation of the Latin word **tornus** meaning a tool for describing a circle or a turner's wheel. In the first half of the seventeenth century, the term was first used for travelling from place to place, a journey, an excursion, a circuitous journey touching the principal parts of a country or a region. Later many definitions of general nature were given for the word **tourist**.

Realising the importance of collecting tourist statistics and of securing international compatibility, the Committee of Statistical Experts of the League of Nations in the year 1937 established the definition. The League of Nations with the concurrence of member countries defined the term foreign tourist as:

Any person visiting a country other than that in which he usually resides for a period of at least 24 hours. The reasons for visiting any other country may be many; for pleasure, domestic reasons, health, business, academics, representative meetings. It also includes persons arriving in course of a sea cruises even when they stay for less than 24 hours.

Unlike foreign tourist, there is no universally accepted definition for the term **domestic tourist**. However, certain parameters need to be kept in mind:

Place of residence: it mostly refers to travel by country's residents within that territory.

Geographical setting: is same as the national territory of the country concerned.

Duration of travel: by analogy, with the accepted definition of international tourist, the domestic tourist is one who spends not less than 24 hours or makes an overnight stay away from his usual residence.

Two more variables may be taken into account:

Distance travelled: may vary between 40-160 kms.

Motivation: for a purpose other than exercising a gainful activity at the place visited.

Q9. Describe the role of visitors and authorities in checking environmental imbalance of a tourist site.

Ans. Role of Visitors: Just as the visitors have the right to get complete enjoyment out of their trips, they have certain duties towards the environment of the place concerned:

- Visitors should be more careful about disposing off their leftovers. This includes eatables, garbage, bottles, etc. This encompasses all the places they visit. This will not only maintain the physical beauty of the place but will be equally enchanting for them, if they visit the place again.
- Visitors should also be cautious about the culture and social traditions of the places they visit. They should not try to interfere with the local customs and traditions. At the same time, they should try to learn the language, social ethos of the places they visit and try to develop friendly links with the people rather than loading upon them as objects of entertainment.
- Visitors should help others which include both the visitors themselves and the local residents to maintain the sanctity of the socio-economic environment of the place and advise and educate them in case of any derelictions or neglects on their part.
- Above all, visitors should develop a broad attitude towards tourism and should consider themselves as active participants in the preservation of the planet as a whole. Such a global and humane outlook would serve a fruitful purpose.

Role of Other Authorities : The state or the authorities concerned with the maintenance and development of tourist destinations should also take certain steps.

- It is now an accepted concept that tourism planning should not be treated as **sui-geneis** but as an integral part of overall physical and economic planning. This should be applied in practice.
- Profiling of tourists both foreign and domestic could play a very effective role in tourism planning and development.
- Control of the number of tourists is also very important for encouraging a healthy guest-host relationship. For example, Bhutan does not allow more than a fixed number of tourists per year, because the Bhutanese feel that a large number of tourists will be a physical as well as a social burden.
- Laws regarding preservation of the environment of tourist sites should be implemented in letter and spirit. Attempts should be made to plug a lucanae in the existing regulations.
- Eco-tourism and sustainable or controlled tourism should be the motto of the authorities. Efforts should be made to restrict/control the number of tourists visiting particular tourist places at any given point of time. This is not restricting tourism but just an alternative approach.
- Efforts should be made through the medium of entertainment – video and audio cassettes, persons of the tourist department – to inculcate an awareness among the visitors and educating them about the need to preserve environment.
- Involving private sector participation can also go a long way in promoting a safe tourism.

Environmental Impacts-1

Q1. Define the term vegetation and wildlife.

Ans. Vegetation : Natural Vegetation can be literally defined as plant communities that grow without human activity in a particular place. The natural vegetation of a particular place varies according to a lot of factors like temperature, latitudinal position, altitude and availability of water body and amount of precipitation in that area. India being a vast country it has various types of natural vegetation which flourish in the different parts of India and each type of natural vegetation has its distinctive features. This is a web page which helps you to glean information on the different types of natural vegetation in India. Preserving the natural vegetation is also ecologically very important. Indian natural vegetation with its wide variety has been elucidated with the help of these ten knock out sites.

Wildlife : Wildlife includes all non-domesticated plants, animals, and other organisms. Domesticating wild plant and animal species for human benefit has occurred many times all over the planet, and has a major impact on the environment, both positive and negative.

Wildlife can be found in all ecosystems, Deserts, rainforests, plains, and other areas – including the most developed urban sites – all have distinct forms of wildlife. While the term in popular culture usually refers to animals that are untouched by human factors, most scientists agree that wildlife around the world is impacted by human activities.

Humans have historically tended to separate civilization from wildlife in a number of ways including the legal, social, and moral sense. This has been a reason for debate throughout recorded history. Religions have often declared certain animals to be sacred, and in modern times concern for the natural environment has provoked activists to protest the exploitation of wildlife for human benefit or entertainment. Literature has also made use of the traditional human separation from wildlife.

Q2. What are the biographical zone? Describe some biographical zone of India. [Dec 2007, Q9, June 2006, Q10(i)]

Ans. Our country, which occupies just two per cent of the total land mass, harbours a rich biodiversity comprising of about five per cent of the known biodiversity from the world over. The numerical figures of the familiar categories of living organisms would give you a feel of the 'rich biodiversity' that we have in our country. There are about :

81,000 species of animals, including
50,000 species of insects, and
12,00 species of birds,
45,000 species of various other categories of plants, including
15,000 species of flowering plants.

In addition, these species may have several sub-species which in turn may have countless varieties. All these make the wildlife in India one of the richest in the world. The prime reason for such a rich biodiversity is because of the availability of an extraordinary diversity of habitats in India; from the cold and arid high-altitude regions of the trans-Himalayas to the dense, tropical rainforests of south India; from the searingly hot Thar desert in the west to the lush mangrove forests of the eastern coastal areas and several variations in between. In fact, an entire life time would be inadequate to see the entire range of habitats.

The country has been divided into ten biogeographic zones: Trans-Himalayas, Himalayas, Indian Desert, Semi-Arid, Western Ghats, Deccan Peninsula, Gangetic Plains, North-East India, Islands and Coasts. This classification was developed at the Wildlife Institute of India by Rodgers & Panwar (1988) and it is being largely followed. What are these biogeographic zones? These represent the major species groupings. In addition, each of these ten zones indicates a distinctive set of physical, climatic and historical conditions. The Himalayas and Gangetic Plains are examples of two adjacent but obviously extremely different zones.

Q3. Discuss about the impact of tourism on wildlife. [Dec 2008, Q8, June 2008, Q9]

Ans. Tourism impact on vegetation and wildlife: The impacts of tourism an wildlife is a mixed one some positive and some negative. Let us take up the positive impacts first. The most impatient positive impact is that it aids in making the tourists ecologically aware, often encouraging them take up conservation measures and initiative to minimize pollution. It has also led to the main finance of sense environment such as of historic sites. Movements and also the wildlife. Another positive feature of tourism is that it has promoted research and environmental impact studies.

Tourist Behaviour: This is one of the most crucial factors that affect the wildlife directly and indirectly in a number of ways:

(i) **Indiscriminate collection of wild plants and flowers:** Unorganized and carelessly conducted botanical and zoological excursions lead to mass proofing of wild plants and capture of wild animals, thereby, affecting the established wildlife population in that area.

(ii) **Disturbance of wildlife:** Tourism has affected the feeding and breeding habits of many wild animals.

(iii) **Souvenirs from wildlife:** It is quite natural for tourists to being souvenirs from the place they had visited.

(iv) **Sports:** Careless handling of scuba and boat equipment, surf riding patrol driver vehicles and other recreational vehicles leave harmful remains in water.

Q4. Discuss about the different perception of the mountains.

Ans. Himalayas in the North and the Nilgiris in the South are the prominent Indian mountains. Environmental attitudes and the ideological perceptions about these mountains have varied considerably in the social systems that held ascendance in the subcontinent.

(1) The Hindu World-View: In the Hindu world view, the Himalayas had religious rather than aesthetic or geographical significance. Let us quote a passage from Bharati to make this perception of the Hindu world view clearer. Bharati perceives that, "to all Hindus except those who live there, the Himalayas tend to be ascriptive rather than actual". Mount Kailash was renowned as the abode of Lord Shiva than as a potential place of settlement. Bharati further elaborates: "The Himalayas of the Rishis (priests) and Yogis is more important as an ideal to (Hindus) than are the actual rocks and the miserable huts of the people there."

Hindu world-view is drawn out sharply in the following extract from an article written by a scholar Anthony D King:

According to Hindu philosophy a spot of beauty is no place for social enjoyment or self-indulgence. It is the place for self-restraint, for solitary meditation which leads the mind from Nature to God. Nowhere else is this concept more exemplified than in the Himalaya. Thus, religious cities have developed around the famous holy shrines which have been set up by saints at sites of exquisite natural beauty where devotees could perform their penance and meditation in a calm and serene and sublime atmosphere."

Emergence of Badrinath, Kedarnath, Kailash Mansarovar, Vaishno Devi, Tirupathi (Terumala Hills in the South) were the reflection of this ideological trend. Pristine beauty of the mountain region with its local habitat was largely left imtact.

(2) The Perceptions of the Medieval Rulers: During the medieval times, Indian sub-continent witnessed the upsurge of the Turkish and Afghan rulers. Under Tughlaqs, Kangra region in the lower Himalayas was brought under imperial control. It was the first impulse to tamper with the indigenous communities settled in the mountaineous region. In the North-West region, hardy hill tribes constantly fought against the imperial excursions. Under the Mughals, first efforts were made to set up a summer retreat at Srinagar. Mughal ruling elite, however, largely sought to mitigate the excessiveness of heat in the Indian plains through 'developmental' decisions and not through 'locational' decisions. These 'developmental' decisions entailed creation of underground Taikhanas, use of open-walled pavilions and light-repellent white marble, large expanse of water and well-irrigated gardens, instead of moving up the hills.

(3) The British Perceptions: Indian hills were subjected to the developmental onslaught during the nineteenth century with the advent of the British empire. Thus began the transformation of the hills from the places of pilgrimage to the resort stations. In the European world-view, attitudes towards the mountains changed from one of awe to the one filled with new adventurous and acquisitive spirit, which signified the seventeenth century Europe. Advances in science, technology and philosophy over the centuries brought about profound ideological changes. Mountains came to acquire certain beneficial qualities. Refreshing air and the purity of the physical environment arrested the attention of the travellers and the seekers of the picturesque. Environmental changes introduced during the course of the nineteenth century were shaped both by the European world-view and their experiences of the Indian climate. It led to the emergence of a new type of settlement, the 'hill stations', in the mountain regions. More than 200 such hill settlements came into existence during the colonial times.

(4) European Romantic Perceptions : In the European world-view, the hills had both ideological and practical connotations. 'Romantics' of the Eighteenth Century Europe excited the imagination about the Himalayas. Pristine purity and unscaled and virgin terrain of the hill country fascinated the 'romantics' wary of the industrial Europe. Romantics and the seekers of the picturesque found the hill environment an idyllic setting for the creation of the countryside retreat. They were delighted by the image of the "wild", the "quaint" and the "exotic" in the Himalayas. Emily Eden described the Simla hills as "so beautiful and purple and such masses of white clouds sailing along the valleys. About Jacko, the highest of the Simla hills, she wrote:

"A sea of pinkish white clouds rolling over them and some of their purple heads peering through like the islands... The clouds drew up like curtains in massy folds every now and then and there were the valleys, grown quite green..., tinged with sunbeams... and the want of shape for which the hills are to blame on common occasion was disguised by all the vapoury dress."

(5) Military Strategic Considerations Behind Making Settlements in the Hills : D.J.F. Newall, another contemporary Nineteenth Century military officer and the traveller to the Himalayas, was struck by the grandeur of the Kanchenjunga. He wrote :

"Who that has witnessed 'Kanchenjunga', its peaks lighted up by the sinking sun, whilst the grey shadows of night are stealing over the lower mountains, can ever forget a sight almost unique in the world... The grand river scenery impending over the bright flashing rivers of the Rungeet and its tributaris from the western watershed; with the deep green flood of the Teesta - semi - tropical foliage clothing its margin and lateral glands - certainly present glorious objects of admiration to the lover of the picturesque."

Practical exigencies of the imperial state and the experience of Englishmen, women and children with the Indian climate also necessitated the emergence of the hill settlement. Practical exigencies of the Imperial State were related to the safeguard of the frontiers of their Indian colony in the North West. It was essential for the British imperialism to develop hillstations for strategic considerations to counterbalance the Russian influence in Afghanistan and Tibet, on the one hand and to keep Gorkhas under check, on the other.

(6) Curative Aspect of the Mountains, its Importance for the British: European elite found the Indian heat in the plains intense and malignant. Indian plains were seen to be riven with malignant diseases. Summer months, in particular, were times of epidemic and fatal diseases like malaria, cholera, black fever etc., which the European constitution was unable to withstand. Captain Peter Mundy in 1828 found the temperature of Simla peculiarly adapted to European constitution. Current ethno-medical perceptions of the early Nineteenth Century Europe emphasised the merits of 'the air', 'the waters' and the benefits of 'exercise' and 'bathing'. Bracing and salubrious mountain air fitted well within this paradigm. Lloyd found Darjeeling as a place particularly "well adapted for the purpose of sanatorium".

Climate of the Indian mountains provided affinity to the climate at Home, i.e. England. Strong nostalgia and yearning of the 'Home' led to the creation of the 'English enclaves' in the hills. In the hills they felt closest to 'Home'.

Viceroy to India, Lord Lytton in the late Nineteenth Century, was struck by the nostalgia for England on his visit to Ooty. "The afternoon was rainy and the roads muddy, but such beautiful English rain, such delicious English mud. Imagine Hertfordshire lanes, Devonshire Downs, Westmoreland Lakes, Scotch Trout streams and Lusitanian views."

All these factors and new mode of production centering around industrial factory and the urban culture of Europe led to the emergence of the hill 'resorts' in the Indian horizon.

(7) Nostalgic Value of the Mountains of the British: The changing perceptions about the mountains are a significant indicator of the changing environmental impact upon the mountains from the pre-colonial to the colonial times. This reflects easily in the :

- emerging conflict between the development versus picturesque which emerged during the course of making of these hillstations;
- the changing power equations in the mountains;
- the displacement of the indigenous communities, and
- the changing ideological-cultural variable centered around leisure and health.

Q5. Write short note on followings :

(1) Simla Hill Station **(2) Darjeeling Hill Station**

(3) Nilgiris Hill Station **(4) Nainital Hill Station**

Ans. (1) Simla Hill Station : Shimla is the capital of Himachal Pradesh and is the most popular and established hill station of Northern India. It is situated at an altitude of 2,130 m. Shimla (also spelt as 'Simla') derives its name from goddess **'Shayamla Devi'**,which is another manifestation of Goddess Kali. Shimla was the most important British hill station, prior to India's independence. It provides superb panoramic sights of the valleys, and the lofty peaks of the great Himalayan range, on both sides. The colourful local bazaars of Shimla are sprawled over the southern slopes of the ridge. The capital of Himachal Pradesh came into light when the British discovered it in 1819. Till then, it was a part of the Nepalese kingdom. In 1864 Shimla was declared as the summer capital of India. After Independence, Shimla became the capital of Punjab and was later named the capital of Himachal Pradesh.

Attractions:

(i) The Mall: All visitors to Shimla inevitably walk down the Mall, the main promenade that runs along the top of the ridge - a busy shopping area with old colonial buildings, souvenir shops and restaurants. Narrow cobble-stoned paths wind down to the middle and lower bazaars where tribals from the hills around gather to sell their quaint and colorful artifacts. At the top end of the Mall is the Scandal Point, a large open square with a view of the town

- a favourite rendezvous for visitors and the local people.

(ii) Rashtrapati Niwas: About 1 km west of the centre of Shimla, on Observatory Hill, Rashtrapati Niwas was formerly the residence of the British Viceroy. The huge, fortress like building has six storeys and magnificent reception and dining halls. Set in beautiful gardens, it now houses the Institute of Advanced Studies.

(iii) Viceregal Lodge: It once served as the seat of power, from a hillock west of Shimla. The imposing six-storey edifice, with its manicured gardens is today the institute for advanced studies. It overlooks the Shimla State Museum, which is a treasure trove of Pahari art and sculpture.

(iv) St. Micheal's Cathedral: Situated on the Ridge, it is regarded as the second oldest church in north India and is known for its fine stained glass windows.

(v) Annandale: 2 kms below the Ridge in Shimla, is Annandale glade, once the playground of Shimla, where racing, polo and cricket were legendary during the British era. Today, it is still a favourite with fun-loving picnickers, for a leisurely game of cricket or for the more princely game of polo.

(vi) Summer Hill: This is a quiet suburb of Shimla, 5 km from the ridge and on the Kalka - Shimla line. Its peaceful environs and secluded walks were endorsed by a personage no less than Gandhiji, who once made this his retreat.

(vii) Jakhoo Temple : 2 km east of the city on the Jakhoo Hill is the small Jakhoo Temple. Atop the highest point in Shimla, it keeps the visitors in constant company of the playful monkeys, who inhabit the environs of this Hanuman temple in hundreds.

(viii) Chadwick Falls (8 km): At 2149 m this beautiful suberb is surrounded by a thick forest. From here, a track leads down to Sipur which is an exquisite glade shaded by ancient deodar trees. There are old temples on a side and a fair is held here every year in April.

(ix) The Glen: About 4 km from Shimla, a sprightly stream flows through a clearing in dense woods. This is The Glen, a popular picnic spot. It is at a height of 1830 mtrs and is very scenic.

(x) Prospect Hill: At a distance of 5 kms from Shimla, this popular picnic spot is a 15 minute climb from Boileauganj. It has imposing views of the surrounding peaks and valleys. From the temple of Kamna Devi, one can catch a glimpse of the toy train threading through the stretch from Tara Devi to Jatogh.

(xi) Sankat Mochan: About 7 km from the town of Shimla and at height of 1875 mtrs is the scenic spot of Sankat Mochan, with its Hanuman Temple and a lovely view of Shimla.

(xii) Mashobra : Pine and oak woods frame the beautiful retreat of Mashobra, 12 km out of Shimla. Enchanting trails wind through the forest to lovely gardens. Through thick woods, a side road leads to Bekhalty. From the heart of Mashobra, a pedestrian track leads down to Sipur. This is a large and exquisite glade shaded by ancient cedar trees. Streams of cool water gently divide it. The pastoral picture is completed by the temples on the edge. A trek to Shali Peak - the highest in the area, can be made from Mashobra.

(xiii) Kufri : A little hamlet, just 16 km away from Shimla, offers unparalled views of the countryside and the majestic Himalayan mountains. The Winter Sports capital, Kufri is the focal point of a large number of ski enthusiasts who come here to enjoy the fine ski slopes.

(xiv) Fagu : 6 kms from Kufri, it is a place of great natural wealth, with its woods, ferns and apple orchards.

(xv) Naldehra: 23 km from Shimla, at a height of 2044 mtrs, is a mini golf course (9 holes) which must be one of the most picturesque in the world. The surrounding country, bouncy turf and a grove of deodars which are its crowning glory, caught the eye of Lord Curzon, and the golf course was laid under his personal supervision.

(xvi) Tattapani: Tattapani is just 28 kms from Naldehra, along a road winding through the scenic countryside. The hot sulphur springs here, are noted for **their invigorating and curative powers.**

(xvii) Narkanda : An enchanting 64 km drive from Shimla, brings you to Narkanda, which is a popular skiing resort in winter. It has a choice of ski slopes - a beginner's run and sharper descents for the seasoned foot. Narkanda is well poised to hold out some of the finest views of the inner Himalayas.

(2) Darjeeling Hill Station : The toy train coming from Siliguri is some thing which is liked by the elders and the children equally. The real fun in coming to Darjeeling is on the toy train. It takes six to seven hours to cover a distance of 82 kms and the slow speed gives you enough time to watch and appreciate the beauty which nature has provided it. This train passes through the Forests, waterfalls, over deep valleys and through the mountains and tunnels.

Prime Attractions of Darjeeling

(i) Batasia Loop : This railway loop is an interesting example of engineering. At this loop the toy train takes a very unique turn. This loop is just five kilometer from the main town of Darjeeling. This place also has a very good market where you can buy the purses, bags and other decorative items made by the local women at very reasonable price.

(ii) Bhutia Busty Gompa : With the back drop of the Kanchenjunga range stands a monastery called the Bhutia Busty Gompa. This monastery was shifted from the observatory hills to the present place. The Gompa is a branch of the Nyingmapa sect's Phodang Monastery in Sikkim. The monastery is not far from the chowrasta and is very tastefully decorated. It also has a library which has a copy of the Tibetan Book of the Dead.

(iii) Botanical Gardens : This place is worth a visit for its exotic and exclusive collection of a variety of Himalayan plants, flowers and orchids. This place is near the taxi stand. The gardens also has a green house.

(iv) Chowrasta : This is one of the important shopping places in Darjeeling . Here the Nehru Road and the Mall Road Intersect each other. The snow capped peaks of Kanchenjunga are visible from this place. Near Chowrata are several Hindu and Buddhists temples. This place is over flowing with foreign tourists. You can also enjoy a pony ride form this place.

(v) Dhoom Gompa : About 8 kms from Darjeeling is the Dhoom Gompa. Here a very beautiful statue of the Maitrayie Buddha (prospective Buddha) is established. The Monastery has also preserved some of the rare handwritten Buddhist manuscripts.

(vi) Happy Valley Estate : Here the tea from the gardens is processed. One can spent a few hours here. Entry is only allowed to persons who have permission from any officer of the estate.

(vii) Himalayan Mountaineering Institute & Museums : The Himalayan Mountaineering Institute is on the West Jawahar road. The institute runs courses for training mountaineers as well as has the very good collection of mountaineering equipments which have been used in various mountaineering expeditions and other wise. Specimens of Himalayan flora and fauna are also kept here. The record of attempts made to conquer Mt. Everest has been kept in the Mt.Everest Museum. The institute also screens short films on mountaineering. You can also view the Himalayan peaks through the Zeiss Telescope given to the Nepalese Maharaja by Hitler. Sherpa Tenzing Norgay was the Director of this institute for many years and he was cremated near the institute after his death in 1986. Near the institute is Srabri which gives a very good view of the Single valley and the Kanchenjunga range. One can sit at Srabri and feel the cool breeze from the valley.

(viii) Kanchenjunga View : From Darjeeling one can have the best, uninterrupted view of the worlds third highest peak. Bhan Bhakta Sarani provides one of the enthralling views of these snow capped peaks. The Chowrasta also gives you a good sight to the Kanchenjunga peak.

(ix) Kurseong : Kurseong is mid way between Siliguri and Darjeeling. The way from Darjeeling to Kurseong is generally open through out the year. So, the toy train is not coming to Siliguri then you can come up to Kurseong. This place is equally beautiful and is full of natural splendour.

(x) Natural History Museum : The museum has a collection of over 4300 specimen . Established in 1903, this natural history museum packs in its folds a rich collection of fauna found in the Himalayas and in Bengal. Among the attractions are included the estuarine crocodiles. This unique museum also has a good collection of butterflies. The mineral forms of various stones are displayed in a very attractive manner in the museum.

(xi) Observatory Hills : This point provides one of the breathtaking views of Kanchenjunga peaks. This place is also very sacred for the Hindus and the Buddhists as there are temples and the monasteries at this place. The Kali temple is decorated with the colourful flags. Be aware of the monkey groups as some of these are very aggressive.

(xii) Passenger Ropeway : Another tourist attraction in Darjeeling has been the ropeway. This was the first ropeway in India. It connects the North point (7000 ft) to the Singla Bazaar (800 ft). The rope covers a distance of 8 kms in 45 minutes. The seats in the rope way is limited and it is better to get the tickets in advance. The ropeway is exciting and unique for any one visiting Darjeeling.

(xiii) Rungli Rungliot : Where the road from Gangtok to Darjeeling takes its great bend high above the Teesta river, directly opposite Kanchenjunga, a Buddhist monk many years ago is believed to have proclaimed "Rungli Rungliot" This pious benediction which, literally translated, means "thus far and no further" is alive and well today in the shape of one of the most celebrated tea gardens in the Darjeeling hills. The village is steeped in legend.

(xiv) Senchal Lake : A scenic place near the tiger hills. This place has popularly come up as a picnic spot among the tourists. The lake supplies drinking water to the town of Darjeeling.

(xv) Siliguri / New Jalpaiguri : The twin Cities of Siliguri and New Jalpaiguri are the departure point to Darjeeling, Sikkim and the North Eastern States. Being the nodal point this place has become very busy and crowded. This area has got population over 2.5 lakh people. Siliguri also acts as a transit point for Nepal. This place is not very pleasant to stay as there are always long lines of buses and trucks. These trucks and vehicles might be good for business but they provide very ugly sight. Tourists come to Siliguri and New Jalpaiguri mainly to change bus or catch trains. If you have time then visit the almost forgotten wild life sanctuary of Jaldhapara. The best season to visit this park is between October and May. This is the time when the new grass has come up and animals are out there. The sanctuary has elephants, dears, tigers and other animals but the main attraction is the Rhinos which are threatened by the poachers. Elephant Safari can be taken from Hollong.

(xvi) Snow Leopard Breeding Programme : Nowadays the zoologists and the environmental scientists are trying to protect the endangered species by breeding them in captivity. Following this trend is Kiran Moktan who has devoted his life in breeding program of snow leopards. The snow leopards are not known to have bred in captivity but in this center thanks to the efforts of Kiran Maktan these animals have given birth in captivity. Snow leopards are animals who have to be kept in large enclosures. Visitors are allowed in the center but they have to watch the animals in utter silence.

(xvii) Tibetan Refugee Self-Help Center : In 1959 was established a center for the refugees who had fled Tibet with the Dalai Lama after the Chinese invasion. This self help center has been developed as workshop for the manufacture of handicrafts. The fine and superb carpets, woollens, woodcarvings and leather work form this center has been very popular among the tourists. The money collected after the sale of the products goes to the Tibetans who work here. The variety Tibetan Curios on sale are also attracting the visitors in a big way. This center has established it self in the International scenario as place for hard work, self esteem and truth.

(xviii) Zoological Gardens : The zoo is situated two kms form the main town. This zoological garden houses some of the rare species of animals and birds. This is only zoo in India having the Siberian Tigers. Apart from these the rare Red Panda is also there. The Snow Leopards, Great Grey Birds, Snow Yaks are some the animals which are attracting tourist in great numbers. The entry in the zoo is by tickets which are also valid for the natural history museum and the mountaineering institute & museum.

(3) Nilgiris hill station : Nilgiris- The Blue Mountains

Nilgiri means “Blue Mountains”. The entire area of the Blue Mountains constitutes the present district of Nilgiri. The height of the hills in the Blue Mountain range varies between 2,280 and 2,290 metres, the highest peak being Doddabetta at a height of 2,623 metres.

It’s Location and Boundaries : High above the sea level, situated at the junction of the two ghat ranges of the Sahayadri Hills, Nilgiri district provides a fascinating view. Kerala on the west, the Mysore State on the north, and Coimbatore district on the east and south bound it. Headquarters of Nilgiris district is Udhagamandalam (also called as Ooty).

The beauty of Nilgiris : Nilgiris derives its charm from its natural setting. The steep hills and fantastically narrow valleys with numerous rivers and rivulets running in all directions with a few fine waterfalls here and there provide beautiful scenery. The temperate and most equable climate further heightens the attractiveness of the place. The major tea growing areas in the South are the Nilgiris and these tea gardens are beautiful to watch.

Adventure and trekking in the Nilgiris : The Nilgiris are a trekker’s paradise. Landscaped by nature, the hills abound in trek for lovers of nature. There are treks and treks in whichever direction you turn and from whichever point you start. A trek can be full of thrill, excitement and adventure and a way of seeing and enjoying nature in all its beauty and splendour.

Trekking pamphlets are available with the Nilgiri Wildlife and Environment

Association (NWLEA). There are guides who have sound knowledge of certain areas. If necessary, their services may be hired. And for further details contact the Tourist Information Office at Charing Cross, Ooty.

(4) Nainital Hill Station- A small town in the hills of Kumaon, Nainital is a lovely hill station surrounded by mountains on three sides. Once this area had many lakes and it was called the City of 60 lakes or 'Chakta'. Most of the lakes in the region have disappeared and whatever remains is just a glimpse of what they might have been in the past. Today the life of Nainital revolves around the lake of Naini. But there are few other lakes around Nainital which are equally beautiful and attractive as the Naini lake.

River Ramganga originates from the Doodha Tauli ranges in district Pauri Garhwal. It enters into district Nainital, before re-entering into district Pauri Garhwal. Nainital was discovered in 1841 by a Britisher called Lord Barron. The weather, the surrounding and the mesmerising beauty of this area attracted the British administrator who turned this place into the summer capital of the United Province. Being a major tourist place Nainital is always bustling with visitors and it is always better if accommodation and other facilites are prearranged. The nearest railway station is that of Kathgodam which is connected by trains from Delhi and Howrah. The narrow gauge trains come from Lalkuan which is 55 kms from Nainital. From Lalkuan and Kathgodam regular taxi and bus services are available for Nainital. Nainital is well connected by buses with other parts of the state. Inter state services are also available. The state transport corporation as well as the private operators have their buses on this route.

Q6. How was the architecture a symbol of power in the mountain?

Ans. Mountains exude might in the length and breadth of their spread. In the Hindu world-view, as mentioned before, Himalayas were sacred abode of the Hindu gods and goddesses. In this respect the Himalayas were also worshipped as the part of Hindu religious system. Indigenous hill tribes were largely ignored by the spiritual leaders in search of salvation. During the medieval period, under the Tughlaqs and later on under the Mughals, sovereignty was asserted on the hill tribes and local Rajput rulers in the Himalayan ranges.

Power machinations came to acquire ascendance only during the colonial times. British imperial machinery had at its disposal technical, scientific and industrial resources to pierce through the uncertain terrain and virgin forests. In the process, it disrupted the ecological balance in the hills. The question of power assumed importance of the ambience of the advanced Imperial administration. Bureaucratic authority was introduced into the hill habitat.

Ideology of legitimacy of power, dominance and subordination were introduced into the hill society which previously exhibited an absence of sharp class divisions. Power dimensions were reflected in the large scale colonization of the hill-tracks. British imperial interests, strategic concerns for defensive security and trade led to the simultaneous process of environmental and ecological changes. British monopoly through arms and tight administration, checked the previously existing close interaction between the local tribes and nature.

In this section we confined to the political motives of the Imperial State. Political motives which started the 'exodus' of the imperial and provincial governments to the hills were directly related to the question of power. By 1860s, British had consolidated their hold over India. Move towards the hills was a part of Imperial British policy to assert their superiority vis-a-vis the Indian rulers and the foreign potentiates. Sir Bartle Frere focussed upon this grand imperial design in his observation that "every great Oriental ruler, with any pretensions to civilization has his summer and winter residence."

Few months stay in the summer season in the hills was seen as conducive to efficient administration. Moreover certain strategic and political issues were also at stake. Himalayas in particular were of values for frontier trade and their rich wood.

Imperial architecture revealed another significant aspect of the power in the hills. Architecture is one of the main evidences man leaves upon the face of this earth. Architectural work involves "intellectual beauty" that is sharing in artist's imaginative process than a crude surface representation. Besides this, architecture reflects upon the material culture of the empire. In the case of British architecture in India, architectural works reveal the Imperial vision at work. Viceregal Lodge at Simla, the various Government houses of the Lieutenant Governors and Governors, the Imperial offices such as the Secretariat, suggests the impression of invincible strength and grandeur of the Raj. Indigenous, small-sized thatched huts were replaced with the huge structures of iron and mortar with a lot of plasters.

Viceregal Lodge, atop the Observatory Hill, was one such gigantic structure built at an extensive scale after levelling down a large area upon the mountain too. Under Henry Irwin, the work was begun in 1886 and it was completed in 1888. Viceroy Lord Dufferin was the first occupant. It is Tudor in design, built chiefly of grey stone from the neighbouring quarries. The house consists of a main block of three storeys, a wing called East wing of two storeys and the Kitchen wing of five storeys. Specialised provision for Kitchen, bakery, scullery, larders, wine cellar, plate room, China and glass room, pantries and store were made. Besides separate space was allotted for bedrooms, boudoir, special staircase, ball-room and an electric lift in keeping with the modern conceptions of the nineteenth century Europe.

Ootacamund Government House was built in 1877, under the patronage of Duke of Buckingham, then the Governor of Madras. It had a pillared portico copied from his ancestral seat in Stowe in Buckinghamshire. Fairly commodious, it had a beautiful bathroom and tasteful apartments.

'Shrubbery', the summer residence of the Lieutenant Governor of Bengal, at Darjeeling, was renowned for its artificially laid out garden. It gave the look of an English countryside house to the official residence. An impressive Darbal Hall was attached to it later.

In Simla large scale extensive project of constructing the public works was undertaken in 1880s. Secretariat buildings, Army Headquarters, Post Office, Public Work Secretariat, Telegraph office, Foreign office were the manifestations of the Imperial power in the hills. Hill environment was modified to suit the needs and the tastes of the colonial elite of the urban-metropolitan England. Foreign office was built on the Prospect Hill, after levelling down the surface. It was designed in Chalet style. Snowdown, the official residence of the Commander-in-Chief was purchased in 1973. Barnes Court, the official residence of the Lieutenant-Governor of Punjab, was bought by the Punjab Government in 1800.

To enable the upper echelons of the colonial elite to avoid excessive contact with members of their own community, hierarchical distance was introduced into the hill station environment. Thus both the Viceroy and Commander-in-Chief enjoyed the residence atop the highest ranges in the Simla hills to maintain the rigid imperial hierarchy. Rudyard Kipling observed this power structure in evidence at Simla. He wrote: "Simla was another new world. There the Hierarchy lived and one saw and heard the machinery stripped bare. There were the Heads of the Viceregal and Military staffs and their aides-de-camp,..." Viceregal Lodge in Simla symbolised in scale, elevation and form, the authority of the dominant culture.' There can be few places in the world where the upper ten were so literally upper; the Viceroy and Commander-in-Chief naturally had the best peaks. Extensive modifications of terrain were carried out to accommodate the distinctive military, religious and recreational needs of the dominant Imperial culture.

Ecclesiastical establishments provided both for the spiritual needs of the rulers and also helped the Imperial rulers in the task of colonising the minds of the local tribes. They complemented and sometimes preceded the Imperial efforts on their march to spread 'civilization and progress' into the virgin soil. In Ootacamund, Saint Stephens Church, Saint Thomas Church, Roman Catholic Church and the Convent and Union Chapel and Zion Chapel were erected. In Darjeeling, Saint Andrew Church was built in 1887, belonging to the Church of England. Union Chapel of non-conformists was built in 1869. In Simla, Christ Church occupies the central position atop the Mall. Its centrality in the imperial power structure was evident from the coronation ceremonies and other Imperial services being performed in its precincts.

Schools and educational institutions were also central to the power structure being formalised into the hill environment. Education offered an effective channel for discrimination and the control over the knowledge by the colonial rulers. Hill environment also provided perfect setting for the nurturing of the delicate constitution of the children. The 1907 Darjeeling gazetteer observed: "The thin, pallid and peevish child is not long in the Darjeeling before becoming fat, rosy and active, while the child who constantly suffered from bowel complaint or intermittent fever in the plains below becomes a different being, regaining health, strength and restless energy of an English child." Education in the hills became a popular phenomenon leading to substantial modification of the hill environment. Breeks Memorial School in Ootacamund, Bishop Cotton School affiliated to Calcutta University in Simla; Saint Paul's School, St. Joseph's and Loretto Convent in Darjeeling and Sherwood School in Nainital were set up.

We thus find that the environment of mountains was so modified that the facts of European dominance tended to be inscribed into both the social structure and the physical environment.

Q7. How did the leisure activities of the visitors affects the landscape of the mountain?

Ans. Some of the practices, habits and leisure activities of the colonial settlers brought about significant changes in the environment of the mountains. You have already learnt about how the construction of buildings, creation of new roads and railways, the new architecture and the buildings of schools and churches inevitably affected the existing landscapes and the environment. The intrusions by the colonial settlers also displaced the local communities. Apart from all this, some of the leisure activities of the British rulers also took their toll on the environment. This was, in some ways, a part of the process of the Indian mountains being developed as full fledged centres of tourism.

For instance, 'Shikar' and other gamesmanship were the favourite recreation of the adventurous Europeans. Infact, 'the hunt' formed an important part of the activities in all hill stations. Shooting trips were organised for the tourists in the thick mountain forests, inhabited by rich wild life. Pheasant hunting, woodcock, snipe, solitary snipe, quail, pea and spur fowl were chased by the more adventurous and energetic people. As a result, a significant part of the wildlife in the mountains got wiped out.

Similarly, natural scenic beauty of the hills was sought to be replaced by the artificial conservation of the gardens and botanical parks for the touristic interests. Public gardens were laid out. In Ootacamund a gardener from Kew was specially imported to supervise the laying out. Annandale Garden at Simla was carefully cultivated for the orchard plantation. Both Annandale and the Ridge at Simla were out of bounds for the common people. Lloyd Botanical Garden of Darjeeling was cultivated as the breeding hot-house for cryptomaria, Birch, alders, maple, oaks, rhododendrons, glossy leaved pipli, scarlet blossomed Erythrins, dahlias, lilies, hydrangeas and primrose.

Thus, we find that the provision for the recreational needs of the colonial community, required extensive modifications of the hill station environment. Horse-racing and polo required the construction of a suitably even plane sports. Cricket required the smoothening of uneven terrain. Sailing and boating needed the creation of a lake or diversion of existing water source. Reading, a favoured pursuit among an educated and leisured elite, meant the provision of well-stocked libraries. Skating rinks and icing rinks were planned out for the winter amusements at Simla, Mussourie and Darjeeling. Environment was so modified as to give greater access for social interaction and entertainment. Thus, Mall, the centre of social activity during the colonial times, was so carved out, that it typically ran mid-way through the station, giving access to the major institutions of the church, principal hotels, library, club and the few European stores.

Environmental Impacts-2

Q1. What are the wetlands? Discuss their importance and functions.

Ans. Wetlands are areas lying along the banks of rivers and lakes and the coastal regions. They are life-supporting systems providing fish, forest products, water, flood control, erosion buffering, a plant gene pool, wildlife, recreation, and tourism areas. Though they are endowed with a rich biodiversity, yet of late they are being greatly exploited.

Many wetland species have become threatened and endangered because of their dependence on a particular type of wetland ecosystem, which has become seriously degraded or destroyed. Such is the case with the swampy grasslands and the flood plain wetlands of the Ganges and the Brahmaputra river valleys. Large areas here have been converted to agricultural land or there has been widespread overgrazing. Removal of sand, gravel, and other material from the beds of rivers and lakes has not only caused destruction to the wetlands but have led to sedimentation, which has affected other areas.

The introduction of exotic plants has had an adverse effect on these areas. The water hyacinth, a native of South America, is now a major pest in many areas forming a vast floating shield over the surface of the water and clogging up rivers and canals. A number of factors have been responsible for the depletion of wetland areas mainly the mangrove forests, along the coasts of India. Intensive aquacultural development, deforestation, pollution from tankers, domestic waste, agricultural run off and industrial effluents are some of the factors. Most of the surviving mangroves are now confined to West Bengal and the islands in the Bay of Bengal.

The Ramsar Convention for the preservation of wetlands of international importance especially as Waterfowl habitat, was held in Iran in 1971. An Asian Ramsar group was thereafter formed in 1990 consisting of members who were a part of the Ramsar Convention. In 1981, Chilika Lake, India's largest brackish water lagoon, was designated a Ramsar Wetland of International Importance. But its fragile ecosystem has of late come under threat due to both anthropogenic and natural factors. It provides refuge to thousands of migratory birds and the balance in the ecosystem has to be maintained to ensure safe habitat for the birds.

Q2. Write a note on the impact of tourism on wetlands.

Ans. Tourism has been considered a major issue by environmentalists so far as environmental damage to natural tourist sites is concerned. Poor planning of tourism schemes and alarming growth of the industry are major factors responsible for the damage. For example, the Dal lake which was twenty five square kilometres five decades ago is only ten square kilometres today, presumably due to tourist pressures.

Chilka in Orissa is considered a tourist paradise. It is a vast expanse of water surrounded by small green hillocks and thousands of migratory birds. There are a large number of spots around the lake which can be developed into tourist spots. The government of India has identified four sites namely Samala islands, Rambha, Barkul and Satpada. Works for establishing a water sports complex at Barkul has already started and at Satpada there are plans to develop tourist lodges. There is a famous temple called the Kalijai temple which attracts a large number of tourists. Besides there are other three interesting but not widely known tourist attractions in and around Chilka: dolphins, black buck and oysters. There are around fifty dolphins which move around the area between Satpada and Arakhud i.e., where the lake meets the sea. Secondly, some wild black bucks stay in the narrow area between the Bay of Bengal and the lake. And lastly, there is scope for having not only pleasure tourism but also adventure, religious and eco-tourism.

However, when the number of tourists increases the limit that the environment can tolerate, there is trouble. Mass tourism brings with it hordes of people wanting to make quick money out of it without the much needed sensitivity. Hotels and lodges are constructed near or on the banks of the lakes. Their refuse leftovers and sewer water get into the lake waters polluting it. At times, jetties are constructed for the boats. This construction does not always take into account the wave pattern of the lake and may have adverse effects on the lake as silt may start getting deposited next to it. Country boats are in course of time, replaced by mechanised boats which not only create a lot of sound but also leave traces of oil/diesel/petrol into the waters. Besides insensitive tourists may damage the rare flora and fauna of the ecosystem. All these problems are faced not only by Chilka but by almost all lakes. While it is agreed whole-heartedly that attention should be paid to the development of tourism, it should be in conformity with the environmental requirements and must merge harmoniously with the overall action plan for conservation and development of wetlands.

Q3. Describe the importance of island and beaches for tourism. [Dec 2007, Q10]

Ans. India, with such a diversified physiography, has much to offer by way of tourism; the Himalayas are perfect for skiing, skating, hiking and trekking. India's temples, forts, palaces, sculptures, paintings, monuments and archaeological ruins are over 3000 years old. The temples of Khajuraho, the Sanchi Stupa, the Ajanta and Ellora caves, the forts at Delhi and Agra and many others are the best bet for those interested in history and architecture. For wildlife enthusiasts there are National parks and sanctuaries with a variety of wildlife. Similarly India is also rich in beaches and islands. The tourists from colder climates looking for sunshine and warm water beaches constitute one of the largest segments of present day tourism. The pleasure periphery of European and American tourists which ended at the Mediterranean and Caribbean now extends to the beaches of Asia and Pacific. India plays a major role in this regard. The beaches along the Arabian sea coast are ideal for bathing, surfing and sailing. The white sand beaches and warm conditions along the Puri-Konark region in the East can draw millions of tourists from freezing Europe. The Andamans and Lakshadweep are ideal for scuba diving and snorkeling. Underwater life can be interesting to naturalists and photographers. It is no wonder that sand, sea, surf, water and wind together with the background in a beach could be fascinating for anyone. It is more so for Indians many of whom living in far interior places would not have seen them before. As far as the domestic tourists are concerned, survey reveal that Beaches are the best attractions followed by temples/pilgrim centres, historic places, Hill resorts, cities, wildlife etc. The beaches and islands therefore have a special importance for foreign as well as domestic tourists.

Q4. Write a note on Andaman & Nicobar Island and Lakshadweep Island. [Dec 2007, Q10]

Ans. Andaman and Nicobar islands are popularly known as the . Emerald Isles. The erstwhile 'Kaala Paani' or the Cellular Jail, now a museum is the most popular tourist spot. Other places of tourist interest include National Memorial, Marine Museum, Naval Marine Museum, Smrithika Museum, Haddo Zoological Garden, Corbyn's Cove, and other beaches, and Humphrey Gunj

Memorial. Andaman Water Sports Complex at Port Blair. Chatam Saw Mill (largest in Asia), Chidiya Tapu, Marine Museum, the island of red Skibn, and Havelock are the other attractions. Corbyn's Cove, Wandoor beach, Sippighat water sports complex, Cinque island, and Jolly Buoy island are some adventurous spots on the island.

Capital	Port Blair
Area ('000 sq.km)	8,249 Sq. Km.
Population ('000 in 1991)	280,661
Principal Languages	Bengali, Hindi, Tamil, Malayalam

The Andaman and Nicobar Islands, home to a number of aboriginal tribes, lie in the Bay of Bengal, approximately 1,220 km south east of the coast of West Bengal and 1,190 km east of Madras. The main islands in the Andamans are Land Fall Island, Middle Andaman, South Andaman, Port Blair and Little Andaman. Nicobar, lying to the south, comprises of Car Nicobar, Great Nicobar, Chowra, Teresa, Nancowrie, Katchal and Little Nicobar.

The two groups of Islands, Andaman and Nicobar, are separated by a deep ten degree channel. 12 of the islands, particularly Car Nicobar in the north, are inhabited, while Great Nicobar, the largest and southernmost island in the group, is virtually uninhabited. The capital of this Union Territory is Port Blair, on the Andaman Islands.

Lakshadweep is one of the worlds most spectacular tropical island systems. Thirty- two sq. km of land spread over 36 islands surrounded by 4200 sq. km of lagoon rich in marine wealth. The precious heritage of ecology and culture is supported by an extremely fragile ecosystem. Committed to the cause of Eco tourism Union Territory of Lakshadweep has consciously followed a middle path between tourism promotion and environmental conservation. The Administration is carefully monitoring the environmental impact of coastal tourism and has taken steps to promote tourism in a way that is consistent with ecological concerns. As an effective strategy to avoid pressure on ecological environment, the efforts to promote tourism have been synchronized with the carrying capacity of the islands.

Though all the islands are endowed with the beauty of coral reef, sandy beaches, unpolluted and clear water and hospitable settings, most of these differ in terms of facilities and services offered. Some islands have been promoted for diving and water sports; still others have been developed so that people enjoy the charm of relaxation and natural enjoyment. Since the land is precious and scarce it is avowed policy of the Administration to relieve pressure on land and promote water based tourism. The motto being admires and not exploits that natural beauty.

The dispersed Island situations and small size of Islands put unavoidable constraints to physical development. Islands are forced to support independent infrastructure and amenities and import almost all requirements to develop such facilities besides items of daily need. However, Lakshadweep has used the situation as an asset rather than a constraint through promotion of quality tourism. To enhance tourism that has significant positive social impact and negative environment impact, and extreme low volume and high value added specialized tourism in the basic thrust to make tourism development environmentally sustainable. The policy thrust is very much evident from the fact that only 3587 tourists visited the islands during the finical year 1998-99.

In pursuance of the above policy, an environment impact assessment of 9th five-year Plan of Lakshadweep Administration for the period 1997-2002 was conducted. While environmental impact assessment of project is now a well-established practice, environmental impact assessment of policies or plans is a relatively new concept. It was for the first time in the country that Five Year Plan was subjected to environmental impact assessment. In the environmental analysis of the Department of tourism, it has been observed that preservation of environment is the cherished goal of Lakshadweep. In fact environment is the basic raw material for tourism for these islands.

Q5. Write a note on the Indian beaches at the eastern and western coasts.

Ans. The beaches on the coastline of the southern peninsula stretch for over 7500 kms. Thus we find beaches both along the western and eastern coast of India. However, more developed beaches, particularly useful for tourism are found along the western coast because of a stronger wave action there and a regular coastline. Thus water sports is a regular feature of the beaches on the Western coast where as beaches along the eastern coast are more noted for their physical beauty.

(1) Beaches Along the Western Coast: The Western coast covers the states of Maharashtra, Gujarat, Goa, Karnataka and Kerala. Out of these, Maharashtra does not have very developed coasts. The Chowpatty and Juhu beaches of Bombay town open spaces and cater mainly to the resident population.

(i) Goa: It has the most comprehensive beach resort in the country. Goa's coastline provides endless sun drenched crescents of sand. Vagator, Anjuna, Aguada, Baga, Calanghute and Candolin stretch out in an unbroken palm fringed Pine. Other Beaches are at Miramar and Colva. Parasailing, yachting, windsurfing and deep sea diving are some of the popular water sports, facilities for which are available. In addition, every sort of accommodation fringes the beaches, from deluxe resorts to budget lodgings.

(ii) Diu: A tiny island off the extreme south of the mainland, it is even now a secluded beach resort near a colonial town of great charm, with whitewashed churches and tile roofed villas.

(iii) Gujarat: The state of Gujarat is endowed with lovely beaches. One of them is Ahmedpur Mandvi whose chief attraction is the ethnic beach resort. Cottages modelled on rural Gujarati architecture look out onto a secluded beach, one of the state's chief centres for water sports.

(iv) Kerala: Just 16 kms away from Trivandrum is one of the most popular beaches in the country; Kovalam.

(2) Beaches along the Eastern Coast: India's long eastern cost bordering the Bay of Bengal presents a charming scene of sun-drenched golden beaches stretching endlessly over hundred of miles in exotic wilderness. It covers the states of Orissa, Andhra Pradesh and Tamil Nadu.

(i) Andhra Pradesh: The coastal fringe of Andhra Pradesh in particular bound by sea and the lush green Eastern Ghats is a beach lovers paradise. Against the backdrop of low hills, one would find curvaceous shore lines dotted by secluded creeks and cover where the idyllic waterfronts are caressed by dazzling white surf. The fast developing modern port-city of Vishakhapatnam or Vizag as it is popularly called, offers tourists and travellers a unique opportunity to explore and enjoy rare views of Gopalpur in Orissa. Bheemunipatnam, just 24 kms away from Vishakhapatnam, is a tranquil beach resort with its aquamarine waters and green groves.

(ii) Orissa: Puri, about 60 kms away from the capital city of Bhubaneswar, is a beach that has been relatively overshadowed by the religious importance of the place. Gopal-on-Sea is a quiet beach resort 95 kms away from Bhubaneswar.

(iii) Tamil Nadu: The Marina Beach is regarded as one of the longest beaches in the world.

Q6. In what ways the environment of the Island and Beaches is effected by tourism.

Ans. The environment of the islands and beaches is threatened, on the one hand, by human activities and encroachment, and on the other, by natural calamities. Natural calamities include cyclones, excessive rains, local upheavals and the presence of certain predator plants like Acathanster which have destroyed the massive corals of minicoyatol. The human encroachment has been mainly in the form of industrialisation, urbanization, construction, dredging and tourism. Here we will concentrate mainly on the impact generated by tourism and tourist industry. The degradation of the islands and beaches caused by tourism is of two kinds. The first is pollution caused directly by increasing human presence at the sites. The second is degradation caused infrastructural expansion. This includes construction activities in the main. Let us look upon both these aspects.

(1) Pollution caused by tourists : Leaving behind leftovers. Bottles, cans, polythene packs dumping of human wastes etc. is a problem faced by almost all the places concerned. To derive maximum pleasure out of the visits, the tourists (both international and domestic) bring along with them eatables, most of which are left behind indisposed after the 'fun' is over. The leaflets, coconut wastes, polythene packs, cans, bottle lie strewn all over the beaches. This does not only give a dirty look to the landscape but also destroys the scenic beauty. Some of these materials are not bio-degradable and take a long time to decay. (polythene packs are non-bio-degradable while glass objects take a long time to decay). These pose a grave threat to the environment. The nature of leftovers varies from place to place. Thus puri being a centre of pilgrimage, gets leftovers which are primarily religious in nature. In Goa, on the other hand, beer bottles and can constitute leftovers. Similarly Bhelpuri leaflets adorned the chaupati beach at Bombay till very recent times.

Likewise pollution of beaches by dumping of human wastes as well as defecation is a major problem in many parts of the country. The atolls of Lakshadweep perhaps stands foremost in this regard. Lack of sanitary facilities coupled with an inherent reluctance to avail even the extending facilities by many make beaches unhygienic. Needless to say that clean beaches will eradicate the causative agents of many contagious diseases from our fishing villages.

(2) Degradation caused by Infrastructure : This will include those activities in which human being is not a direct contributor, although this classification between direct and indirect human interference should not be seen as rigid as ultimately human beings are at the root of both. This incorporates activities which are, in some way or the other are related to the promotion of tourism, for example building resorts, hotels, laying down transport and communication lines, developing golf courses, setting up of small handicraft and consumer industries, eating joints near the coasts. These destroy not only the physical landscape but also seriously affect the ecology of the region cornered.

(i) Building and construction activities either intended to make guest houses, restaurants, hotels almost invariably flay the 500 meter distance from the tide time.

(ii) Besides governments instruction that no building near the beach should be higher than the coconut tree is grossly violated, in some cases by the government agencies themselves.

This is clearly exemplified if you visit Kovalam. At times construction activities also involve dredging. This has a disastrous effect on the ecosystem. The death of benthic organisms at the site of dredging is a natural corollary. The after effect of dredging is even more severe as it causes stirring up of sand and its transport downstream. The situation results in the death of many filter feeding animals either by clogging of their digestive tracts altogether or by total burial of the animal. Sedentary animals like lobsters and scallops, are the worst victims of the situation. The drastic change in the ecosystem and the mass mortality of these corals due to continuous dredging of lagoons and blasting of the reef flat has enhanced the sea erosion of the coast and large scale shifting of bottom sand towards the southern half of the atoll. Dredging is done in many atolls in Lakshadweep and other parts of the country. Somewhere the once beautiful underwater gardens of the atolls with rich and varied fauna and floor are being totally depleted and lagoons found barren. This affects present tourist sites and also the potential ones.

Another factor which affect the concerned ecosystem is deforestation. Deforestation is closely connected with tourism. Removing forests either to develop beach resorts, or set up consumer and handicraft industries, to lay down lines of transport, to develop fishing farms, beach side dwellings etc. has been major problem affecting the ecosystem of the islands land beaches.

Thus removal of evergreen ramified tropical forests in Andaman and Nicobar islands by the proponents of timber/plywood industry presents a grave threat to the forests of the region. Also proposed airstrip in Lakshadweep for small aircrafts like Avro has earned the wrath of the environmentalists. It is said that about one lakh trees will have to be cut down. Further, once the ground is exposed to direct sunlight because of large expanse of clearing, a con-comitant temperature escalation would result which would ultimately lead to the depletion of ground water level. This would also affect surrounding coconut plantations which in turn would be detrimental to the economy of the local inhabitants. Similarly clearing of the coastal Mangrove forests being resorted to in Andhra, Kutch and Western coastal region may have long term effects on the ecology of the region.

Water and adventure sports add new paradigms to the already existing problem. Scuba diving or deep sea diving, if done on a massive scale and at particular spot affect the habitat of many marine organisms. Marine life is also affected by high speed cruising tourist boats. This is particularly true of Andaman and Nicobar islands and Lakshadweep both of which have a sensitive ecosystem. Fishing, or properly speaking overfishing in the form of sports, also affects the marine ecosystem. While talking about sports, golf deserves a special treatment. Golf industry which has a lucrative business proposition, a massive tourist attraction though bringing in million of rupees has a disastrous effect on the regional environment. Golf boosts tourism with it sun-dappled forests and grassy meadows along with their endowments. But Golf courses with rolling turf, engaging waterways, sandy stretches, and trimmed trees imply a severe threat to the biodiversity of the region concerned. Thus plans to set up golf courses at Goa, Puri-Konark region and Andaman and Nicobar islands are not bereft of problems. The 'deceptive greens' will have to be planned carefully.

Q7. Write a note on adventures sports.

Ans. Adventure sports are outdoor activities and India's vast geographical diversity provides a conducive field for outdoor adventures. Natural and artificial landscapes of India are ideally suited for trekking, mountaineering, rock climbing, skiing, hot air ballooning etc. India provides a suitable space for international tourists inclined towards adventure sports not only because of an immense variety of outdoor thrills but also low prices by international standard.

(1) Trekking, Mountaineering and Rock Climbing: Given its rich topographical range, India offers trekking, mountaineering and rock climbing opportunities in states apart from Jammu and Kashmir and West Bengal. In summer the focus is on the mountains in the northernmost states. Jammu and Kashmir, Himachal Pradesh, Uttar Pradesh and Sikkim, all in the lap of the great Himalayan range, provide trekking facilities where the trekking and mountaineering season is roughly from July to mid-October, August and September being the best months. Normally the altitudes range from 9000 feet to 14,500 feet above the sea level but some passes commonly encountered during a trek are as high as 18000 feet above the sea level. The majority of trekking trails in India as well within the 'inner line' which falls within a certain distance of the external boundaries of the country. In a few circumstances if a trekker wishes to cross the inner line, a prior permission is required.

(2) Skiing: Skiing is a wintersport and starts by the end of December and lasts till the end of March. Wintersports are centred around Kashmir, Himachal Pradesh and Uttar Pradesh. Skiing has become a prime attraction in recent years because India provides the cheapest ski holiday anywhere in the world. Beginners are given individual or group coaching and have a variety of gentle slopes with short ski runs to choose from. On the other hand, there is much for the advanced skiier as well.

(3) Hot Air Ballooning and Gliding: These are relatively new sports in India which were earlier limited to elite sports clubs in the cities and had limited following. But now these are fact catching on in popularity. Hot Air Ballooning has been introduced between Rishikesh, Hardwar and the adjacent valley of Dehradun. The best time for ballooning is from October to March when the surrounding temperature is cool. This makes the hot air inside the balloon lighter and enables it to rise. Suspended in a basket under a giant, colourful balloon with a pilot, a maximum of four passengers are allowed at a time in the balloon. In hand gliding the person flies while hanging from a frame like large kite, called glider, controlled by one's own movements. Paragliding is a combination of parachuting and hang gliding. For beginners the ideal terrain is a gently sloping hillock. After safely gliding a few feet off the ground and learning how to control and manoeuvre the paraglider, one can move on higher and steeper slopes. Once the controls have been mastered, one can start from a cliff or steep summit and soar thousands of feet above ground. Auli, Pithoragarh, Manali are ideally suited for hang gliding and para gliding.

Q8. Write a note on water sports.

Ans. India's geographical diversity provides the scope for a number of water sports and most of them may be termed as adventure sports. Each of India's coastal states – Gujarat, Maharashtra, Goa, Karnataka, Kerala, Tamil Nadu, Andhra Pradesh and Orissa – provide perfect beach holidays. A few of these offer wind surfing and yachting while Lakshadweep offers excellent wind surfing, snorkelling and scuba diving in the crystal clear waters of the lagoons which surround each island. The perennial rivers that flow through Uttar Pradesh are home to popular sports like rafting and canoeing.

(1) Sailing: In India, sailing has a long and colourful history, dating back to 1830 when the first yacht race was held in Bombay, for a prize of one gold coin. Since then the sports has came a long way. There has been a noticeable, upsurge in yachting activity. This can be judged by the growth of different varieties of sailboats. For solo sailors are available 'Cadet' and 'Optimist' and for sailing crenes, the 'Enterprise', 'Lightening' and 'Seabird'. India is blessed with abundance of beautiful coastline, fine sailing weather and some of the world's best sailing harbours – like Bombay and Goa.

(2) Wind Surfing: This adventurous water sport is not very old but it has become so popular that most good seaside resorts offer it as a part of their standard recreational fare. These, together with water sport clubs and good hotels, provide the main source of access to this immensely rewarding solo sport. Wind surfing is essentially a riding on a surfboard with a sail. Freestyle wind surfing is essentially a solo sport. Its growing popularity has been supported by a new technology and new materials. Once the rudiments of wind surfing have been learned, it up to the windsurfer to develop his own technique and methods.

(3) Canoeing: The canoe developed from the seagoing dugouts of the Carib Indians of the Caribbean islands. These dugouts were made from large tree trunks, which had been sharped and hollowed out. The word 'canoe' comes from 'Kanu', the Carib word for such dugout.

Canoeing as a recreational activity has grown rapidly in recent years. Essentially a solo sport, canoeing is more participative and more skilful than river rafting. In India, the abundance of natural waterways and the growing number of canoe camps and holiday packages have witnessed a rapid burgeoning of this sport.

(4) River Rafting: Rafting is done in inflatable, synthetic rubber rafts which vary in length from eight to sixteen feet. Rafting usually involves groups of six to twelve persons. For those who like to combine scenic beauty with a hint of danger, river rafting is the ideal choice. The ideally suited spot for this sport is in norther Uttar Pradesh along a seventy km. stretch of water from Devaprayag to Rishikesh. From the middle of October to May is the best suited season for river rafting. Leading river rafting experts have opined that the Ganges, Alaknanda and the Bhagirathi have the potential of developing into some of the most exciting stretches of river rafting in the world.

(5) Scuba Diving and Snorkelling: Scuba diving is deep sea diving with the help of sophisticated breathing apparatus while snorkelling is sea diving with the help of not so sophisticated breathing apparatus and not going very deep into the sea. These sports provide the diver the enjoyment of the scenic beauty under the sea. The study of flora and fauna under the water can also be done through scuba diving and sea diving but adventurous people practise it for recreational activities. Lakshadweep provides the best opportunity to scuba divers and snorkellers because of its vast and rich marine wealth.

Q9. Discuss about the impact of sports on environment. Suggest some measures to check adverse effects. [June 2006, Q9]

Ans. Though these sports are certainly a catalyst to tourism and tourism is a very important contributor to the economy, they are also proving to be hazardous to the environment in many ways. The most negative aspect of these sports has been pollution, environmental injury, degradation of the landscape and more often a disturbance in the eco systems.

Trekking, mountaineering, rock climbing and skiing affect the environment of mountainous regions. Trekkers, mountaineers and rock climbers often disturb and destroy the flora and fauna of the area by trampling. The growing number of such tourists can also lead to various erosions in the region. Littering of toxic wastes, canes, broken glasses etc. by such adventurous persons is a serious threat to the environment. South Col near the Mount Everest has been termed as world's highest dustbin because of the littering by trekkers and mountaineers. They can also damage the local flora and fauna by campfiring. Skiing in India is done mainly on natural landscapes but sometimes artificial landscapes are also prepared for different levels of skiiers by drilling and blasting of rocks and destroying natural flora and fauna. For better skiing, the bulldozing of banks to encourage snow-accumulation may accelerate erosion and cause damage to the environment.

Golf is a sport which affects the environment very severely. Making of a golf course needs high cost and a vast tract of land. To avoid high cost of making a golf course sometimes fertile land is also used which affects the food production for the sale of recreation. Sometimes, when a golf course is made in hilly areas, mountains are blasted off for landscaping. Land of hilly areas which otherwise may have been used for growing fruits is used to make golf courses. Specific landscaping of golf courses is another environmental hazard. Artificial hill, slope, pond, sand area create an artificial environment at the cost of natural flora and fauna. To make the turf of international standard sometimes the grass is imported from abroad which needs high cost of maintenance. To maintain the grass turf and the exotic foliage, chemical fertilizers, insecticides and pesticides, selective herbicides and plant hormones are used in a large acreage continuously. Due to natural rain and underground percolation, these chemicals run-off from the golf course and affect the adjoining land and water systems polluting them and causing harm to the environment as well as flora and fauna. Water sports such as sailing, canoeing, river rafting, scuba diving etc. affect seacoasts, rivers and other island waters. These sports also cause littering, erosion of banks, disturbance of birds, destruction of aquatic vegetation and marine lives, noise and oil pollution etc. Though sailing itself enhances the beauty of the landscape, but causes several other harms to the aquatic lives.

Besides these environmental impacts other adverse impacts of tourism on environment are also accelerated by these sports. Making of hotels, resorts and camping in these areas where these sports are played are the factors which harm the environment. Making of roads to promote these sports and vehicular pollution take their toll on the environment. In these circumstances it is necessary to check the adverse impact of these sports on the environment. Environmental impact assessments, with special reference to impact assessment of flora and fauna, should be done before developing and establishing skiing resorts, golf course resorts, water sports resorts and beach resorts etc. In golf courses the use of insecticides, pesticides, herbicides should be minimised and instead biofertilizers, bioherbicides and biopesticides should be used. Waste land, instead of fertile lands, should be used to make golf courses and in hilly areas smaller golf courses should be made. Natural slopes should be promoted for golf courses and skiing and artificial slopes should be avoided. Heavy tourist influx causes more harm to the environment which should be regulated. The governments should also bring strict legislations against those who harm the environment by their activities. In India diving people are indulging in coral smuggling which causes immense damage to the marine life. These practices can be checked through monitoring and legislations. Besides the government can also resort to educate the tourist and sport enthusiasts.

Q10. What are the different types of hotels? Why hotels and resorts are important components of touristic infrastructure?

Ans. The word hotel derives from the French hôtel, which referred to a French version of a townhouse, not a place offering accommodation (in contemporary usage, hôtel has the meaning of "hotel", and hôtel particular is used for the old meaning). The French spelling (with the circumflex) was once also used in English, but is now rare. The circumflex replaces the 's' once preceding the 't' in the earlier hostel spelling, which over time received a new, but closely related meaning.

Services and facilities: Basic accommodation of a room with only a bed, a cupboard, a small table and a washstand has largely been replaced by rooms with en-suite bathrooms and, more commonly in the United States than elsewhere, climate control. Other features found may be a telephone, an alarm clock, a TV, and broadband Internet connectivity. Food and drink may be supplied by a mini-bar (which often includes a small refrigerator) containing snacks and drinks (to be paid for on departure), and tea and coffee making facilities (cups, spoons, an electric kettle and sachets containing instant coffee, tea bags, sugar, and creamer or milk).

In the United Kingdom a hotel is required by law to serve food and drinks to all comers within certain stated hours; to avoid this requirement it is not uncommon to come across "private hotels" which are not subject to this requirement. However, in Japan the capsule hotel supplies minimal facilities and room space.

Classification: The cost and quality of hotels are usually indicative of the range and type of services available. Due to the enormous increase in tourism worldwide during the last decades of the 20th century, standards, especially those of smaller establishments, have improved considerably. For the sake of greater comparability, rating systems have been introduced, with the one to five stars classification being most common.

Boutique hotels: "Boutique Hotel" is a term originating in North America to describe intimate, usually luxurious or quirky hotel environments. Boutique hotels differentiate themselves from larger chain or branded hotels by providing an exceptional and personalized level of accommodation, services and facilities.

Boutique hotels are furnished in a themed, stylish and/or aspirational manner. Although usually considerably smaller than a mainstream hotel (ranging from 3 to 100 guest rooms) boutique hotels are generally fitted with telephone and wi-fi Internet connections, honesty bars and often cable/pay TV. Guest services are attended to by 24 hour hotel staff. Many boutique hotels have on site dining facilities, and the majority offer bars and lounges which may also be open to the general public.

Of the total travel market a small percentage are discerning travelers, who place a high importance on privacy, luxury and service delivery. As this market is typically corporate travelers, the market segment is non-seasonal, high-yielding and repeat, and therefore one which boutique hotel operators target as their primary source of income.

Unusual hotels : Many hotels can be considered destinations in themselves, by dent of unusual features of the lodging and/or its immediate environment:

Treehouse hotels : Some hotels, such as the Costa Rica Tree House in the Gandoca-Manzanillo Wildlife Refuge, Costa Rica, or Treetops Hotel in Aberdare National Park, Kenya, are built with living trees as structural elements, making them treehouses. The Ariau Towers near Manaus, Brazil is in the middle of the Amazon, on the Rio Negro. Bill Gates even invested and had a suite built there with satellite internet/phone. Another hotel with treehouse units is Bayram's Tree Houses in Olympos, Turkey.

Cave Hotels: Desert Cave Hotel in Coober Pedy, South Australia and the Cuevas Pedro Antonio de Alarcón (named after the author) in Guadix, Spain, as well as several hotels in Cappadocia, Turkey, are notable for being built into natural cave formations, some with rooms underground.

Capsule hotels : Capsule hotels are a type of economical hotels that are quite common in Japan.

Ice hotels

Main article: Ice hotels, such as the Ice Hotel in Jukkasjärvi, Sweden, melt every spring and are rebuilt out of ice and snow each winter.

Snow hotels : The Mammut Snow Hotel in Finland is located within the walls of the Kemi snow castle, which is the biggest in the world. It includes The Mammut Snow Hotel, The Castle Courtyard, The Snow Restaurant and a chapel for weddings, etc. Its furnishings and its decorations, such as sculptures, are made of snow and ice.

There is snow accommodation also in Lainio Snow Hotel in Lapland (near Ylläs), Finland.

Garden hotels: Garden hotels, famous for their gardens before they became hotels, includes Gravetye Manor, the home of William Robinson and Cliveden, designed by Charles Barry with a rose garden by Geoffrey Jellicoe.

Underwater hotels: As of 2005, the only hotel with an underwater room that can be reached without Scuba diving is Utter Inn in Lake Mälaren, Sweden. It only has one room, however, and Jules' Undersea Lodge in Key Largo, Florida, which requires scuba diving, is not much bigger.

Hydropolis is an ambitious project to build a luxury hotel in Dubai, UAE, with 220 suites, all on the bottom of the Persian Gulf, 20 meters (66 feet) below the surface. Its architecture will feature two domes that break the surface and an underwater train tunnel, all made of transparent materials such as glass and acrylic.

Other unusual hotels : The Library Hotel in New York City is unique in that its ten floors are arranged according to the Dewey Decimal System.

The Rogers Centre, formerly SkyDome, in Toronto, Canada is the only stadium to have a hotel connected to it, with 70 rooms overlooking the field.

The Burj al-Arab hotel in Dubai, United Arab Emirates, built on an artificial island, is structured in the shape of a sail of a boat.

The RMS Queen Mary in Long Beach, California is the only 1930s ocean liner still in existence. Its elegant first-class staterooms are now used as a hotel. The Oriental Pearl Tower in Shanghai houses an extremely expensive hotel with only 20 rooms.

World-record setting hotels Tallest : The tallest hotel in the world is the Burj al-Arab in Dubai, United Arab Emirates at 321 meters (1,053 feet). However, this title may be taken by the less illustrious Ryugyong Hotel in Pyongyang at 330 meters (1,083 feet), pending its (perhaps unlikely) completion; it has been under construction since 1987 and was abandoned in 1992.

Largest : The current largest hotel in the world is First World Hotel in Genting Highlands, Malaysia. It has a total of 6,118 rooms, and is part of the Genting Highlands Resort and Casino. The First World Plaza which is adjoined to the two hotel towers boasts 500,000 square feet of indoor theme park, shopping centres, casino gaming areas, and eateries. Previously, the largest hotel in the world was the MGM Grand Las Vegas in Las Vegas, Nevada, USA with 5,044 rooms in the main building and a total of 6,276 rooms.

Oldest: According to the Guinness Book of World Records, the oldest hotel still in operation is the Hoshi Ryokan, in Awazu, Japan. It opened in 717 CE, and features hot springs.

Q11. Certain sectors of hotel industry need to be improved. Comment.

Ans. The problems afflicting hotels may relate to the service sector or the enterprise of hoteliering. Tourist inflow is directly influenced by the problems in the service sector and hence is important from a tourism point of view. Hotels and resorts are a part of hospitality industry. It is a personal service business that requires maximum attention to people as human beings and on this industry falls the responsibility of matching a tourist's dreams to his experiences. House keeping activities which include room cleaning, tidy and sanitary conditions, linen supply, electrical and water services, furniture, room supply and services attract the sight of the tourists. Unsatisfactory house keeping activities tarnish the image of hotels and resorts.

In India, many hotels and resorts are developed without any regard to landscape or location. Landscape is a dominating element in the hotel design; particularly so in the case of a resort-cum-transit hotel. Unplanned hotel structure not only obstruct the city look but also create ugly skyline. Also meteorological conditions should be taken into consideration: glare/sun-shine, day and night temperatures, rain/humidity and storm, etc. Image problem seriously affects the hotels and resorts. It is held that quality of hotels in India cannot be as good as in advanced countries. The general perception is that unless booked in advance, no accommodation can be available in good cities. The hoteliers' perception, on the other hand, is that their establishments are first rate whereas, in fact, quality of services is not even comparable to second class hotels in the West.

Nearly 75 per cent of the problems of tourists on land are connected with unsatisfactory hotel accommodation and services. Sargent Committee in 1945 was the first to point out the dearth of hotels and resorts for foreign and domestic tourists. In 1956, an appraisal of the hotel accommodation was made by the Tourism Department, which recommended the increased number of rooms. Estimate Committee on tourism, in the same year opined that the situation was far from satisfactory. Surveys conducted by Administrative Staff Training College, Hyderabad in 1977 and the Indian Statistical Institute, Calcutta in 1982-83 have also considered lack of good accommodation as one of the most important growth inhibiting factors of the Indian tourist industry. Thus, it can be stated that for almost four decades the same perception of hotel accommodation persists.

Certain tourists have a shoe-string budget. In other words, many of the tourists may have low per-capita income and they cannot afford costlier accommodation. Cheaper private hotels often do not meet the requirements of this category of tourists. A study of comparative growth of hotel industry from 1963 to 1984 shows that the number of hotels has increased from 186 to 427. However, most of the increase has taken place in 3, 4 and 5 star hotels. The number of domestic tourists has also increased due to government incentive in the form of Leave Travel Concession, etc. Though, there are low tariff hotels, popularly known as 'Janta Hotels', their number is few. Also, the services provided are not satisfactory. Several steps should be taken to develop low tariff hotels with minimum amenities but clear atmosphere and prompt services. An important beginning has been made with the construction of Janta Hotel (Ashok Yatri Niwas) at New Delhi, which provides low cost accommodation to low budget tourists.

Some problems of hotel industry affecting entrepreneur include non-availability of suitable land, shortage of funds, shortage of man power, etc. Hotel sites should be earmarked in general developmental plans and these should be made available at reasonable cost to hoteliers. Financial institutions such as **IFCI, IDBI, ICICI,** etc. should give concessional credit to the hotels. Also, hotels and resorts should generate income through shops etc. so that they can afford a bigger man power.

Q12. How does hotels and resorts degrade the environment?

Ans. Hoteliering is a lucrative industry but has its responsibilities too. The development should not only be quantitative but also qualitative and environment friendly. The ministry of environment has stipulated explicit norms in this respect, but often these are disregarded for monetary considerations.

Touristic and recreational activities affect environment in a number of ways. If the visit of tourists to a certain place is periodic, it does not have much impact and can be controlled. However, hotels and resorts are permanent structures which make the recreational activities perpetual. Good siting and design minimise impact on landscape, but there can be severe local pest problem from waste and feedings left over by visitors. It may affect rare vulnerable species. Some of the tourists who stay in hill resorts are often found littering cans, milk bottles and cleaning tissues. Resorts located in Nainital, Kulu-Manali, Shimla, Mussorie and other parts of the country should provide the tourists with a list of instructions about do's and don'ts to preserve the environment around them. Water resorts not only disturb the tranquility on the beaches but a lot of waste is dumped in the water. Beaches in Kerala, Puri and Goa, etc. are used by tourists who throw litter and play portable stereos. Their activities not only lead to erosion of the banks but also disturb aquatic vegetation. Forest resorts can become potential threat to endangered species. Touristic movement in the forests may frighten animals. The use of torches and sound stereos disturb the forest environment. Organized coach tours by the forest resorts may result in severe trampling of forest area. The idea behind development of the forest resorts is to enable tourists to enjoy the natural and peaceful environment. However, quantitative development of forest resorts may consequently lead to gradual deforestation.

Hotel buildings in the places of tourist interest are often built in haphazard, unplanned and congested manner. A trip to a hill station like Mussorie shows the hill slopes dotted with ugly concrete structures. It not only destroys the scenic beauty but also adds to already constrained hill-resources. The construction material used in development of hotel buildings is also dumped in the nearby areas. Hotels which are located near river banks dump waste material and drain sewage in the river. River Ganges is of pilgrimage interest. Towns located on the banks of this river like Varanasi have a lot of hotels which exemplify the above problem. Small hotels in big numbers develop around already congested railway stations and inter-state bus terminuses in India. Tourists prefer these accommodations because of their locational importance.

Q13. What are the short and long term consequence of environmental degradation by hotels and resorts?

Ans. The responsibility of hotels and resorts in the environmental degradation is well manifest. However, the implications may not be physically visible immediately or remain invisible for some time. Some of the implications realised in the short run may be as follows:

Development of unhygienic conditions: Unhygienic conditions may follow due to clumsy practices of hoteliers as well as the recreationist groups. The draining of sewage, dumping of solid construction materials, unplanned and unclean vicinity and untidy services create an uncomfortable atmosphere. Also, the activities of the recreationists including throwing of feeding, litter, viz. cans, milk bottles, cleaning tissues, trampling of the area and noise pollution due to loud blaring stereo-system produce an unhealthy scenario.

Ugly structures and congestion: During the tourist seasons, hotels and resorts work to their capacity. However, tourists with shoe-string budget look for cheaper accommodations. In the last two decades, there has been a mushrooming of small hotels, either converted from residences or built in unapproved and haphazard manner. These ugly structures not only give the city a bad look, but also congest the lanes and by-lanes in the old cities. The hotels located near the New Delhi Railway Station prove the point. Similar examples can be found in cities like Varanasi, Calcutta, etc.

Decline in the occupancy curve: Although visitor behaviour is mainly determined by the provision of services, the reputation and exterior of hotels are also important factors. Hotels whose reputation become questionable due to their reported and established violation of environmental norms are bound to suffer a decline in the occupancy. Similarly, the haphazard and ugly exterior of a hotel/resort may attract very few visitors. Other than immediately visible implications there may be implications of a more serious nature. Hotels and resort may not be solely responsible for some of these implications though they play an important role. These are as follows:

Environmental degradation and tourism: Hotels and resorts are an important component of tourism. If this component becomes weak, it will certainly affect the tourism industry. As had already been discussed, in the short run occupancy may slide downwards. However, in the long run the defaulting hotels and resorts may face forced closure. The location of a hotel in a beautiful and healthy environment may enhance its reputation and earnings. Similarly, hotels and resorts may contribute to beautifying the environment. Hotel development and opening should be such that unsightly views are screened and environment is upgraded. Plantation of trees, plants, shrubs and flowers would enhance the beauty of the surrounding landscape.

Soil Loss: Unplanned and unchecked development of hotels and resorts may have very harmful effect on the soil. Some areas are reserved by the government as protected ridge areas. A hotel under construction at Bagor in Himachal Pradesh was accused of causing soil erosion recently. As soon as the construction starts, the closed system of nutrient cycling is disrupted and the nutrients escape. This causes loss of the valuable and scarce nutrients in the soil. Soil loss is particularly dramatic when it takes place on steeply sloped areas. Hill resorts are usually built on slope areas.

Deforestation and species loss: Sariska incident which brought to the fore the issue of land leasing to a private hotel company in tiger reserve area may just be tip of the iceberg. Because of local endemism and gradual deforestation, diverse and sparse population of the species, may face extinction. A complex mass of interactions and inter-relationship weave together all the eco-systems in the forest and snapping off even a single link in the chain can have a serious effect on all the others and a chain reaction of extinctions may get started. Once the wild species of a crop or animal become extinct, the genetic material for the survival of their domesticated varieties is also lost.

Climatic change and aridity: If the forest area is cut to develop hotels and resorts, it will contribute to the process of deforestation. Deforestation reduces the leaf area, which in course of time significantly decreases evapo transpiration and, therefore, rainfall. Deforestation gradually leads to the increase of more arid vegetative types.

Loss of aquatic vegetation: Resorts which are located on the sides of lakes, rivers and seas directly contribute to the loss of aquatic vegetation. Recreationists who stay at these resorts throw litter and create sound pollution by playing blaring stereo systems. They also indulge in spear-gun fishing, canoeing and rowing, sailing, motor-boating, speed-boating, water shilling, angling, etc. which disturbs the aquatic vegetation. Draining of sewage and solid waste leads to sedimentation and silt. Many lakes of our country have reduced in their pondage area. A visit to Dal Lake, Srinagar testifies to this problem.

Cultural Loss: Development of hotels and resorts in certain areas like forests and tribal habitation may disturb the ethnicity of the people. Many such areas can be located in the North-East India. Hotels and resorts are permanent structures. They also make the touristic movement in such areas permanent. Interaction of the tribal or forest people with the tourists may not help in the real development of these people as the purpose of the tourists is recreation and not education.

Q14. How can hotels and resorts be stopped from degrading the environment?

Ans. The awareness of environmental degradation by hotels and resorts is gradual. However, it is enough to activate government and various categories of people to find means and ways to check it. The onus lies on every agency and everybody who is related to hotel tourism. It may be a tourist, a hotel employee or an agency like tour operators, etc. Vigilance and efforts by several categories of people who can help check the environment degradation are as follows:

(1) Role of the Government: Role of the government is most important. Government should pass strict laws and see to it that they are implemented. Sariska incident would not have happened if the Forest Protection Act and Environment Protection Act were strictly enforced. Ministry of Environment should get pollution control devices installed at hotels and resorts, as was done in hotels at Park Street, Calcutta and in Digha. Ministry of Environment should earmark certain areas which fell in higher zones of Seismic Map. Recently, a hotel at Bagor was asked to pay Rs. one lakh to enable the experts of Forest Research Institute, Dehradun to examine whether the hotel construction could lead to soil erosion. In brief, there exists a network of rules and regulations to ensure that hotels and resorts do not encroach upon the fragile environmental zones. What is needed is adequate sensitivity and will power to implement the already existing rules.

(2) Role of Hoteliers: Hotel industry is a lucrative enterprise. Since the accommodation demands from the tourists are increasing, hotels, with no regards for environmental norms, are being developed. Hoteliers can play an important role here. Firstly, hoteliers should locate a site where construction of buildings in environment friendly and does not spoil the landscape. Secondly, they should be careful about disposing the sewage or any other kind of waste. Thirdly, they should provide the employees as well as the tourists a list of instructions of do's and don'ts. Fourthly, hoteliers should seek the help of plantation companies who plant environment friendly trees.

(3) Role of Media and the NGOs: The awareness of the environmental degradation is largely promoted by the media and NGOs. It is only after the reports are published that other agencies become active. Non-Governmental Organisation should conduct research and surveys on the environmental degradation. Centre for Science and Environment, New Delhi and other NGOs are working hard in this direction.

(4) Role of Recreationists: Undisciplined behaviour of the recreationists is responsible to a large extent for environmental degradation. Recreationists cannot be seen separately from resort hotels whose chief aim is to provide recreation and pleasure. Recreationists should keep themselves disciplined and should not throw litter, trample and pollute the area in any manner.

(5) Role of City Planners and Administrators: City Planners should allocate land to hoteliers in such a manner that there is enough spacing and the city does not become congested. Also the hotel should not destroy the city skyline. Administrators should see to it that unauthorized construction of hotels or its extension in any form is not allowed. They should also see that hotels and resorts do not pollute the city environment in any way.

≈≈≈≈≈≈≈≈≈≈≈≈≈≈≈≈≈≈

Question Papers
TS-5

≈≈≈≈≈≈≈≈≈≈≈≈≈≈≈≈≈≈

TS-5: ECOLOGY, ENVIRONMENT AND TOURISM
December, 2001

Note : Answer any **five** questions in about 600 words each.

Q1. Write an essay on the scope of Environmental Tourism in India.

Q2. Discuss the relationship between environment and development.

Q3. How can regional assets be effectively utilised in promoting environmental tourism in India? Elaborate.

Q4. Discuss main laws and Acts for protecting environment in India. How state has protected environment?

Q5. Evaluate the politics of environment in the context of tourism activities in India.

Q6. How is visitor behaviour important for environmental tourism? Discuss.

Q7. Describe the importance of wildlife for tourism promotion in India.

Q8. Assess the potential of Islands and Beaches for the growth of tourism in India.

Q9. Write a detailed note on any one of the following :

(a) Biomass of the world

(b) Indian philosophy and environment.

Q10. Write short notes on any two of the following :

(a) Responsible tourism

(b) Infrastructure and environmental tourism

(c) Visitor behaviour

(d) Wetlands

TS-5: ECOLOGY, ENVIRONMENT AND TOURISM
June, 2002

Note : Answer any **five** questions in about 600 words each.

Q1. **Write an essay on the biomes of the world and their significance.**

Q2. **Discuss the practices of environmental conservation in pre-modern world.**

Q3. **Examine the concept of Responsible Tourism and discuss the benefits that emerge from it.**

Q4. **Assess the significance of Multiplier Effect for environment friendly tourism.**

Q5. **How can tourism be used as a tool for environmental conservation? Analyse critically.**

Q6. **Discuss the main features of Tourism Policy that have a bearing on environment.**

Q7. **Write an essay on the vegetational variety of India as an important feature of environmental tourism.**

Q8. **Do you see an inevitable conflict between environmental conservation and development? Examine in detail.**

Q9. **Write short notes (in about 300 words each) on any two of the following:**

(a) Visitor behaviour and environmental tourism

(b) Islands and Beaches

(c) Environmental Laws in India

TS-5: ECOLOGY, ENVIRONMENT AND TOURISM

December, 2002

Note : Answer any **five** questions in about 600 words each.

Q1. **Describe the distinctive features of abiotic environment of the world.**

Q2. **Write an essay on Indian philosophy and environment.**

Q3. **What do you understand by the term Responsible Tourism? Explain in detail?**

Q4. **Assess the impotence of regional assets for environmental tourism.**

Q5. **What is the utility of infrastructural facilities in environmental tourism?**

Q6. **Describe main pressures on environment and also suggest measures to overcome them.**

Q7. **How can mountains be developed for environmental tourism? Suggest a plan?**

Q8. **Write short notes:**

(a) **Biodiversity**

(b) **Multiplier effect**

(c) **Pressures on Hosts in Tourism Development**

(d) **Wetlands**

Q9. **Write an explanatory essay on any one of the following:**

(a) **Environment and Development**

(b) **Islands and Beaches**

TS-5: ECOLOGY, ENVIRONMENT AND TOURISM
June, 2003

Note : Answer any **five** questions in about 600 words each.

Q1. What do you understand by the term "ecosystem"? Explain. Also describe the components of ecosystem.

Q2. Write a descriptive note on the terrestrial biomes of the world.

Q3. Examine the relationship between environment and developmental issues. Also give your opinion as a tourism professional on this relationship.

Q4. Examine the salient features of physical planning for hill and coastal resorts.

Q5. What is multiplier effect and what are its positive and negative impacts?

Q6. How can tourism help in the process of conservation? Elaborate?

Q7. Discuss in detail the importance of tourism laws and regulations that relate to environment.

Q8. Write an essay on visitor behaviour in the context of environmental tourism.

Q9. Write short notes (in about 300 words each) on any two of the following:

(i) Abiotic Environment

(ii) Responsible Tourism

(iii) Adventure Sports

(iv) Islands and Beaches

Q10. Write an essay on the negative impacts of tourism on wildlife.

TS-5: ECOLOGY, ENVIRONMENT AND TOURISM
December, 2003

Note : Answer any **five** questions in about 600 words each.

Q1. **Write an essay on communities in nature.**

Q2. **Discuss the relationship between Indian philosophy and environmental conservation.**

Q3. **Examine the importance of tourism planning in relation to environment.**

Q4. **Discuss the causes of regional imbalances in the context of tourism development.**

Q5. **Describe the major pressures on environment and the role of tourism.**

Q6. **Discuss the impact of tourism on the finance and economy of a country.**

Q7. **Examine the importance of any two biogeographic zones for tourism.**

Q8. **Discuss the role of hotels and resorts in environmental conservation.**

Q9. **Why is it important to preserve the ecology of islands and beaches? Examine critically.**

Q10. **Write notes of about 300 words each on any two of the following:**

(i) Regional Assets

(ii) Adventure Sports

TS-5: ECOLOGY, ENVIRONMENT AND TOURISM
June, 2004

Note : Answer any **five** questions in about 600 words each.

Q1. Write an essay on the biomes of the world.

Q2. Describe the history of environmental conservation.

Q3. Is there an inevitable conflict between development and environmental protection? Discuss.

Q4. What do you understand by the term Multiplier Effects? Elaborate.

Q5. Can planned tourism help conserve environment? Discuss in detail.

Q6. Discuss the utility of tourism regulations and laws.

Q7. Define the relationship between environmental protection and local population.

Q8. Examine the importance of mountains in the context of environmental tourism.

Q9. Why is it important to conserve wetlands? Discuss with reference to environmental tourism.

Q10. Write notes on about 250 words each on any two of the following:
- **(i) Linkages in Nature**
- **(ii) Responsible Tourism**
- **(iii) Tourism impact on vegetation and wildlife**

TS-5: ECOLOGY, ENVIRONMENT AND TOURISM
December, 2004

Note : Answer any **five** questions in about 600 words each.

Q1. **What do you understand by abiotic environment? Explain.**

Q2. **What is the place of environment in Indian philosophy? Elaborate.**

Q3. **Is there an inevitable conflict between the requirements of development and environmental conservation? Analyse critically.**

Q4. **Discuss the role of physical planning in hill tourism.**

Q5. **Write an essay on tourist site and locational planning.**

Q6. **Analyse the fiscal and economic impacts of the National Action Plan, 1992.**

Q7. **Discuss some of the major pressures on environment.**

Q8. **Describe the wildlife of the Himalayan zone and the Indian desert.**

Q9. **Discuss the main forms of water sports in India and their importance for tourism.**

Q10. **Write short notes on any *two* of the following (300 words each):**
(i) Terrestrial Biomes
(ii) Responsible Tourism
(iii) Wetlands

TS-5: ECOLOGY, ENVIRONMENT AND TOURISM

June, 2005

Note : Answer any **five** questions in about 600 words each.

Q1. **What is an ecosystem and what are its components? Discuss.**

Q2. **Discuss the impact of tourism on environment and suggest a few solutions for any adverse impacts.**

Q3. **Development of tourism may also help in the preservation of nature – Give your views in support of this statement.**

Q4. **How can regional assets be used for tourism promotion? Describe.**

Q5. **Discuss the causes of regional imbalances in tourism.**

Q6. **Examine the importance of tourism infrastructure.**

Q7. **Elaborate the meaning and significance of environmental thresholds.**

Q8. **Discuss the impact of tourism on wildlife in India.**

Q9. **What are the main adventure sports in India and how can they help promote tourism? Discuss.**

Q10. **Write short notes on any *two* of the following (300 words each):**

(i) Aquatic Biomes

(ii) Multiplier Effect

(iii) Acts and Laws

TS-5: ECOLOGY, ENVIRONMENT AND TOURISM

December, 2005

Note : Answer any **five** questions in about 600 words each.

Q1. **What do you understand by communities in nature? Explain by giving suitable examples.**

Q2. **Define conservation and give a brief history of conservation in modern times.**

Q3. **Discuss the concept of responsible tourism and elaborate the benefits of responsible tourism.**

Q4. **Examine the positive and negative impacts of multiplier effect in tourism development.**

Q5. **Write an essay on uneven regional planning in tourism.**

Q6. **Describe the salient features of Indian Tourism Policy, 1982 and Perspective Plan, 1988.**

Q7. **Discuss the role of visitor behaviour in environmental tourism.**

Q8. **Write a detailed note on the value of Indian wildlife for tourism.**

Q9. **Examine the importance of islands and beaches for promoting tourism in India.**

Q10. **Write short notes on any *two* of the following (300 words each):**

(i) Abiotic environment

(ii) Indian philosophy and environment

(iii) Hotels and environmental conservation

(iv) Major pressures on environment

TS-5: ECOLOGY, ENVIRONMENT AND TOURISM
June, 2006

Note : Answer any **five** questions in about 600 words each.

Q1. Write an essay on the 'abiotic environment' and environmental changes.

Refer to Dec-2006, Q.No.-1

Q2. Elaborate the importance of biodiversity.

Refer to Chapter-1, Q.No.-15

Q3. What is the place of development in environmental tourism? Discuss with the help of suitable examples.

Refer to June-2007, Q.No.-4

Q4. Bring out the significance of planning for tourism.

Refer to June-2008, Q.No.-6

Q5. Examine tourism's potential for environmental conservation.

Refer to June-2008, Q.No.-8

Q6. Discuss the importance of acts and laws for environmental tourism.

Ans. Customs and conversations of a society differ from region to region and country to country. These are rooted in the histories and cultures of the concerned society. Thus for a tourist or a tour operator it is important to know not only the kind of a culture a region has but also how the institutions of that society have drawn upon to create lanes for its governance. To take an example: A tour operator is algarising a tour to a pilgrimage site in Maharashtra i.e. Pandharpur. Here customs and conversations have evolved a rule that specialized functions of worship are performed by local community while that state administration looks after the law and order and health administration. However with the haoparikar report (1972), this distinction was sought to be blurred and the government undertook the responsibility of conducting the catirepuoudings. This led to considerable disputes. Therefore a tourist operator today needs to be sensitive to these issues while taking his group to the pilgrimage site. After rule based on customs and conversions tend to be disputed. Here a sensitivity to local context and concerns are important.

Any nation state today is founded on the bed rock of lanes enacted by the state itself. Depending on the nature of state, whether democratic or authoritarian these cones vary. Tourism industry needs to take this fundamental fact into account in shaping is agenda. Restrictive Rules and enqulations can create havoc with a planned tour. Ex-countries with restriction an freedom of movement like S. Arabia can bed to fairly restricted kind of tourism. Whereas countries like India facilitate interaction with Indian ethnicity and culture in a more in depth fashion. However even democratic countries impure restrictions. In India inner line permits are needed for accessing parts of North East India. To take another country's example Mauritius government imposes a number of constrains on the tourist arrival to see to it that mainly high subject tourists visit Mauritius. These rules and laws in Mauritius are ostensibly designed to protect the environment to Mauritius. The ministry of environment in Mauritius is clear that "To this effect the ministry of tourism is preparing in the first instance, draft legislation directly connected with the various sectors of tourism industry to regulate Hotel operations. Travel agencies and tour operators. Beach operators, boats for hide etc. An overall legislation should be capable of giving the ministry legal part in its challenging crusade to regulate all activities falling under the umbrella of tourism and at the same time controlling its impact on environment now. The need for such a legal structure is considered still more crucial if our tourism industry is not limp into the next century."

There are also specific acts regarding conservation and preservation which relate to both environment and heritage. These establish rabious environmental and heritage zones, after special facilities to visitors and regulate visitors behavior.

(i) Installation of water supply sewage treatment systems in tourism areas.

(ii) Development of proper earitary disposal of solid waste generated by Hotels and other tourist facilities.

Q7. How can local population help develop and promote environmental tourism? Elaborate.

Ans. Tourism, if well planned and controlled can help maintain and improve the environment in many ways. For instance, tourism can help justify and pay for conservation of important natural areas and development of parks and reserves including the establishment of national and regional parks, because, they are tourist attractions.

The negative impact of tourism on environment however offsets these advantages. Moreover as far as India is concerned (one can also read, third world as a whole) there are no adequate facilities to deal with environmental stress of any kind, let alone from tourism. Thus in most of the tourist destinations we find the following :

Water Pollution : Resulting from bad sewage disposal management in hotels and resorts, because it is normally connected to nearby river, lake or sea.

Air Pollution : Resulting from excessive use of internal combustion vehicles (cars, buses and motor cycles) used by and for tourists in particular area, especially at tourist attraction sites that are accessible only by road.

Waste Disposal Problems : Cutting of debris, improper disposal of solid waste from hotels, restaurants and resorts can generate both litter and environmental health problems from vermin, disease and pollution as well as being unattractive.

Ecological Disruption : It is generally observed that an overuse of fragile environment by tourists leads to an ecological damage. For instance the local paths of the community get damaged from the trampling of horses used for re-creational riding in certain coastal and mountain areas. Deforestation of ski-slopes may lead to erosions, landslide and avalanches. Animal behaviour pattern gets disturbed by uncontrolled photography and regular feeding of the animal behaviour pattern gets disturbed by uncontrolled photography and regular feeding of the animals. Their habitats can be disrupted or reduced by excessive encroachment of tourism development into them. The coastal and mountain environment is particularly vulnerable to overuse and unsuitable development.

Such environmental damage makes the host area/region, apprehensive to any tourist development, though they still invite tourists for limited economic benefit. The discussion above amply reflects the fact that in the name of limited economic protection and benefit, the hosts go on to bear the immense social and environmental cost.

Q8. Write an essay on the making of the hill stations in India.

Refer to Chapter-8

Q9. How can adventure sports be developed for attracting tourism in India? Discuss.

Refer to Chapter-9, Q.No.-9

Q10. Write short notes on any *two* of the following in about 300 words each :

(i) Biogeographic zones

Refer to Chapter-8, Q.No.-2

(ii) Ecology of islands & beaches

Refer to June-2007, Q.No.-8

(iii) Regional assets

Ans. Every place has its regional resources in the form of landscape, ecological settings, historical monuments and other places of interest. Wood Tourism throws light upon the various assets of the different ecosystem :

(a) **Coastal areas, including beaches, marine areas and wetlands:** Well developed beaches have the appeal and the carrying capacity for tourism volume. Marine parks and wetlands with their fragile ecosystem are better suited for adventure and special interest tourism.

(b) **Mountains and wilderness areas:** High mountains, forests, moors, deserts, lakes and rivers are mostly visited by various tourists interested in nature or special activities such as climbing, trekking and country skiing.

(c) **Inland rural areas:** Agricultural lands, terests, lake shores and riverbanks can provide appropriate tourism location for country side retreats and special tourism such as farm and village stays.

(d) **Urban areas:** Culture, monuments, special went and special facilities for conventions and exhibition can attract great number of tourists.

(e) **Small islands:** Natural resources such as coral reef, mangrooves, seagrass beds and forests in addition to the coastal and wilderness aspects of a small area may make islands especially attractive destination areas.

Here we are going to look at the mountain resort as a case study of a regional asset with both touristic and environmental significance.

(f) **Mountain Resorts:** Nature reposes in all its majestic glossy in the Himalayan and Nilgiri Mountains in India. Most of the hill resorts were developed during the colonial period mainly as a reseal from the summer heats for the British. Most of the mountain resorts of India are known for the three T's:

- Tourism
- Teaching and
- Tea

Variety of herbs and wild flowers are plants mushrooming in abandon, covering the mountain in thick foliage, add to the natural beauty and richness of the mountains. In order to preserve this rich foliage and plant life, many hill stations have mentioned botanical gardens.

Mountain's refreshing air also has natural regenerative power to attract the tourists and the invalids. It is not without reason that the mountain places are considered natural sanatoriums. For foreign tourists, these hill stations have the climate akin to the temperate climate of Europe. If the heat of the Indian plains becomes unbearable for those from cooler environs, then the hills are the natural choice. It was one major reason why the colonial rulers of India set up summer capitals up in the hills at Simla, Darjeeling, Nainital, etc.

A number of educational institutions with boarding facilities at various hill resorts have added to the tourist traffic. The local communities are devising new ways to exploit these natural resources for tourism - the latest being opening of remote hill tribal areas to tourist.

(iv) Pressures on environment

Ans. Tourism is one of the fastest growing industries in India and natural area tourism is an important segment of this industry. However, opening the flood gates of tourism is likely to disturb the fragile eco-system of the earth. The increased number of tourist have been a subject of debate as to their negative impact of losing the delicate balance of our ecosystem. The major pressures on environment are in context of tourism development are:

(1) Wildlife: National parks for wildlife and conservation increase the levels of tourism and recreation. The regulating authorities of tourism sector believe that with proper regulation a delegate balance can be retained between nature and tourism. But the fact suggests otherwise. Even forest resorts have caused a lot of damage. Cottage for the tourist have resulted into forest clearance - 'Mollen' - Mahavir Wildlife sanctuary is a case in sight. The same is the case with Pitchanaram mangrove forests at the month of Vella River in Tamil Nadu. The mangrove which acts as resistant to coastal erosion, tidal erosion and cyclones, has already disappeared on the eastern coast which is rich in different species of flowers and fishes.

(2) Beaches and Seas: The ecology of Seas and Beaches is very fragile. It is because here two ecosystems-land mass and water mass-interact. The balance between these two should be maintained as cultures surviving along sea coasts are very deliate. Tourism developed along sea coasts is basically tourism. The hotel company acquire vast stretches of village land. It cut the dense forest around to construct the road which disturbed the natural system of the region. These development have drastically changed the region. Also endanger the safety of exquisite rain forests and untapped gene pool of medicinal and herbal plants. Most of the island till have a forest cover of nearly 85%. But the tourist activity like trampling, littering, overturning of coral blocks and scuba diving has spelt death to these delicate polyps, damaging the sect which has been built over hundred of years.

(3) Mountains: Mountains are not exempt from the tourist devastation. Ladakh especially has all trails choked in garbage and filth, left by trekkers it is found that mountains and valleys are strewn with skins of potatoes and fruits, cooked and uncooked vegetables, shells of eggs packing of medicines and noodles, as a result vegetation is sparse in upper altitude. Dal Lake is another example that is dying slowly due to the sewage and grins in its waters. The most dangerous pollutants are the 8000 house boats which have no proper sewage disposal facilities and so flush the waste into the water; consequently bacteria and the entire range of virus thrive. As a perfect example of the saying "Tourism destroys tourism", we can see the plight of hill stations. Building construction in addition to denuding the forest cover, has brought the mono-culture of urban sprawl to these much louded townships. Apart from these short term social, economic problems, uncontrolled tourism is taking the environment to the thresholds of destruction.

TS-5: ECOLOGY, ENVIRONMENT AND TOURISM
December, 2006

Note : Answer any **five** questions in about 600 words each.

Q1. What are the abiotic components of our environment?

Ans. We know that the biological world lives within and depends on the abiotic environment. These are some of the important features of abiotic environment :

(a) Atmosphere	**(b)** Light	**(c)** Temperature
(d) Wind	**(e)** Humidity	**(f)** Water
(g) Soil		

(a) Atmosphere : Our current atmosphere is a mixture of many different gases and suspended particles. This gases in the lower atmosphere is almost the same everywhere upto the attitudes of 80 km. The atmosphere contains minute liquid and solid particles. These are known as aerosols. Most of these are found near the earth's surface and originate as a result of soil erosion due to wind, forest fires, salt crystals from oceanic sprays and volcanic eruptions.

(b) Light : The first and foremost requirements of life is energy and sunlight. Solar radiation is the chief source of energy on this planet. Sunlight evaporates water that later falls as rains. Plants that are fundamental to all life on earth have the ability to trap some of the solar radiation the strikes the earth. It is also important in the life of animals.

(c) Temperature : All living organisms are influenced by temperature. Most organisms survive within a narrow temperature range. Infact, each species tends to have its own range of temperature within which it can function normally. Maximum temperature is that on which the activity starts, maximum beyond which activity is not possible and optimum at which it is at its highest place.

(d) Wind : The strong moving current of air or wind determines weather conditions and becomes an important environmental factor for some organisms. Plants are highly influenced by wind. One of the physiological activities such as evapo-transpiration is directly affected by strong or slow wind.

(e) Humidity : Amount of water vapour or moisture in the atmosphere is known as humidity. When atmosphere holds the maximum quantity of moisture at a fixed temperature and pressure then it is known as absolute humidity. It directly regulates the rate at which water evaporates from the body surface of land organisms by various physiological actions such as transpiration, perspiration etc.

(f) Water : Water is essential requirement of life. The requirement of water differs from one organism to another and the distribution of organisms depends upon the extent of the need and special adaptation for conserving water.

(g) Soil : Soil is chief reservoir of mineral elements required by the plants and other organisms. Plants take the macro and micro nutrients from the soil in soluble form. The quantity of available nutrients, the water holding capacity and the aeration of soil play major roles in determining soil fertility. All the environmental features as sunlight, temperature, humidity etc. do not function is separation. These is close linkage between these factors.

Q2. How has the environment been understood in the Indian philosophical traditions?

Ans. Environment in Indian thought is not conceived as a physical, lifeless entity; it is very living mechanism where humans are one of the many living creatures. The Indian textural tradition conceived environment as a system with life which has synchronized the complex internationship of numerous living and non-living entities. Even the biotic world has been perceived as a living creature with a soul. It was a very significant concept as it placed man as equal to every other element of the Environment. The Indian thought greatly emphasizes upon very cordial relationship among all the elements of our world. To highlight the importance of various components of our Environment, various rituals has been institutionalized. These ritual ensured that we treated even the non-living world with great care and maintain a harmony.

For example, Fire is conceived as a messenger of God. Earth has been considered as mother goddess. Sky is worshipped as father. Earth worship manifested itself even in stone worship. The non human living world has also been given a very kind attention in Indian philosophic thought. There is a whole tradition of anthropomorphism, where various kinds of plant and animal life have been ascribed special position. The ancient tradition of worship of Pasupati is one such example.

Cutting across historical, philosophical debates, the one principle which underlies and provides unity in Indian Philosophy as also continuity of vision and perception is the assertion that man is only among all living matter. Man's life depends upon and is conditioned by all that surrounds him and sustain him. It is therefore, Man's duty to constantly remind himself of the environment and the ecology. We now know that resources exist within Indian philosophical traditions for the elaboration of an ethnic suited to environmental problems. To sum up we can say that man is related to nature the elements and animals and plant life. The environment in which he lives is not an alien environment. The tales of Panchatantra also highlight the special position which is given to living world. Animals are given human characteristics of not only language but also faculty of feelings and rationality. It tries to give lessons to mankind by highlighting the problem through animal world's characteristics. Different attributes of animals have been identified and are very beautifully utilized in these tales. Cow is worshipped, Trees are worshipped. Various animals are allotted to different Gods and Goddesses are their mode of transportation to highlight their utility and enhance their positions. Indian philosophical though also highlights the numerous species of flora and fauna and their special position vis-a-vis environment and a Master giving creature. This totalistic view is a great achievement of the Indian Philosophy.

Q3. What is the nature of relationship between environment and development?

Ans. The earth is facing an environmental crisis. There is now a worldwide consensus on this. There is little doubt that this crisis can be attributed to the manner in which the industrial and technological development has taken place in the world. The crux of the problem is, that the extent of human reproduction is infinite while the resources of the Earth to support human life are finite. Thus, technology based development confronts modern civilization with a challenge to make a decision or rather, a series of decisions about how the enormous power now available to society will be used. The need to control the development of technology be regulating its application to creative social objectives makes it ever more necessary to define these objectives and modify the existing relationship between Environment and Development based on technology.

Population : The world will have to come to grips with the population problem before the end of the present century if life is to remain tolerable on the planet Earth in the next century. The problem can be tackled in two ways, both the approaches drawing on the resources of modern technology.

Social Difficulties : The suggested solution for the population problem will bring to the fore secondary social problems associated with a way of life based upon large scale technology. These are clearly visible in the advanced industrial countries, but they are likely to reach out to other societies as well. The cities of many industrial nations are already afflicted by urban blight.

Ecological Problems : The third and the most important problem area of modern technology based development in the society is the ecological problem of preserving a healthy environmental balance. Although man had used the natural resources for centuries, there was no threat to the environment until the down of the industrial era.

Imperialism, colonialism, flight for supremacy, market economy, mad race for profits, world wars etc. threatened the environment in their own ways. Today, once again, it is the exploitation of the nature for mass industrial production with the help of modern technology that has created a global environment crisis. Although, some protective measures, such as the establishment of natural forests and wildlife sanctuaries were taken decades ago, yet a great increase in population and in the level of industrialization has caused a public crisis. The great public concern with pollution in the advanced nations in both overdue and welcome. Once more, however, it needs to be said that the fault for this waste making abuse of development lies with man himself, rather than with the technology he uses. For all his intelligence, man behaves in communities with a certain thoughtlessness for the environment that is potentially suicidal. It is debatable, then, whether technology based development is a blessing or a bane.

Q4. What are the ways in which tourism related activities can affect the traditional community life?

Refer to June-2008, Q.No.-5

Q5. How can tourism be developed as a tool for conservation?

Refer to June-2007, Q.No.-5

Q6. Visitor behaviour can play a crucial role in the preservation or the destruction of the environment. Discuss.

Refer to June-2008, Q.No.-8

Q7. Write a note on the 'Politics of Environment'.

Ans. First Refer to Chapter-7

Awareness of the political dimensions of tourism, and more particularly the uneven allocation of power in a society or a community, should caution us about the outcomes of tourism planning exercises. Certain interests are often better able to achieve their objectives than others not only because of their greater resources but also because of their ability to influence the direction of tourism planning and policy. In tourism planning and policy making, often, power politics becomes the order of the day.

Public participation in tourism planning at times is more a form of demonstration than actually of giving power to communities to form their own decisions. In addition, participation ought not to be assumed to affect planning outcomes. Alternatives may have already been defined before public participation began, while any changes which do occur may simply be changes at the margin.

Therefore, notions of representation and responsiveness in tourism planning and policy making need to be assessed in the light of the reality or unreality of participation. According to **Fischer** (1990), genuine political participation requires "a political system... in which each citizen is able to authentically engage in the political processes of policy decision making. Speech and argumentation are the basic media of these processes; each citizen must, therefore, have significant voice in them.

The outcome of the deliberative process, a democratic decision, must be founded on the most persuasive argument".

However, this approach is still in the minority in tourism planning and policy analysis. The dominant approach is to ignore such participatory values. In order to achieve a sound base, tourism policy analysts and planners will need to be both proactive in their design of planning systems as well as understand the political structures they are operating in. Urban planners have described such systems as 'participatory design' or 'advocacy planning'. In the case of urban planning, 'advocacy planning' means speaking for those who will actually use the building, instead of doing research for those who hold the power. It means helping people in a community do their own planning. Such an approach will challenge many ideas about the role of government in the tourism planning and policy process, particularly with respect to the roles of the 'bureaucratic' expert and interest groups.

Q8. What is the difference between a mountain and a hill-station? Discuss with reference to their relationship with tourism.

Refer to Chapter-8

Q9. W hat are Wet-lands? What impact does tourism have on them?

Refer to June-2008, Q.No.-10

Q10. Write short notes on any *two* of the following in about 300 words each :

(i) Ecosystem

Ans. The ecosystem is what we choose it to be. It can be the biosphere, earth, forests, rivers, ponds, island etc. Ecosystem is, thus, a handy operational term that can be applied at any scale. In tourism it is often applied in the context of a destination i.e. the ecosystem of a destination. Also we can say ecosystem is an intricate network consisting of biotic and abiotic factors, connected through complex interactions that arise between the biotic and abiotic components.

The components of Ecosystem: In addition to the wide range of biotic forms found on the island, abiotic components such as soil, water, air and light too constitute an integral part of the island ecosystem. The complex interactions between these factors create conditions suitable for the existence of life. Both abiotic and biotic components together form the ecosystem. The living organism require energy for their life processes and materials for the formation and maintenance of body structure. The energy and materials are obtained from food taken up by the organisms. All living beings in an ecosystem are related among themselves through food. Organisms are broadly divided into two categories producer and consumer. The green plants are producers as they there the capacity to manufacture their own food from existing supplies of water and carbon dioxide utilizing sunlight as a source of energy. This process is known as photosynthesis. Not only big trees are efficient in this solar energy fixing process but diatoms, green algae and phytoplankton also produce food.

Therefore animals and most microorganism unlike plants cannot capture energy from the such as plant do. To obtain energy and nutrition they eat plants directly or feed on plants indirectly by eating other organisms. Therefore animals and most microorganism are consumers. Consumers may belong to one of the four class on the basis of their food. There are :

- Herbivores
- Carnivores
- Omnivores and
- Detritus feeders.

A consumers that eat only plant is a herbivore and the animals which prey on animals are known as carnivore. A consumer that eats both plants and animals is an omnivore. Detritus feeds are decomposers. The deer on partially decomposed remains of plants and animals and obtain both energy and nutrients from dead organic matter helping in recirculation of the materials on the environment. Numerous kinds of bacteria, fungi, earthworms are all examples of decomposers.

(ii) Master Plan in Tourism

Ans. First Refer to Chapter-6

The development of a tourism master plan provides a structural framework for development, management and monitoring with the aim of pre-empting problems, mitigating impacts and fostering/maintaining equitable relationships between the various stakeholders (all key components of sustainable resource management). It also provides for intersectoral cooperation to mutual benefit. If the goals of local stakeholders are incorporated into the planning, development, management and monitoring stages, then an effectively managed, supply-led system may evolve within which many of the problems exhibited by unplanned and unregulated demand-led tourism may be avoided. In terms of the wider management process a tourism master plan can be developed in the following way:

(a) environmental audit: biophysical, socio-economic and cultural resource assessment,

(b) stakeholder feedback through a 'Rolling programme' of stakeholder consultation,

(c) structural framework for tourism master planning,

(d) implementation and development,

(e) management and monitoring: stakeholder representation and policy adjustment.

In points (1-5) above, it is the tourism master plan that represents the central element. By incorporating the data generated during steps 1 and 2, it seeks to balance the various stakeholder interests, generating a comprehensive framework for development, management and monitoring. However, in order to successfully follow the above approach it is also necessary to have in place a number of additional components:

– community support and commitment,
– political support and commitment e.g. policy,
– integration of planning frameworks at all levels,
– assembly of appropriate expertise/skill-base,
– access to necessary resources,
– financial support.

In conclusion, if the approach outlined above can be successfully adopted, then it may be possible for a destination/area to develop a quality tourism product without degrading the resource base upon which tourism, and other industries (e.g. fishing) ultimately depend. In this way, tourism may function as a platform for sustainable rural development and conservation through intersectoral cooperation for the mutual benefit of all.

(iii) Wildlife

Refer to Chapter-5, Q.No.-1(3)

(iv) Environmental Thresholds

Refer to Chapter-7, Q.No.-2

(v) Tourism Infrastructure

Ans. Tourism needs accommodation, transport and attractions to enlarge its outreach. The new approach of the government to this issue is that the state has made a substantial contribution to the development of services in the country and now the time has come to encourage the private sector and foreign investment for accelerated growth of tourism. It is developing a model which identifies weakness of infrastructure as the main hurdle in increasing India's share of the world tourism. The action policy therefore wants to develop areas on a selective basis for intensive development and to identify destinations which already have tourist attractions so that optimal use can be made of such areas, like DELHI-AGRA-JAIPUR.

(1) Accommodation : Hotels form an important and vital segment of tourism infrastructure. The present capacity stands at 55,000 rooms in the approved category which needs to be doubled by the end of the decade if we have to double our share of the international tourist market. The government has drawn up a fiscal concession scheme to draw investment to this segment including tax holidays and exemptions as well as loan waivers. The regions which get the highest state subsidy will be rural areas, hill stations, pilgrim centres and island and beach resorts. The heritage hotel scheme is also going to take tourism development into the hinterland of major tourist circuits. Accommodation for domestic tourists is to be strengthened by establishing camping sites, tented accommodation and paying guest accommodation. Apartment hotels are also being envisaged.

(2) Transport : Tourists use air and surface transport to reach their destination. We therefore have to develop an inter-modal mix of transport where tourists come to India by air, link to a special tourist train, take a coach tour or follow a part airport surface itinerary. We therefore need to enlarge our wayside facilities and transport systems. This includes importing state of the art coaches and cars, improving the conditions of national and state highways and the facilities required to access attractions. Subsidy schemes are being envisaged for the implementation of this plan so that an important need of the travel trade can be met. In the field of air transport two new schemes that have been implemented are the open-sky or liberalised charter policy and the establishment of six private airlines. The Directorate General of Civil Aviation (DGCA) automatically grants permission for charter flights and in one year of its liberalisation, 50% of tourists coming to India are now using charters. The private airlines will play the role of linking them to their different tourist destinations.

For rail transport, other than the use of air-conditioned coaches on the major trunk routes, special tourist trains are being developed along the lines of the palace on wheels, which are to link major tourist circuits outside of Rajasthan like the Gujarat-Rajasthan circuit and the Mysore-Goa circuit. Water transport by hydrofoil as is being developed on the Bombay-Goa link and luxury cruises are also being introduced to India for the incentive tourist market. Cruise ships run by Shipping Corporation of India are already on the Lakshadweep and Andaman and Nicobar Islands routes. Indian tourists are also to be encouraged to take international cruises with the liberalization of the foreign exchange regulation.

TS-5: ECOLOGY, ENVIRONMENT AND TOURISM
June, 2007

Note : Answer any **five** questions in about 600 words each.

Q1. Write a note on the history of conservation with special reference to Indian philosophical traditions.

Ans. Conservation of natural ecosystems and animal inhabitants has a long and complicated history. Modern conservation attitudes and practices have evolved largely in the context of western society. They have been modelled definitely by the major political, economic and intellectual revolutions that western society has experienced. A fundamental Judeo-Christian belief is that nature was created to serve the human all. Hence, the exploitations of nature is a legitimate and natural pursuit. Until beginning of 18th century however, the rights and records of exploitations of the nature of largely in the hands of an elite aristocracy. The democratic revolutions of the late 1700's including the American revolution of 1775-1783 and the Frenet revolution of 1789, triggered a restructuring of the from work of most western societies. With this change came increased access of individuals an enormously expanded ability to exploit resources and create material wealth.

By the middle decade of 19th century biology was undergoing a revolutionary change in its view of the natural world i.e. the replacement of a static, creatiorist view of life by an evolving mechanistic view. This change is best exemplified by the emergence of the theory of evolution by natural selection, presented jointly by Charles Darwin and Alfred Wallace. The concept of natural selection replaced the creationist view of the original giving species with a mechanistic process of interaction within nature. The evolutionary view also opened the eyes of many to the fact that change in the environment, including changes caused by humans, could bring about the extrication of many kinds of organisms, as the fossil record demonstrated.

World War II - suddenly diverted attention from conservation issues. It also initiated an era of unparalleled economic expansions and explosive growth of technology and human population. Technology provided synthetic fibres, plastics, inorganic pesticides, leaded fuels and many of the products that sooner or later caused the introduction of toxic and biological topic and biologically active materials into the environment. To this explosion of industrial technology was added that of the human population. The result was exponential growth in the pollution of air, land and water by chemicals and chemical wastes. Soon, natural mechanism of detoxifications of pollutants and static adjustments to this effect were overwhelmed by these inputs.

The ecological situation today has become quite critical today so critical that if we do not take urgent steps, things will go out of control and beyond redeem. Man's various activities in all fields of daily life, particularly the industrial and agricultural ones, are rapidly destroying nature. By destroying it, man is creating conditions for self destruction. Environment in Indian thought is not conceived as a physical, lifeless entity; it is very living mechanism where humans are one of the many living creatures. The Indian textural tradition conceived environment as a system with life which has synchronized the complex internationship of numerous living and non living entities. Even the biotic world has been perceived as a living creature with a soul. It was a very significant concept as it placed man as equal to every other element of the Environment. The Indian thought greatly emphasizes upon very cordial relationship among all the elements of our world. To highlight the importance of various components of our Environment, various rituals has been institutionalized. These ritual ensured that we treated even the non-living world with great care and maintain a harmony.

For example : Fire is conceived as a messenger of God. Earth has been considered as mother goddess. Sky is worshipped as father. Earth worship manifested itself even in stone worship. The non human living world has also been given a very kind attention in Indian philosophic thought. These is a whole tradition of anthropomorphism, where various kinds of plant and animal life have been ascribed special position. The ancient tradition of worship of Pasupati is one such example. Cutting across historical, philosophical debates, the one principle which underlies and provides unity in Indian Philosophy as also continuity of vision and perception is the assertion that man is only among all living matter. Man's life depends upon and is conditioned by all that surrounds him and sustain him. It is therefore, Man's duty to constantly remind himself of the environment and the ecology.

We now know that resources exist within Indian philosophical traditions for the elaboration of an ethic suited to environmental problems. To sum up we can say that man is related to nature the elements and animals and plant life. The environment in which he lives is not an alien environment. The tales of Panchatantra also highlight the special position which is given to living world. Animals are given human characteristics of not only language but also faculty of feelings and rationality. It tries to give lessons to mankind by highlighting the problem through animal world's characteristics. Different attributes of animals have been identified and are very beautifully utilized in these tales. Cow is worshiped, Trees are worshipped. Various animals are allotted to different Gods and Goddesses as their mode of transportation to highlight their utility and enhance their positions.

Indian philosophical though also highlights the numerous species of flora and fauna and their special position vis-à-vis environment and a Master giving creature. This totalistic view is a great achievement of the Indian Philosophy.

Q2. What do you understand by tourism planning? Give concrete examples of how it influences tourism.

Ans. The importance of planning in tourism areas has emerged as an effort is made to create a balance between the tourist environment and the local environment. This is critical particularly in developing countries like India where the impact is the strongest because of lack of a necessary infrastructure to preserve the existing environment. However it should be remembered that tourism and environment are complementary and supplementary to each other. The controlled and uncontrolled endeavour of the societies all over the world to harvest the profit potential of growing magnitude and changing structure of tourist traffic have, on the one hand, enhanced the magnificence of some selected tourist spot and areas. But on the other, they have also stimulated the ugly growth of hutments, slums etc. The unkindly use of resources to commercialization taking precedence over the protection of landscape and environment has resulted in insufficient infrastructure and inappropriate superstructure. The destruction caused by trade and haphazard development has awakened the societies to the paramount need for planning of tourism development based on scientific research of requirements of the travel market and absorptive capacities of the tourist destination spots.

The process of planning inevitably involves identifying certain areas or locations with a long term tourist potential. Mass tourism demands environmental resources in a big way and with the problems of mass tourism arises the issue of protecting and conserving the ecological system which the tourists erode unintentionally. It is therefore necessary that while planning the construction of new hotels, buildings etc. due consideration should be paid to the fragile beauty and unique natural settings. Every new constructions in that are a should be environmental oriented and adequate facility for garbage and dirt disposal should be made. Once the public is made aware of the benefits of a sound ecology and environment then there would be an overall change in the attitude of tourists. It should be environment that must be highlighted that tourism be considered an ally and not an adversary in conserving ecology. Finally, these should be the introduction of planning procedures and controls to ensure good management of the environment. Once the site become a tourist spot, the popularity of its attractions demand management controls which might have seemed necessary without tourism.

Q3. Make an assessment of Indian Government's Policy on tourism.

Ans. Current national policies and tourism policies of various states and union territories in India priorities infrastructure driven tourism, and rarely address issues of impacts, regulation, and management.

Environmental regulation in tourism is weak, and even what exists is flouted with impunity, by both policy makers themselves and the tourism industry

We demand that national and state government reclaim their regulatory role by :

Seriously considering the negative and destructive impacts of tourism on the environment and indigenous & local communities and incorporating these in tourism policies and planning frameworks

Setting up mechanisms that involve local communities and local governments to monitor the impacts of tourism. We ask that research and monitoring for such impact assessment be privileged.

Regulating tourism growth taking into consideration ecological and social carrying capacity of locations.

Adopting people-centred tourism planning and policy formulation to reduce environmental impacts of tourism;

Formulating policies that are geared to preserving and conserving the natural environments rather than opening them up for relentless exploitation by development activities including tourism; In the light of unchecked proliferation of tourism into newer and fragile areas, taking steps to check access and growth, including moratoriums wherever required on the entry of tourism;

Strengthening regulation and laws to ensure the protection of ecosystems and customary rights of indigenous & local communities; in this regard :

Disallowing proliferation of tourism establishments on the peripheries on forest, protected areas strengthening the CRZ Notification, 1991, dealing sternly with violations and scrapping the proposal to replace the CRZ Notification, 1991 with the CMZ Notification reinstating tourism in the list of the developmental activities that require environmental clearances under the EIA Notification, 2006

Now Refer Chapter-6

Q4. What are the various aspects of environment's relationship with development?

Refer to Dec 2006, Q.No.-3

Q5. Tourism and conservation are not inherently incompatible with each other. Critically examine.

Refer to June 2008, Q.No.-6

Q6. Elaborate the meaning and significance of environmental thresholds.

Refer to Chapter-7, Q.No.-2

Q7. Discuss the impact of tourism on vegetation and wild-life in India.

Ans. Tourism impact on vegetation and wildlife : The impacts of tourism an wildlife is a mixed one -some positive and some negative. Let us take up the positive impacts first. The most impatient positive Impact is that it aids in making the tourists ecologically aware, often encouraging them take up conservation measures and initiative to minimize pollution. It has also led to the main finance of sense environment such as of historic sites. Movements and also the wildlife. Another positive feature of tourism is that it has promoted research and environmental impact studies.

Tourist Behaviour : This is one of the most crucial factors that affect the wildlife directly and indirectly in a number of ways:-

(i) **Indiscriminate collection of wild plants and flowers :** Unorganized and carelessly conducted botanical and zoological excursions lead to mass proofing of wild plants and capture of wild animals, thereby, affecting the established wildlife papulation in that area.

(ii) **Disturbance of wildlife :** Tourism has affected the feeding and breeding habits of many wild animals.

(iii) **Souvenirs from wildlife :** It is quite natural for tourists to being souvenirs from the place they had visited.

(iv) **Sports :** Careless handling of scuba and boat equipment, surf riding patrol driver vehicles and other recreational vehicles leave harmful remains in water.

Q8. How are islands and beaches affected by excessivc tourism?

Ans. Tourism and environment are mutually inter-related. While tourism requires a good natural environment, not to speak of socioeconomic environment, for it to flourish, the existence of the latter pre-supposes, a controlled, disciplined and regulated tourism. India with such diversified physiography, has much to offer by way of tourism, the Himalayas are perfect for sking, skating, hiking an trekking. The tourists from colder climates looking for sunshine and warm water beaches constitutes one of the largest segments of present day tourism. The pleasure periphery of European and American tourists which ended at the Mediterranean and Caribbean now extends to the beaches of Asia and Pacific. India plays a major role in this regard. The beaches along the Arabian sea coast are ideal for bathing surfing and sailing.

These days the environment of the islands and beaches is threatened, on the one hand, by human activities and encroachment, and on the other, by natural calamities. Natural calamities include cyclones, excessive rains, local upheavals and the presence of certain predator plants like Acathanster which have destroyed the massive corals of minicoyatol. Like wise pollution beaches by dumping of human wastes as well as defecation is a major problem in many parts of the country. The human activities like building and construction activities either intended to make guest houses, restaurants, hotels almost invariably flag the 500 meter distance from the tide line. At time these construction activities also involve dredging. This has disastrous effect on the ecosystem. The death of benthic organism at the sick of dredging is a natural corollary. The after effect of dredging is even more severe as it causes stirring up to sand and its transport downstream. The situation results in the death of many filter feeding animals either by clogging of their digestive tracts altogether or by total burial of the animal. The drastic change in the ecosystem and the mass mortality of these corals due to continuous dredging of lagoms and blasting of reef flat has enhanced the sea erosion of the coast and large scale shifting of bottom sand. Another factor which effect the concerned ecosystem is deforestation.

The removal of every green ramified tropical forests in Andaman and Nicobar island by the proponents of timber industry presents a grave threat to the forests of the region. Also proposed airstrip in Lakshasweep for small air crafts has earned the wrath of the environmentalist. These are the happenings around the environment including island and beaches also. It we want to conserve or preserve our natural beauties we have maintain the norms regarding preservation. By the foregoing discussion we can say that it is very important to conserve or preserve the ecology of island and beaches.

Q9. What is the relevance of hotels and resorts in tourism?

Ans. The democratization of leisure and growth of tourism as a mass movement in recent years is indisputably important for development of tourism as an industry. The stay and travel factors and their mutually accelerating interaction and primordial relationship, it is said, have primarily contributed to tourism emerging as a mass phenomenon. Tourism can be seen as the sum of the relationship resulting from travel and stay of non-residents to the extent that the stay does not need a permanent residence and does not come from a paid activity.

Hotels, thus can be seen as a basic element of tourism industry. All the national scenery, all its climatic virtues and all the sporting and recreational facilities of a country cannot suffice to sustain a good volume of tourist trade without an adequate development of hotels and resort resources. So much is the significance of hotels/resorts as infrastructural component of tourism industry that it is remarked, "No hotels no tourism". Basically, infrastructure includes all forms of construction on and below the ground required by any inhabited area in intensive communication with the outside world and as the basis for extensive human activity within. When we talk about touristic infrastructure it not only includes the accommodation sector, but also transport system, touristic sports, travel agencies, tour operators, the entertainment industry, art and crafts, the souvenir industry and so on. The acceleration of economic growth requires a prior development of touristic infrastructure. All the developing economies are making a high level investment of capital in building infrastructure. The present inadequate infrastructure in India needs to be expanded and development of hotels and resorts would be a welcome step in the right direction.

If seen in a broader context, the development of tourism is a multi-dimensional phenomenon consisting of many diverse but interdependent activities. It entails co-operations and co-ordination among hoteliers, tour operators, planners and local administrators. The objectives of the whole co-ordination includes generation of social and economic benefits like employment and tax revenue generation and foreign exchange earning, promoting social and cultural cohesion and national integration, augmenting public utilities and social facilities and providing support to local handicrafts and cultural activities.

Q10 Write short notes on any two of the following in about 300 words each :

(i) Biomes of the world

Refer to June 2008, Q.No.-2

(ii) Linkages in Nature

Ans. Linkages in Nature : One, the ecosystem is what are choose it to be it can be the biosphere, earth, forests, rivers, ponds, islands, wheat field, an aquarium, a jar of and water and even a rock with lichens growing an it ecosystem is, thus, a handy operational term that can be applied at any scale. In tourism it is after applied in the context of a destination i.e. the ecosystem of designation.

There is an ecosystem within an ecosystem and yet another ecosystem within it. It is just like the dolls made of head. The whole biosphere is an ecosystem, so are its components the earth and the atmosphere. Which in turn have smaller ecosystems.

There, the ecosystem is a unit of the nature that is in itself an independent functional entity.

Four, the ecosystem is an intricate metalmark consisting of biotic and abiotic factors, connected through complex interactions that arise between the biotic and abiotic components.

Fifth, Ecosystems vary in complexity.

Six, despite the variations in different ecosystems, the underlying basic ecological principles and processes are similar.

In addition to the rule range of biotic forms found on the island, abiotic components such as soil, water, air and light too constitute an integral part of the desired ecosystem. The living organisms require energy for their life processes and materials for the formation and maintenance of body structure. All living beings in an ecosystem are related among themselves through food. Organism are broadly divided in to the categories viz. producer and consumer.

Consumers may belong to one of the four classes on the basis of their food sources :

- Herbivores,
- Carnivores,
- Omnivores

(iii) Multiplier Effect

Refer to Dec 2007, Q.No.-6

(iv) Wetlands

Refer to June 2008, Q.No.-10

(v) Politics of Environment

Environmental Politics is concerned with four particular aspects of the study of environmental politics, with a primary, though not exclusive, focus on the industralised countries.

First, it examines the evolution of environmental movements and parties. Second, it provides analysis of the making and implementation of public policy in the area of the environment at international, national and local levels. Third, it carries comment on ideas generated by the various environmental movements and organisations, and by individual theorists. Fourth, it aims to cover the international environmental issues which are of increasing salience. Its coverage of the developing world does not reach beyond this to the affairs of individual countries, partly because of the journal's chosen focus and partly because of the number of existing journals dealing with development.

Environmental Politics is sensitive to the distinction between goals of conservation and of a radical reordering of political and social preferences, and aims to explore the interface between these goals, rather than to favour any one position in contemporary debates.

Now Refer to Chapter-7

TS-5: ECOLOGY, ENVIRONMENT AND TOURISM
December, 2007

Note : Answer any **five** questions in about 600 words each.

Q1. What is ecosystem? How can it affect the tourism business?
Refer to Chapter-1, Q.No.-4&8

Q2. What are the causes of Bio-diversity loss? Discuss the measures for conserving the Bio-diversity.
Refer to Chapter-1, Q.No.-16

Q3. "Eco Tourism is coming up in a big way". Discuss with special reference to India.
Refer to June 2008, Q.No.-7

Q4. Describe the concept of Responsible Tourism. What role can industry play in this regard.

Ans. Responsible tourism is a kind of tourism which, while safeguarding the experience of travel, would also further mutual understanding between people, prevent environmental and cultural degradation and, most of all, exploitation and dehumanization of the local population. The idea of responsible tourism has its source in two contemporary ideological pre-occupations:

(a) Counter Cultural Responsible Tourism: Counter cultural responsible tourism inverts the values, motives, attitudes and practices of conventional mass tourism, all helps in conservation effects and contributes in environmental protection.

(b) Concerned Responsible Tourism: It has been defined as a just form of travel between members of different communities. It seeks to achieve mutual understanding, solidarity and equality among participants. The principal means of promotion of this type of tourism are various small-scale projects in developing countries, establishes with local consultation and participation. The visitors are understood to pay for their stay and there is no exploitation involved.

Benefits : In these tours there is an effort to encourage and facilitate people to people encounters in an atmosphere where the visitors and the hosts can sit and interact under the same roof. The tour is arranged with positive purpose and includes the orientation lecture in which the visitors sit and listen to what the hosts have to tell about their locality's unique culture, environment and social and economic problems. So that visitors are tuned to the same wavelength.

Role of Governments : Their lies heavy responsibility on the government as regards making the idea of responsible tourism a success. It must be noted that environmental issues cannot be tackled merely by passing laws very often there is no co-ordination among the various government department. This not only leads to confusion but provides loopholes for flouting laws and regulations. These are certain measures must be initiated and implemented by the government. For example :

(a) Carrying capacity of each destination must be defined and there should be specific guidelines in this regard.

(b) It must be ensured that tourism is considered integral to land use planning at the destination and environmental friendly construction guidelines are there.

(c) All types of media should be used extensively for creating environment awareness.

Role of Locals : Besides governments, the local residents at a destination must also share the responsibility for promoting responsible tourism. This is more so because ultimately it is the locals only who tend to lose because of negative impacts or wrong policies some steps regarding are :

- Creating environmental awareness among fellow locals
- Keeping a strict watch over the construction and building activities, land use etc.
- Adopting the use of non-conventional energy resources.

It is through constant interaction between government tourism industry and the local residents that efforts initiated for responsible tourism can become a success.

Q5. Write an essay on Environmental Assets used in tourism.

Environmental assets, which are important for the sustainable growth of tourism in India, should be safeguarded from encroachment and damage by inappropriate development. These assets include special landscapes, important views, good water quality, the setting of historic buildings and monuments, biodiversity and access points to the coast and open countryside.

Anything that impacts on the environment, in which tourism is a stakeholder, is India's concern. The industry is dependent upon the country's natural environment and cultural heritage to sustain the distinctive Indian tourism product and to develop environmentally-based ecotourism products. We must ensure that the beneficial uses to tourism of a range of environmental resources - particularly water - are made clear to those with a responsibility for protecting them. The importance of high quality water for angling, cruising, water sports and bathing cannot be overemphasised. There has been sizable expenditure on infrastructure to clean up India's waters in recent years. However the current situation or the quality of various water resources, show that spending has not always been well targeted at the objective of improving water quality, and that the results of investment were not properly tracked subsequently, in order to learn from experience. Similarly, according to various tourism agencies, the attitudes of overseas visitors to litter have changed very little since 1999 despite various central and local government schemes aimed at litter reduction and control. The importance of accurate and credible data relating to the relationship between tourism and the environment

Many areas which are important to the tourist industry owe their attraction to the exceptional quality of environmental assets like landscape or particular features of the built environment. Examples include Areas of Outstanding Natural Beauty, Conservation Areas and historical and archaeological sites. It is important however to protect the qualities of such areas from unnecessary or excessive development. There is a delicate balance in many cases between exploitation of a natural resource and over development which would destroy its intrinsic character and quality.

I would always recommend that we must use the Environmental assets of any country or place without harming our mother nature. This will be the lovely gift from us to our mother nature in this critical environmental conditions.

Now Refer to Chapter3

Q6. What do you mean by 'Multiplier Effect'? How does it affect the society?

Ans. The term multiplier is used to describe the total effect, both direct and secondary, that an external source of income has on an economy. In the context of tourism, multiplier effect is the way in which total spending done by the tourist filters through the economy and stimulates other sectors as well. In tourism the multiplier effect is usually applied to encompass the direct and secondary effects of tourist expenditures on the economy, although it can be applied to employment or other variables. The term multiplier effect is actually the specialized application of a general economic technique first developed by the famous British economist in 1930.

Positive effect : The socio-economic impacts of tourism have made this field a rather controversial one in recent years, especially where tourism development has been rapid and largely unplanned and uncontrolled, with the result that there have been adverse socio-cultural as well as environmental impacts.

Direct economic benefits include provision of employment, income and foreign exchange, which lead to improved living standards of the local community and overall national and regional economic development. An indirect economic benefit of tourism is that it serves as a catalyst for the development on expansion of other economic sectors. Tourism provides the incentive and helps pay for the conservation of archaeological and historic sites and as attractions for tourist that might otherwise be allowed to deteriorate or disappear, thus resulting in the loss of the cultural heritage of an area. Conservation and revitalization of traditional arts, handicrafts, dance, music, drama and customs and ceremonies and certain aspects of traditional life styles directly feed into tourism.

Negative Impact: If not well planned and controlled tourism may generate negative impacts or reduce the feasibility of multiplier effect on local economy. Tourism is a capital intensive industry and no local involvement is possible at that level. So the large resources, required for immediate tourist facilities, airport, service roads, bridges, sewage etc. Loss of potential economic benefits to the local areas can occur and local resentments are generated if many tourist facilities are owned and managed by outsiders.

Economic distortations can take place geographically if tourism is concentrated in only one area of few areas off country and region, without corresponding development in other places. Considering that the tourism industry is seasonal it inevitably results in underemployment, unemployment and social unrest. Inflation is another direct result of the coming of tourism to an area. Foreign tourists pay for many overvalued goods and services quite gladly since they are cheaper than the same goods in their own countries. If local features such as beaches are closed off to the local population and maintained for the exclusive use of tourists, residents lose access to their amenities and can become hostile towards tourism. Over commercialization and loss of another city of traditional arts and carpets, customs and ceremonies can result if those are over modified to suit tourist demands.

Q7. What are the causes of Regional Imbalances? Discuss the important tips for equitably developed tourism growth.

Ans. Generally it is thought that tourism development creates regional imbalances. The situation however, is somewhat different.

Natural Imbalances : Different regions of a potential tourist area are endowed with uneven distribution of resources-natural, human and other locational advantages. Even regions having similar land resources may differ in landscape, topography, climatic conditions etc. Regions placed in more advantageous position attract development or progress on a preferential scale. Thus the process of development starts first in regions endowed with natural attractions or advantages. As the development process advances, the investment opportunities and mobility of tourists increase due toe availability of infrastructural facilities, markets, skilled labour etc. This gives rise to a curious phenomenon whereby the resources form the regions less developed or not developed of all begin to flow to those sectors where such development has started. The backward regions thereby get their resources drained gradually and the developed regions prosper at the cost of former. The gap between advantaged and unfavorably placed regions gets widened with every stage of development. One of the possibilities, however, is that the advanced regions create stimulus for development in their hinterland. But the gap we are talking about between the two would even then remain.

Created Imbalances : Created imbalances emerge from a willful or otherwise ignorance on the part of policy markers who pay little attention to regional resources while formulating and executing developmental plans. Generally and argument generally put forward by people in support of lopsided policies reads : in view of limited resources and their uneven distribution over space it is not possible to develop every region at the same time on the same line or scale. They further argue that in a developing economy it would be proper to invest limited resources in limited number of developmental centres, which have got better facilities for development. Such investment would create adequate surplus for the development of surrounding backward regions. It would help maintain the economic efficiency on the one hand and maximum utilization of resources on the other hand. Under this system of development strategy some regions are favoured while the development of other regions is put in abeyance for a long time. No serious attempt is made to develop the surrounding backward regions even after complete development of the first selected region. As a result the gap between regions widens giving impetus to regional imbalances.

Historical Factors : Regional imbalances may be created due to historical factors attribute to either the initial advantages enjoyed by some regions or to the ill-conceived public investment programmes effected under colonial rule. The regions which attracted the attention of various rules and administrator grew at a faster rate and thus became developed regions. The development of metropolitan cities like Bombay, Calcutta, Delhi and Madras can largely be attributed to historical factors. As a matter of fact we know that before 1912 Bengal, Bihar and Orissa were collectively known as Bengal province. Bengal attracted the attention of British Government due to some historical reasons but Bihar having rich natural and human resources never got their proper attention. As a result pace of development was much rapid in Bengal in comparison to Bihar and Orissa. This is one the important factors that has still kept Bihar as a backward province of India and so it is one of the least developed tourist cent rein the country despite and extremely rich heritage of natural and historical attraction features.

Q8. "Host and local population play an important role in Tourism

Development." Comment.

Refer to Chapter-7, Q.No.-3

Q9. Discuss the Biogeographic zones and their important wildlife in India.

Refer to Chapter-8, Q.No.-2

Q10. How can islands be formed? Write a note on Andman and Nicobar Islands or Lakshadweep Islands.

Refer to Chapter-9, Q.No.-3&4

TS-5: ECOLOGY, ENVIRONMENT AND TOURISM
June, 2008

Note : Answer any **five** questions in about 600 words each.

Q1. What are the components of an ecosystem? What role can humans play in changing the environment?

Refer to Chapter-1, Q.No-4&8

Q2. What are biomes? Describe the major terrestrial and aquatic biomes of the world.

Ans. First : Refer to Chapter-1, Q.No-9

The major biomes found are :

Tundra: The northern most biome of our planet is the arctic tundra. It lies as a treeless wet circumpolar band between the polar ice caps and the forest to the south. The predominant plants are licens, grasses, sedges and dwarf woody plants Tundra is a very fragile ecosystem as the rate of organic matter decomposition is very slow. Therefore, plants grow very slowly and the tundra takes a long time to recover from any disruptions.

Coniferous Forest and Taiga : As we travel from the Tundra we will enter the circumpolar belt of coniferous forests which stretches across North America to Eurasia, this region is called taiga, a world derived from Russian word meaning "primeval forest". It is a land of lakes, boys and marshes. The climate is cold with long winters and short summers. The dominant trees are conifers like spruce, pines and firs. Typical animals found in this region include moose, wolves, lynx. Many of these rely on their stored body fat for survival during cold month.

Temperate Deciduous Forests : Going south of taiga we would reach the temperate regions of the planet. These regions experiences moderate temperatures on average treat change during four distinct seasons. They have long summer, not to severe winters and abundant precipitation spread over the whole year. These regions are dominated by broad leafed deciduous trees such as oak, hickory, maple, poplar etc.

Temperate Shrublands : These are areas where woody shrubs predominate rather then trees. In regions with a Mediterranean type of climate i.e. hot dry summers and cool wet winters, shrubs grow close together having typically leathery leaves. Remarkably similar shrublands are found in the coastal mountains of California in O.S.A. and a Chile, at the tip of Africa and South Western Australia.

Grasslands : In the northern hemisphere grasslands are found over large areas in huge plains. Such grasslands are known as prairie in North America, steppes in Asia and pampas in South America.

Deserts : It is lying between mountains and grasslands that are too dry and hostile to life. These are the deserts. The words largest desert is Sahara. The animals of deserts are primarily arthropods, reptiles, birds and mammals. Desert soil are rich in nutrients.

Tropical Savanas : It is combination of grassland with scattered or dumped trees. These special kinds of grasslands often border tropical rain forests. The climate is warm having 100-105 an annual rainfall.

Tropical Rain Forests : This tropical region abounds with life and thousands of species of plants and animals can be seen, though no species predominates. Tropical rainforests are found on both sides of equater in South East Asia. Both temperature and humidity are very high and constant. Rainfall exceeds 200 cm a year and is distributed over the year.

Q3. Discuss the inter-relationship between tourism and environment. How can responsible growth of tourism be ensured without causing damage to the environment?

Refer to Chapter-3, Q.No-2&3

Q4. Describe the importance of participatory tourism in development.

Refer to Chapter-3, Q.No-6

Q5. "Tourism brings tension and conflict to the community." Discuss the statement with the help of Indian examples.

Ans. Aspects of tension and conflict comes into focus, when we place the colonial developments against the cultural ecology of the Himalayas in particular and Indian sub-continent in general. Let us take the example of Uttarakhand (the hill tracts in U.P.) to understand this aspect better. Traditionally, the area of Uttarakhand did not witness a shape class classification, unlike the extremely stratifies villages of the Indo-Gangetic plain. This diffused class differentiation prevailed in all the mountainous regions. The absence of sharp class cleavage within the village society, owed its origin to the ecological characteristics of mountain society. The limited extent of the cultivable land restricted the possibility of extensive cultivation. Similarly, the fragility of the soil and poor communication hampered the growth of intensive agriculture for the market.

As a result of these ecological constraints, the agricultural economy of Uttarakhand did not produce much surplus. Also, the small peasant proprietor was the dominant class in Uttarakhand, big land lord and agricultural labourers were very few. Since there was no sustained yield, there was close co-relation between the forests, pastures and the fields. In the permanent hamlets, oak forests provided both fodder and fertilizers. This enabled the hunter gatherers and pastoralists to continue their traditional mode of resource use and helped the pre-colonial communities to track a distinctive path of inter modal cooperation and co-existence.

However, the colonial intervention completely transformed the social, ecological and demographic characteristics of Uttarakhand. The traditional structure was destroyed and the new changes only benefited the Europeans. Colonial exploitation was an important part of capitalism as it emerged in Europe. An important feature of capitalism was that it produced an atomized society which was in conflict with the traditional forms of living based on collective activity and consumption by the entire community.

Similarly, colonial state control too meant a negation of the collective appropriation of nature by the community as a whole. Colonial forest laws recognised only individual rights of users and initiated the fragmentation of social bonds. This process was hastened by commercialization and capitalist penetration. The produce of the forests no longer belonged to the hill villages. Extensive tea and coffee plantations were set up by large-scale deforestation and the appropriated produce benefited the colonial elite. In the process, Lepchas of Darjeeling and Todas of Ooty faced extinction as they were deprived of their sustenance from the forests.

Q6, Why do tourist sites and conservations require special planning? Discuss its advantages.

Ans. Conservation is a method of prevention of waste or damage of our natural resources both renewable as well as nonrenewable. Since natural resources are limited, their reckless use may result in rapid depletion and exhaustion. In recent times mass tourism has been welcomed as a saviour to solve the economic problems of a region. It would also help in the conservation of resources. There we are going to discuss these aspects :

Sense of Belonging : Generally local people are not taken into confidence while formulating any plan or deciding on policies relating to tourism. This has a sense of alienation pervading the local climate on tourism. It the local are involved in the management process, it will surely develop in them a sense of attachment and the results will be fruitful.

Regulatory Measures : Regulatory measures in tourism development are one of the more important aspects in achieving conservation of resources. Haphazard and reckless use of resources have always had negative consequences. Therefore, it is imperative for planners to evolve some regulatory measures in the utilization of resources.

Self Management : The tourism industry is a typical service oriented industry which can attain higher productivity and efficiency through re-unification of workers and employers which is generally known as self management by co-workers. Government can help establish self-managed organizations or jointly managed ones-such organizations have built in bonus system in which the bonus depends on performance and on the other hand tourist can expect a much better service. Once they are warmly treated like family members, they would like to come back or would recommend the facility to other visitors. In this way it will increase this in come substantially. Such facilities do not require huge infrastructure and prove conservation friendly also.

Tourist development should be based on rational utilization of resources. Excessive utilization which leads to exhaustion or destruction of resources must not be allowed under in any circumstances. This interrelationship between growth of tourism and ecology as a whole should be emphasized. Preservation of wildlife, forests, mountains and sea beaches should be given priority.

Proper planning of tourism and a coordination with other related branches in the essence of a property managed tourist development. Constant monitoring and periodic assessment of the situation should be carried out which could alert us to the forthcoming danger. For conservation it is necessary to promote:

- biological and cultural diversity
- decentralized planning
- utilization of multiple value systems
- simple technology and
- use of indigenous management

Application of such strategies would result in social, economic and environmental aspects of life.

Q7. Write an essay on Eco-Tourism.

Refer to Chapter-2, Q.No.-2

Q8. Visitors behaviour has a great impact on environment. Discuss the role of visitors in this regard.

Ans. Behaviour connotes the way a visitor conducts himself, goes about the place, and how he interacts, how he spends, etc. In every aspect of his behaviour, a visitor affects the environment whether in a positive or negative sense.

A visitor by many of his activities and ways may disturb the apparent physical surroundings of a tourist destination. In such situations, the impact felt on the environment depends upon the degree to which such environments are open to outside interference and the degree to which such areas can withstand tourism. In many such unique environment, tourists are only allowed day excursions and are kept away from local communities under controlled conditions. This is the case in the Lakshadweep islands where Bangaram, an uninhabited island was selected for tourism development.

Leftovers and eatables : This includes paper packs, ploythene packs actual eating stuff, bottles, leaflets. This problem has assumed a universal dimension. Visitors carry along with them eatables, the leftovers of which, are strewn behind without caring.

Dumping garbage, other than eatables : This is one of the less noticed but a very common problem with the visitors. Also the visitor is relatively ignorant about the damage his act may bring to the physical surroundings.

Historical Sites : These are also affected by an indifferent visitor behaviour in a variety of ways. One problem is that posed by a special class of visitors; those connected with a film shooting company. If has often been found that film shootings leave behind deep scares that mar the grandeur of the historical monuments. This problem is, however, applicable to other sits also like a forest, an island, a beach etc. Another almost universal threat posed to the historical monuments is the tendency of the visitors to record their visits by scribbling their names.

Wildlife and Vegetation Sites : These sites have their own problems. Thus disturbing or provoking animals in a zoo or in a reserve is a common phenomenon. In addition connivance with the local people to hunt, animals, despite the governmental ban is a major threat. Also plucking branches, making marks on the trunks of the trees has its own set of problems.

Islands and Beaches : We have visitors who can unknowingly threaten the local environment. Thus excessive swimming, scuba diving not only pollutes the water but also affects the marine habitat. In addition nabbing corals which is particularly true of Lakshadweep Islands or taking back sea-shells, pebbles etc. from beaches by the visitors affects the physical environment.

Q9. Indian wild-life is considered a valuable resource for tourism. Discuss the impacts of tourism on wild-life.

Refer to Chapter-8, Q.No.-3

Q10. What is the importance of wetlands? What problems are they facing because of tourism?

Ans. The first international commencing on wetlands of international importance was held in Ramsar in Iran in February 1971. This conference made an inventory of important wetlands at the global level. The two wetlands from India which found place in the first list were chilka and Bharatpur. Gradually, wetland conservation got incorporated in the process of planning and the government of India constituted a National wetland Management committee. However, the key really lies in finding the right level of sustainable development within the carrying capacity of the lake. Long term research needed to provide information for resource management and evaluate management effectiveness in conserving the ecosystem with all its values.

In a remarkable sense, wetlands have become central points of bird observations, the lead example being set by Bharatpur sanctuary. It is therefore proposed at various forms to develop other wetlands as tourist attraction centers after all a sanctuary is not worth its value if human beings and birds cannot communicate with each other.

It is however, important to realise that tourist traffic needs to be strictly regulated. For this the wetland area can be divided into the district games :-

- Activity zones at the peripheral put of wetland
- Buffer gone
- Conservation zone forming the wetlands core where no tourism intervention should be allowed.

Wetland conservation does not mean setting wetlands aside as prohibited areas but use there is a positive manner as an important resource successful management demands much more information on how wetlands actually work so that they can be sustainably for pisciculture, aquaculture environment improvement, education and scientific research. A lot of effect is being made to conserve these ecologically distinct areas including increased public consciousness. It is clear that concept of world conservation strategy of :-

- maintenance of essential ecological processes and life system.
- Preservation of genetic cycles.
- Sustainable utilization of species and ecosystem and
- a cross sectorial approach and anticipatory environmental policies in realising the above three.

Needs to be adopted if such specific ecosystems are to be conserved. The case for perfecting and managing wetlands is based not just on sentimentality or preservation of rare species. Rather if hinges on very Real ecological and economic benefits of this ecosystem.

TS – 5 : ECOLOGY, ENVIRONMENT AND TOURISM
December, 2008

Note : Answer any **five** questions in about 600 words each. **All** questions carry equal marks.

Q1. Explain the meaning of Abiotic Environment with the help of appropriate examples.

Refer to June 2006, Q.No.-1

Q2. Discuss the impact of tourism on environment and suggest measures to reduce adverse impacts.

Refer to June 2008, Q.No.-3

Q3. Write an essay on Responsible Tourism.

Refer to Dec 2007, Q.No.-4

Q4. What is Tourism Master Plan? Explain.

Refer to Dec 2006, Q.No.-10(ii)

Q5. Analyse critically the relationship between conservation requirements and development.

Refer to Chapter-3, Q.No.-5

Q6. Describe Chipko Movement and the debate on building large dams in India.

Refer to Chapter-6, Q.No.-18&19

Q7. Discuss how tourism is both an opportunity to the locals as well as pressure on locals.

Refer to Chapter-7, Q.No.-4

Q8. Evaluate the impact of tourism on wildlife.

Refer to Chapter-8, Q.No.-3

Q9. Discuss the importance of wetlands. Also examine the impact of tourism on wetlands.

Refer to Dec 2006, Q.No.-9

Q10. Write short notes on any two of the following in about 300 words each :

(i) The Aquatic Biomes
Refer to Chapter-1, Q.No.-11

(ii) Indian Philosophy and Environment
Refer to Dec 2006, Q.No.-2

(iii) Visitor Behaviour
Refer to Dec 2006, Q.No.-6

(iv) The Making of Shimla
Refer to Chapter-8, Q.No.-5(1)

(v) Adventure Sports
Refer to June 2006, Q.No.-9

Word Meaning

Abundance – large quantity, plenty

Anchorage – port, waterfront, dock

Biome – a division of the world's vegetation that corresponds to a defined climate and is characterized by specific types of plants and animals, e.g. tropical rain forest or desert. The world's lakes and oceans may also be considered biomes, although they are less susceptible to climatic influences than terrestrial biomes.

abiotic – describes the physical and chemical aspects of an organism's environment

biotic – relating to life and living organisms, or caused by living organisms

biomass – the mass of living organisms within a particular environment, measured in terms of weight per unit of area

Boreal – describes a region that has a northern temperate climate, with cold winters and warm summers

Benign – kind, benevolent, caring, kindly

Crust – coating, outer layer, outside

detritus – debris, accumulation, backlog, silt

Discernible – visible, noticeable

dune – bank, sandbank, hill

detritivores – organism that feeds on detritus, U.K. an organism that feeds on decaying animal or plant material. Detritivores such as bacteria, earthworms, and many insects aid in breaking down soil.

Ecology – natural science, environmental science, natural balance

Epidemiology – study of disease origin and spread, the scientific and medical study of the causes and transmission of disease within a population

Gyre – a circle or spiral

Hawk – a bird of prey that is active in the daytime, typically having broad wings, a short hooked beak, strong talons, and a long tail.

Hibernate – take cover, hole up, overwinter, hide

Helix – coil, curl, twirl, twist

Herring – a small commercially important fish with silvery scales. Native to: northern Atlantic .

Isolation – separation, segregation, loneliness

Morphological – structure of organism, biology the form and structure of an organism or of a part of an organism

Monogenic – describes a characteristic that is controlled by one gene or one pair of genes

Parlance – manner of speaking, phrasing

Pecking – pick something up with beak, to take small bits of food using a beak

Perceived – supposed, alleged, apparent

preying – aggressive, plundering, predatory

Plankton – a mass of tiny animals and plants floating in the sea or in lakes, usually near the surface, and eaten by fish and other water animals

permeate – infuse, flood, saturate stunt – act, exploit

rot – decompose, decay, perish

Tilth – the plowing of land in preparation for growing crops

trample – crush, walk on, step on, walk over

terrestrial – worldly, global, earthly

vertebrate – an animal with a segmented spinal column and a well-developed brain, e.g. a mammal, bird, reptile, amphibian, or fish

remnants – bits and pieces, odds and ends, leftovers

Glaciations – ice over, transitive and intransitive verb to cover something with a glacier, or become covered with a glacier

Clams – to be hungry, or make a person or animal hungry

Crustaceans – an invertebrate animal with several pairs of jointed legs, a hard protective outer shell, two pairs of antennae, and eyes at the ends of stalks. Lobsters, crabs, shrimp, crayfish, water fleas, barnacles, and wood lice are crustaceans.

Amphibians – a cold-blooded vertebrate that spends some time on land but must breed and develop into an adult in water. Frogs, salamanders, and toads are amphibians.

Littoral – on or near a shore, especially the zone between the high and low tide marks, living on or near a shore

Limnetic – relating to or living in the deep open water of a freshwater pond or lake

Plankton – a mass of tiny animals and plants floating in the sea or in lakes, usually near the surface, and eaten by fish and other water animals

Heterotrophy – obtaining nourishment by digesting plant or animal matter, as animals do, as opposed to photosynthesizing food, as plants do

Thermocline – a layer of water, e.g. in a lake, where there is an abrupt change in temperature that separates the warmer surface water from the colder deep water

Trout – a freshwater fish that is typically smaller than the related salmon and has a speckled body, small scales, and soft fins.

Murky – dark, misty, cloudy

Sediments – material, originally suspended in a liquid, that settles at the bottom of the liquid when it is left standing for a long time

Hydrophytes – a plant that will only grow in water or in a very damp environment

Lilies – a perennial plant that grows from a bulb. Flowers: single, large, sometimes trumpet-shaped.

Cattails – a tall, slender marsh plant. Flowers: brown, tube-shaped, in furry spikes

Sedges – a wetland plant that resembles grass and has a triangular stem, leaves growing in three vertical rows, and inconspicuous spikes of flowers.

Spruce – neat, smart, trim

Cypress – a coniferous evergreen tree with dark green leaves resembling scales.

Waders – a person or animal that wades through something

Furbearers – an animal with fur, especially fur with high commercial value, e.g. a fox or mink - a semiaquatic carnivorous member of the weasel family with webbed toes and a bushy tail. fur.

Coral – a marine organism that lives in colonies and has an external skeleton. reafs

Estuaries – the wide lower course of a river where the tide flows in, causing fresh and salt water to mix

Intertidal – occurring within, or forming, the area between the high and low tide levels in a coastal zone

Pelagic – relating to, living, or occurring in the waters of the ocean or the open sea as opposed to near the shore

Abyssal – found in the very deepest areas of the oceans or on the deep ocean floor

Benthic – relating to or characteristic of the bottom of a sea, lake, or deep river, or the animals and plants that live there

Mollusks – an invertebrate with a soft unsegmented body, usually protected by a shell in one, two, or three pieces, e.g. the snails and the octopus. Most mollusks live in or near water

Herbivorous – eating only or mainly grass or other plants, or relating to the eating of such plants

Snails – a small organism with a coiled shell and a retractable muscular foot on which it crawls

Crabs – a crustacean with a broad flat shell, antennae, a small abdomen, and five pairs of legs, the front two of which are in the form of grasping pincers.

Invertebrates – an animal that does not have a backbone, e.g. an insect or worm

Benthic – relating to or characteristic of the bottom of a sea, lake, or deep river, or the animals and plants that live there

Anemones – a perennial flowering plant of the buttercup family with wild and cultivated

Tectonic – relating to the forces that produce movement and deformation of the Earth's crust

Thrive – prosper, succeed, boom, bloom

Polyp – growth, tumor, swelling

Tentacles – a long flexible organ around the mouth or on the head of some animals, especially invertebrates such as squid, used in holding, grasping, feeling, or moving

Massif – a large mountain mass, or a group of connected mountains that form a mountain range

Flanking – neighboring, nearby, next, closest

Swamplands – an area of land that is always moist or that contains swamps

Bluff – trick, fake it, lie

Levees – a natural embankment alongside a river, formed by sediment during times of flooding

Ravine – narrow valley, gully, rift, george

Gully – channel, ditch, culvert, drain

Erosion – wearing away, corrosion, wearing down

Waterfowl – a bird that lives on freshwater lakes and streams

Deciduous – describes trees and bushes that shed their leaves in the fall

Thorn – barb, spine, spike

Riparian – situated or taking place along or near the bank of a river

Girth – restraint, belt, cinch

Resilience – elasticity, flexibility, spirit

Perturbations – disturbance and trouble, a disturbed and troubled state, or the act of disturbing and troubling somebody or something

Noxious – harmful, toxic, deadly, lethal

Decimate – destroy, devastate, ruin

Devour – eat greedily, consume, get through, demolish

Dodo – a large flightless bird with a hooked beak, extinct since the 17th century. Native to: formerly, Mauritius and neighboring Indian Ocean islands.

Roosted – a place where a bird rests or sleeps, e.g. a perch or a building with perches for domestic fowl

Impinge – impose, intrude, interrupt, encroach

Populace – public, population, common people

Chapter-2

pristine – perfect, untouched, unspoiled

poach – steal, thieve, pilfer

premise – idea, principle, basis

sustenance – nutrition, food, rations

Canoeing – the sport, hobby, or activity of paddling a canoe

expatriated – a citizen who has left his or her own country to live in another, usually for a prolonged period

Laissez-faire – lenient, tolerant, liberal

propensity – tendency, inclination, partiality

etymology – the study of the origins of words or parts of words and how they have arrived at their current form and meaning

anthropomorphism – the attribution of a human form, human characteristics, or human behavior to nonhuman things, e.g. deities in mythology and animals in children's stories

Studious – serious, reflective, bookish

assiduous – diligent, persevering, attentive, tireless

Iconographical – the set of symbols or images used in a particular field of activity such as music or the movies and recognized by people as having a particular meaning

Incessant – non stop, never-ending, ceaseless

Penance – self-punishment, forfeit, apology

austerity – strictness, graveness

primal – original, ancient, primitive

Chapter-3

Mores – civilization, society, background, tradition

Warfare – conflict, fighting, combat, war

Trajectory – route, course, flight, path

Transgress – misbehave, disobey, lapse, sin

Causation – the fact that something causes an effect, or the action of causing an effect

Coincidence – accident, chance, luck

Ingenious – clever, resourceful, original, inventive, inspired

Millennial – relating to a millennium

Timescales – a period of time scheduled for something to be completed

Locust – a migratory grasshopper that often swarms and devours crops and vegetation.

Anti-semitic – hating or discriminating against Jews

Pogroms – a planned campaign of persecution or extermination sanctioned by a government and directed against an ethnic group, especially against the Jews in tsarist Russia

Feudal – relating to, typical of, or resembling feudalism

Reverberate – echo, resound, ring

A-field – the first letter of the English alphabet, representing a vowel sound

Polity – a particular form of government that exists within a state or an institution

flux – fluctuation, change, unrest

Resilient – elastic, flexible, tough, durable

Perturbations – disturbance and trouble, a disturbed and troubled state, or the act of disturbing and troubling somebody or something

Brittle – fragile, breakable, weak

Souvenir – memento, reminder

Graffiti – drawings or words that are scratched, painted, or sprayed on walls or other surfaces in public places

Parasailing – a sport in which somebody wearing a parachute rises high into the air from a platform at the back of a moving motorboat or from the water behind the boat and is towed along

Snorkeling – the activity or pastime of swimming with a snorkel

Scuba-diving – the activity or pastime of swimming with a snorkel

Poach – boil, steam, simmer, steal

Preclude – prevent, stop, rule out

Inborn – natural, innate, intuitive, inherited

Lobbyists – somebody who is paid to lobby political representatives on an issue

Pseudo – fake, pretend, artificial

Onslaught – attack, assault, offensive

Endemic – widespread, common

taboo – banned, prohibited, unthinkable

Rucksack – pack, backpack, bag

Protagonist – character, hero, leading role

Embellishments – accompaniments, trappings, add-ons

Ploy – trick, maneuver, plan

Intrusive – disturbing, forward

Preclude – stop, prevent, rule out

Overt – obvious, explicit, evident, open

Ostensibly – apparently, supposedly, seemingly

appease – mollify, conciliate, settle

discerning – discriminating, sharp, perceptive

unabated – still as forceful or intense as before

flouting – breaking, breach

deter – discourage, put-off, prevent

Chapter-4

Spatially – relating to, occupying, or happening in space
Hinterland – surrounding, neighborhood, locality
Terrain – land, topography, territory, ground
Curvature – curve, curving, bend, twist
Multifarious – diverse, varied, assorted, mixed, different
straddle – bestride, sit astride, overlap, stand astride, include
Maritime – marine, novel, sea
Proliferate – reproduce, propagate, grow
Impoverished – poor, broke, insolvent, bankrupt
Stratum – layer, band, level, division, section
Estuary – the wide lower course of a river where the tide flows in, causing fresh and salt water to mix
Mosaic – assortment, mixture, variety
Territorial – defensive, protective
Repairers – to restore something broken or damaged to good condition, restoring relationship
Endogamous – the social practice of marrying another member of the same clan, people, or other kinship group
Negation – cancellation, reversal, contradiction, denial
Goaded – motivated, forced, irritated
Nestle – be situated, be located, lie
Tertiary – the period of geologic time, 65 million to 1.6 million years ago, during which mammals became dominant and modern plants evolved
Aftermath – result, outcome, consequences
Stem-out – the main stalk of a plant that bears buds and shoots, secondary plant branch, narrow connecting part.
Emancipation – liberation, setting free, freeing, freeing, release
Impetus – momentum, force, impulsion
Reef – a ridge of coral or rock in a body of water, with the top just below or just above the surface
Inhibit – slow down, hold back, reduce
tout – advertise, plug, push
construed – transitive verb to interpret or understand the meaning of a word, gesture, or action in a particular way
Bilge – the part of a boat below the water where the sides curve inward to the keel
Resentment – anger, dislike, hatred
Ensue – result, follow, develop

Expatriate – refugee, deportee, emigrant

Chapter-5

plunder – loot, rob, steal, ransack
Exaggeration – overstatement, embroidery, amplification
Woo – encourage, pursue
Bounty – reward, price, payment, gift
Doom – lot in life, kismet, trouble, end, death
Enchanting – Charming, delightful
Foolhardy – rash, foolish, unwise
Sheer – pure, utter, complete, total
Detriment – loss, harm, disadvantage, damage
Deterioration – worsening, decline, weakening, fall
Unkind led – lacking kindness, sympathy, or consideration, or resulting from such a lack, severe, harsh
Precedence – priority, preference, superiority
Abhor – hate, dislike, detest
Tardy – overdue, behind, delay, late
Erode – wear away, wear down, eat into
splendor – finery, luxury, brilliance
lopsided – irregular, uneven, unbalanced
impetus – drive, force

irrational – illogical, foolish, unreasonable
Patrimony - the objects, traditions, or values that one generation has inherited from its ancestors
Conservernism
Pronged – split, divided
Culinary – cooking, cookery
Pronouncement – statement, declaration, announcement
Plank – board, flat timber, piece of wood
Inertia – inactivity, apathy, inaction
Usurp – take, appropriate, assume, take over
Dubious - doubtful
Cajole – persuade, sweet-talk
intervention – interference, involvement
Wake – get up, wake, come around
Alienation – unfriendliness, hostility, isolation, separation
Deprivation – lack, deficiency, denial, withdrawal
Turf – grass, lawn, territory

Truism – saying, maxim

repudiate – reject, deny, not accepted, rebut

contrived – artificial, unnatural, manufactured, fixed

Unsavory – nasty, unpleasant

Transient – brief, fleeting, passing

Deplete – reduce, eat up

Troposphere – the lowest and most dense layer of the atmosphere, extending 10 to 20 km/6 to 12 mi, in which temperature decreases with rising altitude and most weather occurs

Discern – distinguish, tell the difference, separate

Bogey – something that troubles, annoys, or frightens somebody

Prerogative – privilege, right, due, choice

Fodder – food, silage, feed

Fell – cut down, chop down, clear cut

Spontaneously – impulsively, of your own accord, suddenly, unexpected

Hug – hold close, embrace

interpose – insert, introduce, step in

sublimate – redirect, psychology transitive verb to channel impulses or energies regarded as unacceptable, especially sexual desires, toward an activity that is more socially acceptable, often a creative activity

sprout – grow, shoot, develop

denude – strip, uncover

saplings – small tree, a young tree with a slender trunk

egalitarian – open, classless, free, unrestricted

Grave – serious, severe, crucial

Exaggerated – overstated, inflated, blown up

Seldom – not often

Biodiversity – the range of organisms present in a particular ecological community or system. It can be measured by the numbers and types of different species, or the genetic variations within and between species

Gene-pools – the total of all genes carried by all individuals in an interbreeding population

Pauperization – an impoverished person, very poor person

Oblivious – unaware, ignorant

Warbler – a small songbird of the wood warbler family that eats insects and is often brightly colored. Native to: North and South America . Family: Parulidae

Whiskered-tern – a short stiff hair growing on somebody's face, especially on the cheeks, chin, or upper lip

Mangrove – an evergreen tree or bush with straight slender stems and intertwined roots that are exposed at low tide. Native to: tropical coasts. Families: Combretaceae, Verbenaceae,

Waning – declining, weakening, diminishing

Provocation – irritation, aggravation, frustration

Host – crowd, swarm, mass

Panacea – cure-all, universal remedy, solution, answer

Exodus – mass departure, migration

Lopsided – irregular, uneven, unbalanced

Servility – A moral and mental, is as obnoxious as a physical servitude, and not to be tolerated; as the one may, eventually lead to the other

Embellish – decorate, beautiful, make fancy

Avalanche – rush, flood, land slide, storm

Gaze – look, watch, fix your eyes on

Allured – highly attractive quality

Unflinching – constant, steady, persistent

Deity – idol, god, goddess

Prettify – make more attractive, smarten up, pretty up, beautiful

Deodorize – fresh, refresh, perfume

Wedge – fix in place, hold

Circuitous – roundabout, indirect, twisty

Analogy – similarity, likeness, parallel

Ethos – culture, philosophy, nation

Derelictions – neglect of duty

Lacunae – a gap or place where something is missing, e.g. in a manuscript or a line of argument

Glean – garner, collect, pick up

Elucidate – make clear, explain

Arid – dry

Searingly – extremely intense or strong, felt a searing pain

Sprawled – to sit or lie with the arms and legs spread awkwardly in different directions

Cobble – a small rounded stone used for paving streets

Hillock – small hill

Edifice – structure, construction

Manicured – a cosmetic treatment for the hands and nails that usually involves shaping and polishing the fingernails, pushing back the cuticles, and treating rough skin

Trove – a collection of discovered valuable items

Stained – discolored, marked, blemished

Suburb – village, town, colony

Secluded – private, quite

Personage – VIP, celebrity

Sprightly – active, energetic

Glade – clearing, open space

Cedar – a tall evergreen tree with spreading branches, needles, and large rounded upright cones. Native to: Europe, Asia, Africa. Genus: Cedrus

Pastoral – rustic, rural

Hamlet – village, settlement

Orchards – an area of land on which fruit or nut trees are grown, especially commercially

Enthralling – action-packed, absorbing

Estuarine – relating to, formed in, or found in an estuary

Splendor – brilliance, majesty, luxury

Benediction – blessing, approval

Pious – dutiful, moral, religious

Poachers - somebody who hunts or fishes illegally, usually while trespassing

Captivity – imprisonment, custody, detention

Rivulet – stream, brook, gully

Mesmerizing – gripping, compelling

Salvation – rescue, recovery

Sovereignty – rule, power, control

Machinations – plotting, scheming, intrigues

Ascendance – succeeding or rising to a powerful position

Terrain – land, ground, territory

Exodus – mass departure

Potentate – royal leader, monarch, ruler

pretension – affectation, posturing, self-importance

Invincible – unbreakable,

Grandeur – splendor, dignity

Thatched – a plant material used as roofing on a house, e.g. straw or rushes

Gigantic – huge, enormous, massive

Tudor – relating to or belonging to the English royal family that ruled between 1485 and 1603, or to this period of English history. The period is spanned by the reigns of Kings Henry VII, Henry VIII, and Edward VI, and Queens Mary I and Elizabeth I.

Sallery – a small room for washing and storing dishes and utensils and doing other kitchen chores

Larder – store, store room, food store

Cellar – basement, vault

Echelons - a level of authority or rank in an organization or system

Stripped – naked, nude, exposed

Ecclesiastical – church, clerical, religious

Coronation – the ceremony or act of crowning a monarch

Precincts – grounds, area, confines

Pallid – white, pale, colorless

Peevish – irritable, cross

Bowel – a section or part of the intestine, especially the part of the intestine that connects to the anus - the opening at the lower end of the alimentary canal through which feces are released

Pheasant – a large bird, the male of which often has a long tail and brightly colored feathers. Pheasants are often bred for shooting. Native to: Asia, Europe, North America. Family: Phasianidae

Woodcock – a medium-sized ground-dwelling game bird related to the snipe, with short legs and rounded wings, a stocky body and a long beak. Native to: North America, Europe, Asia. Genus: Scolopax

Quail – draw back, recoil, shrink back

Pea – a round green seed that grows in a pod, eaten as a vegetable

Fowl – chicken, hen, rooster, pullet

Maple – a deciduous tree with winged seeds and lobed leaves producing attractive fall colors. Native to: northern temperate regions. Genus: Acer

Alders – a deciduous tree or bush with male catkins and cone-shaped fruits, common in wet places. Native to: northern temperate areas. Genus: Alnus

Rhododendrons - an evergreen tree widely grown in temperate regions. Flowers: brightly colored. Native to: South Asia. Genus: Rhododendron

Scarlet – red, ruby, crimson

Dahlias – a tall perennial plant with tuberous roots. Flowers: large, brightly colored. Genus: Dahlia

Hydrangeas – an erect or climbing evergreen or deciduous bush. Flowers: white, pink, or blue, in large clusters in a variety of shapes. Native to: Asia . Genus: Hydrangea

Primrose – U.S. , Australia, New Zealand a flowering plant from the family that includes the cowslip, cyclamen, and pimpernel. Native to: northern temperate regions. Family: Primulaceae

Rinks – a smooth, enclosed, and often artificially prepared ice surface used for ice-skating, hockey, or curling

amusement – delight, enjoyment

Chapter-9

Swampy – marshy, boggy, muddy, wet, moist

Sedimentation – the process by which particles in suspension in a liquid form sediment

Hyacinth – a cultivated plant of the lily family. Flowers: fragrant pink, white, or blue, in spikes. Native to: northeastern Mediterranean. Latin name: Hyacinthus orientalis

Clogging – blockage, obstruction, congestion

Brackish – salt, salty

Anthropogenic – relating to or resulting from the influence that humans have on the natural world

Horde – crowd, mass, gang

aboriginal – original, native

Avowed – affirmed, stated, confirmed, declared

Drenched – socked, wet, saturated

Secluded – private, quite, isolated, out of the way

Endowed – gifted, able, brilliant

Curvaceous – curvy, rounded

Idyllic / tranquil – peaceful, calm

Caress – stroke, touch, pat

Mini-coastal – smaller version of something

dredge – search, scour

Defecation - intransitive verb to expel feces from the bowel through the rectum

Atoll - island

Causative – casual, contributory

contagious – infectious, catching, communicable

Flay – criticize, condemn

Benthic – relating to or characteristic of the bottom of a sea, lake, or deep river, or the animals and plants that live there

Corollary – consequent, result, effect, outcome

Stirring – inspiring, moving, emotive

Clogging – blockage

Tract – area, territory, zone

Sedentary – inactive, sitting

Lobsters – a hard-shelled sea crustacean with a pair of large pincers, five pairs of limbs, eyes on stalks, and long antennae. Native to: Atlantic coasts of North America, Europe. Family: Homaridae

Scallops – a sea bivalve mollusk that has a fan-shaped shell with radial ribs and wavy edges. Family: Pectinidae

Grave – serious, severe,

Wrath – anger, rage, fury

con-commitant – to cheat somebody dishonestly, usually out of money or property, by first convincing the victim of something that is untrue

Bereft - deprived of somebody or something loved or valued

deceptive-greens – liable or meant to deceive or mislead somebody

canoeing – going by canoe, the sport, hobby or activity of paddling a canoe

Burgeoning – growing, mushrooming, escalating

Acreage – land, home, house

Percolation – pass through filter, transitive and intransitive verb to make a liquid or gas pass through a filter or porous substance, or filter through in this way

Enthusiast – fan, devotee

circumflex – diacritic, acute accent,

Quirky – original, individual

Discerning – sharp, sensitive

Boast – possess, have, blow your own horn

Eateries – restaurant, a place where food is cooked and sold

Dearth – lack, shortage, scarcity, drought

Vulnerable – helpless, open to, expose

Tranquility – calm, quite

Trample – crush, walk on, step on, stamp on, walk over

Exemplify – demonstrate, represent

Clumsy – ungainly, awkward, inept

Blaring – loud, piercing

Shoe-string – an outer covering for the foot, usually made of leather, fabric, or plastic, with a stiff sole and usually not reaching above the ankle

Endemism – restricted to one place, medicine describes a disease occurring within a particular area

Extinction – death, extermination, destruction

Ridge – edge, point

Aridity – dryness

Spear-gun – a gun designed to shoot a barbed spear underwater, used to catch fish

Shilling – a former subunit of British currency

Ethnicity – civilization, society, mores

Onus – burden, obligation, duty

Seismic – relating to or caused by an earthquake or earth tremor

Trample – crush, walk on, stamp on

PAPERS

Circumpolar – in polar regions, located or living near one or both poles of Earth or another planet

Sedges – a wetland plant that resembles grass and has a triangular stem, leaves growing in three vertical rows, and inconspicuous spikes of flowers. Genus: Carex

Coniferous – any tree that has thin leaves needles and produces cones. Many types are evergreen. Pines, firs, junipers, larches, spruces, and yews are conifers. Order: Coniferales

Eurasia – the land mass consisting of the continents of Europe and Asia

Taiga – the subarctic coniferous forests located south of the tundra in North America, northern Europe, and Asia

Marsh – bog, swamp, fen

Conifers – any tree that has thin leaves needles and produces cones. Many types are evergreen. Pines, firs, junipers, larches, spruces, and yews are conifers. Order: Coniferales

Wolves – plural of wolf

Hickory – the hard light-colored wood of a North American walnut tree. Use: tool handles, sports equipment, furniture.

Maple – a deciduous tree with winged seeds and lobed leaves producing attractive fall colors. Native to: northern temperate regions. Genus: Acer

Prairie / steppe / Pampas – plain, pampas, grassland

Arthropods – an invertebrate animal that has jointed limbs, a segmented body, and an exoskeleton made of chitin, e.g. an insect, arachnid, centipede, or crustacean. Phylum: Arthropoda

Tract – area, territory, zone

Cleavage – a split, division, or separation of something

Fragility – weakness, tenderness

Pasture – meadow, grazing land

Pastoralists – somebody who has a pastoral way of life

Negation – cancellation, reversal

Hasten – hurry, rush, speed up

Lepchas – a member of a people who live in the northeastern Indian state of Sikkim

Savior – somebody who rescues somebody or something from harm or danger

Alienation – isolation, separation, division

Pervade – saturate, encompass, spread through

Strewn – scattered, sprinkled

Mar – ruin, spoil

Grandeur – splendor, majesty, dignity

Provoking – irritating, annoying, frustrating

Connivance – involvement, responsibility

Pisciculture – the controlled breeding, hatching, and rearing of fish, especially for scientific or commercial purposes

Alga-rising – a photosynthetic organism of a group that lives mainly in water and includes the seaweeds. Algae differ from plants in not having true leaves, roots, or stems.

Blurred – unclear, hazy

Ethnicity – civilization, mores, society

TS–5 : ECOLOGY, ENVIRONMENT AND TOURISM

June, 2009

Note : Answer any five questions in about 600 words each.

Q1. Describe in detail the nature of terrestrial biomes of the world.

Q2. How is environment described in the Indian philosophical tradition? Discuss.

Q3. Does tourism activity always affect environment adversely? Examine.

Q4. Examine the importance of regional assets in tourism development.

Q5. Discuss the role of locals in tourism development.

Q6. Examine the nature of wild life in any two biogeographic zones of India.

Q7. Describe how the hill-stations of Darjeeling and Nilgiris were established?

Q8. Examine the character of beaches in India. What are the possibilities of tourism promotion there?

Q9. Write an essay on the water sports in India.

Q10. Write short notes on any two of the following in about 300 words each:

(a) The Ecosystem and its components

(b) Sustainable Development

(c) Importance of Tourism Master Plan

(d) India Tourism Policy-1982

(e) Visitor Behaviour and Environment.

TS–5 : ECOLOGY, ENVIRONMENT AND TOURISM
December, 2009

Note : Answer any five questions in about 600 words each.

Q1. What are the different components of the abiotic environment? How have they changed with time?

Q2. Explain main elements of Indian philosophical views on environment.

Q3. Write an essay on the relationship between environment and development.

Q4. What is multiplier effect? How does it affect the economy of an area?

Q5. How does tourism affect environment? Discuss critically.

Q6. How did the National Action plan of 1992 affect tourism? Describe.

Q7. How would you identify pressures and assess thresholds on environment in the context of tourism?

Q8. Write a note on the process through which various mountains were transformed into hill stations?

Q9. What are wetlands? How does excessive tourism affect them?

Q10. Write short notes on any two of the following in about 250 words each:
(a) Hotels and Resorts
(b) Wildlife
(c) Politics of Environment
(d) Tourism Master Plan

TS–5 : ECOLOGY, ENVIRONMENT AND TOURISM
June-2010

Note : Answer any five questions in about 600 words each.

Q1. What are biomes? Describe some of the terrestrial biomes of the world.

Q2. How has the environmental question been understood in the Indian philosophical tradition?

Q3. Write a note on the nature of relationship between environment and development.

Q4. Define 'Community'. How have local communities been influenced by tourism?

Q5. Write a note on tourism as a tool for conservation.

Q6. Write an essay on the politics of environment.

Q7. What are the ways in which the local physical environment is affected by visitor behavior?

Q8. Write a note on wild life? How does it get affected by tourism?

Q9. Write an essay on the role of different kind of accommodation in promoting tourism.

Q10. Write short notes on any two of the following in about 250 words each:
(a) Tourism Master Plan
(b) Wet Lands
(c) Hill Stations
(d) Multiplier Effects

TS–5 : ECOLOGY, ENVIRONMENT AND TOURISM
December-2010

Note : Attempt any five questions in about 600 words each. All questions carry equal marks that are mentioned against each question.

Q1. What are some of the main features of the abiotic environment?

Q2. What is the place of the environment in the Indian philosophical traditions?

Q3. Write an essay on the relationship between tourism and development.

Q4. How does mass tourism affect the nature and environment of any destination? Pick up example from your local place.

Q5. Does tourism necessarily lead to a destruction of the environment? Discuss with examples.

Q6. Write an essay on the politics of environment.

Q7. What do you understand by visitor behaviour? How does it affect a tourism site?

Q8. What is the difference between mountain and hill station? Discuss with reference to a major hill station.

Q9. What are wet lands? What major ecological functions do they play?

Q10. Write short notes on any tow of the following in about 300 words each:

(i) Hotels and Resorts

(ii) Tourism and local population

(iii) Indian Tourism Policy of 1982

(iv) Tourism Master Plan

TS–5 : ECOLOGY, ENVIRONMENT AND TOURISM
June-2011

Note : Answer any five questions in about 600 words each. All questions carry equal marks which are mentioned against each question.

Q1. Describe in detail the nature of terrestrial bioms of the world.

Q2. What is conservation? What has been its significance through the ages?

Q3. Critically discuss the relationship between environment and development.

Q4. What is the significance of a Master plan in the development of tourism?

Q5. How can tourism be used on a tool for the conservation of the environment?

Q6. What do you mean by tourism infrastructure? How does the development of tourism infrastructure land to ecological imbalance?

Q7. Discuss the role of local population in the conservation of environment and tourism development.

Q8. What is wild life? Discuss the nature of wild life in any two biogeographic zones of India.

Q9. How is the environment affected by adventure sports? Give examples.

Q10. Write short note on any two of the following in about 300 words each:
(a) Wet land
(b) Shimla as a Hill station
(c) Debate on the building of Dams
(d) The eco system and its components.

TS–5 : ECOLOGY, ENVIRONMENT AND TOURISM
December-2011

Note : Answer any five questions in about 600 words each.

Q1. What do you understand by Abiotic Environment? Explain with examples.

Q2. Discuss the impact of tourism activities on environment and suggest some possible solutions to check/mitigate these impacts.

Q3. What do you understand by Alternative Tourism? What are the problems and benefits associated with the same?

Q4. Discuss the positive and negative socio-economic impacts of Tourism. Give relevant examples from Indian context.

Q5. Write short notes on any two.
(a) Politics of Environment.
(b) Biodiversity.
(c) Carrying Capacity.

Q6. Discuss the importance of planning in Tourism Development. How does it help particularly in the preservation of environment and ecology?

Q7. Explain in detail how the visitor behaviour affects the local behaviour. Give appropriate examples from your city.

Q8. Explain the characteristics of the Biogeographical zones of India.

Q9. What do you understand by Adventure Sports? Explain the classification of adventure sports.

Q10. Discuss the National Action Plan 1992 and its impact on India Tourism management and marketing.

TS–5 : ECOLOGY, ENVIRONMENT AND TOURISM
June-2012

Note : Attempt any five questions in about 600 words each.

Q1. List the terrestrial biomes of the world with their distinct characteristics.

Refer to June-2008, Q.No.-2

Q2. Write an essay on Indian Philosophies on environment and its conservation.

Refer to June-2007, Q.No.-1

Q3. What do you understand by sustainable development? How can you link conservation and preservation of environment with development?

Refer to Chapter-3, Q.No.-7&4&5

Q4. Compare the environmental planning required for Hill Tourism with that of Coastal Resorts.

Ans. Today most of the hill stations are overcrowded and all types of scarcities have emerged because of the unplanned growth of tourism. It is time to realise that tourism can play a positive role in the socio-economic development of the hill areas and hill towns of the Himalayan and Sub-Himalayan region.

A scientific approach to tourism planning in the hill regions and the habitat would require analytical studies relating to:

- likely impacts of development on the local environment and the hill habitat,
- evaluating the tourist resources and infrastructure needs,
- establishing certain developmental thresholds consistent with the carrying capacity of the area and similar aspects.

The focus in all development programmes, particularly tourism related development, should be primarily on:

- the upgradation of the quality of life,
- safeguarding and maintaining their socio-cultural identity, and
- a general improvement in the town's economy.

Coastal Resorts

Now Refer to Chapter-4, Q.No.-4

Q5. Write short notes on any two:

(a) Community Tourism

Ans. Community tourism is 'sharing the natural resources of a local community with visitors from home and overseas for the sustainable benefit of that local community whilst conserving the natural environment and respecting the way of life.' Community tourism is a growing market, as new generations of travelers worldwide seek more meaningful experiences from their leisure time. Integrated community participation between the local people, the local government and national level plan makers has to be adopted.

Some principles of the community tourism are as follows:

(1) Community tourism should involve local people. That means they should participate in decision-making and ownership, not just be paid a fee.

(2) The local community should receive a fair share of the profits from any tourism venture.

(3) Tour operators should try to work with communities rather than individuals. Working with individuals can create divisions within a community. Where communities have representative organisations these should be consulted and their decisions respected.

(4) Tourism should be environmentally sustainable. Local people must benefit and be consulted if conservation projects are to work. Tourism should not put extra pressure on scarce resources.

(5) Tourism should support traditional cultures by showing respect for indigenous knowledge. Tourism can encourage people to value their own cultural heritage.

(6) Operators should work with local people to minimise the harmful impacts of tourism.

(7) Where appropriate, tour operators should keep groups small to minimise their cultural and environmental impact.

(8) Tour operators or guides should brief tourists on what to expect and on appropriate behaviour before they arrive in a community. That should include how to dress, taking photos, respecting privacy.

(9) Local people should be allowed to participate in tourism with dignity and self-respect. They should not be coerced into performing inappropriate ceremonies for tourists, etc.

(10) People have the right to say no to tourism. Communities who reject tourism should be left alone.

(b) Environmental Laws and India

Ans. In India, there are a number of laws which deal with various aspect of environment protection regulation, conduct of environmentally harmful activities and provide for remedies in case of their breach. Some of them are general, having an "indirect" bearing on environment protection, while others are special, (viz. Water, Air and Environmental Acts, Forest Act, etc.) being "directly" concerned with environment protection. Some of the environmental laws are The Insecticide Act, The Wildlife (Protection) Act, The Water (Prevention and Control of Pollution) Act, The Air (Prevention and Control of Pollution) Act, The Environment (Protection) Act, etc.

The Insecticide Act: Being aware of the prime responsibility of protecting the health citizens and the environment, the Government of India enacted the Insecticide Act in 1968. This was enforced from 1971 to regulate import, manufacture, sale, transport, distribution and use of insecticides with a view to preventing risk to human beings and animals. Several agencies, such as the Central Insecticide Board, the Pesticide Registration Committee, the Pesticide Environment Pollution Advisory Committee, the Central Insecticide Laboratory, the Committee to Ban/Restrict the use of Pesticides, were created for effective enforcement of this Act.

The Wildlife (Protection) Act: Realising the importance of the wildlife resource and in order to prevent the gene erosion, our country or Wildlife Parks and Sanctuaries, enactment of an All India Wildlife Protection Act (1972), becoming a party to the Convention of International Trade in Endangered Species of Fauna and Flora (CITES, 1976), launching a national component of the UNESCO's Man and the Biosphere Programme (1972) and by starting conservation projects for individual endangered species like Hungal (1970), Lion (1972), Tiger (1973), Crocodiles (1974) and Brown-antlered Deer (1981).

The Water (Prevention and Control of Pollution) Act: The Water Act defines water pollution, prescribes penalties and establishes an administrative machinery, called the Water Pollution Boards, at the Central and State level in order to control and prevent pollution of water.

More importantly, Boards are entrusted with the task of monitoring the state of water pollution in the country and laying down standards of permissible and impermissible levels of pollution.

The Water Act prohibits dumping of poisonous, noxious or polluting matter into streams and wells, as well as any activity which impedes the proper flow of the water of a stream causing aggravation of pollution due to other causes.

The Air (Prevention and Control of Pollution)Act: The Central Boards for the Prevention and Control of Water Pollution is authorised to implement and enforce the Act also. This body lays down standards for the quality of air. Under Section 19, the Central Board is given powers mainly to coordinate the activities of the state Boards. After consultation with the state Board, the state government may declare any area within the state as "air pollution control area," and prohibit the use of any fuel other than approved fuel in the area causing air pollution.

The Environment (Protection) Act: The Act refers to the Stockholm Conference of 1972 and is based on Article 253 of the Constitution. By virtue of this Act, the Union Government has armed itself with considerable powers deemed necessary for the prevention, control and abatement of environmental pollution. The powers include, coordination of action by states, planning and execution of nationwide programmes, laying down environmental quality standards, specially those governing emission or discharge of environmental pollutants, placing restrictions on the location of industries and so on. The powers claimed are indeed comprehensive; the coverage includes handling of hazardous substances, prevention of environmental accidents, research, inspection of polluting units, establishment of laboratories, dissemination of information, etc. A whole set of administrative procedures and structures are envisaged under the Act.

(c) Alternative Tourism

Refer to Chapter-3, Q.No.-8

Q6. What role can tourism play in the conservation of environment?

Refer to Chapter-3, Q.No.-5

Q7. Discuss the impact of tourism activities on the local/host population. Give appropriate examples.

Refer to Chapter-7, Q.No.-7

Q8. How does hotels and resorts development affect the local environment?

Refer to Chapter-9, Q.No.-12

Q9. What is meant by Politics of Environment? Explain with examples from India vis-a-vis global affairs.

Refer to Dec-2006, Q.No.-7 and Chapter-6, Q.No.-16&18

Q10. Discuss the impact of tourism activities on the wildlife.

Refer to Chapter-8 Q.No.-3

TS–5 : ECOLOGY, ENVIRONMENT AND TOURISM
December-2012

Note : Attempt any five questions in about 600 words each. All questions carry equal marks.

Q1. What is meant by Abiotic Environment? Explain with the help of appropriate examples.

Ans. The abiotic environment is the non-living part. Included are all the physical elements of an organism's existence, especially the intersecting roles of the sun and solar energy, weather and climate, soil, and water. The basic dependence of biotic life on the abiotic environment is the need for solar energy to be transformed, by green plants through the processes of photosynthesis, into a form of energy used by living organisms. Climate is widely considered a major determinant of life patterns on planet earth. And, climate of course is driven by earth-sun relationships.

Now Refer to Dec-2006, Q.No.-1

Q2. Define Biomes. Enumerate the terrestrial biomes of the world.

Refer to June-2008, Q.No.-2

Q3. What do you understand by multiplier effect? What role does it play in the economy?

Refer to Dec-2007, Q.No.-6

Q4. Analyse critically the relationship between conservation requirements and development.

Refer to Chapter-3, Q.No.-5

Q5. What are wet lands? What major ecological functions do they play?

Refer to Chapter-9, Q.No.-1

Q6. Write an essay on Responsible Tourism.

Refer to Dec-2007, Q.No.-4

Q7. Enumerate how the local physical environment is affected by the visitor behaviour.

Refer to June-2008, Q.No.-8

Q8. Discuss the role of accommodation sector in promoting tourism.

Ans. Tourism needs accommodation, transport and attractions to enlarge its outreach. The new approach of the government to this issue is that the state has made a substantial contribution to the development of services in the country and now the time has come to encourage the private sector and foreign investment for accelerated growth of tourism. It is developing a model which identifies weakness of infrastructure as the main hurdle in increasing India's share of the world tourism. The action policy therefore wants to develop areas on a selective basis for intensive development and to identify destinations which already have tourist attractions so that optimal use can be made of such areas, like DELHI-AGRA-JAIPUR.

Accommodation: Hotels form an important and vital segment of tourism infrastructure. The present capacity stands at 55,000 roms in the approved category which needs to be doubled by the end of the decade if we have to double our share of the international tourist market. The government has drawn up a fiscal concession scheme to draw investment to this segment including tax holidays and exemptions as well as loan waivers. The regions which get the highest state subsidy will be rural areas, hill stations, pilgrim centres and island and beach resorts. The heritage hotel scheme is also going to take tourism development into the hinterland of major tourist circuits. Accommodation for domestic tourists is to be strengthened by establishing camping sites, tented accommodation and paying guest accommodation. Apartment hotels are also being envisaged.

Now Refer to Chapter-6, Q.No.-5

Q9. Evaluate the impact of tourism on wildlife.

Refer to Chapter-8, Q.No.-3

Q10. Write short notes on any two of the following:

(a) Indian philosophical views on environment.

Refer to Chapter-2, Q.No.-7

(b) Tourism Master Plan.

Refer to Dec-2006, Q.No.-10(ii)

(c) Hill Stations.

Ans. A hill station is a town located at a higher elevation than the nearby plain or valley. The term was used mostly in colonial Asia (particularly India), but also in Africa (albeit rarely), for towns founded by European colonial rulers as refuges from the summer heat, up where temperatures are cooler. In the Indian context most hill stations are at an altitude of approximately 1,000 to

2,500 metres (3,500 to 7,500 feet); very few are outside this range. The Indian subcontinent has seven principal mountain ranges and the largest of all is the Himalayas that lies in the northern part of India. Then there is Shivalik range that also lies within the same region has some famous hill stations that include Dalhousie, Kullu, Shimla, Nainital and many more.

Most of the hill stations in India were developed by the British, around a central mall, to get respite from the oppressive summer heat. Many have picturesque lakes as their focal point, making them excellent places for boating activities.

Most of the hill stations in India are located in Jammu and Kashmir, Himachal Pradesh, Uttarakhand, Sikkim, West Bengal, Arunachal Pradesh and Meghalaya in the Himalayas and in Maharashtra, Karnataka, Tamil Nadu and Kerala in Western Ghats.

Since all these hill stations are world famous they are frequently visited by tourists on a summer vacation tour. Due to this almost all of the above hill stations are well connected by rail, road and air services to major Indian cities.

(d) Politics of Environment.

Refer to Dec-2006, Q.No.-7

TS–5 : ECOLOGY, ENVIRONMENT AND TOURISM
June-2013

Note : Attempt any five questions in about 600 words each. All questions carry equal marks.

Q1. Define ecosystem. Explain the various components of ecosystem and their linkages.

Refer to Dec-2006, Q.No.-10(i)

Q2. How does mass tourism affect the nature and environment of any destination? Explain with the help of an example.

Ans. Mass tourism refers to the global tourist industry involving hundreds of thousands of tourists visiting both developed and developing countries of the world.

Now Refer to Chapter-4, Q.No.-12

Q3. What do you understand by politics of environment? Discuss.

Refer to Dec-2006, Q.No.5

Q4. Analyse critically how tourism is both an opportunity as well as pressure on the local community?

Refer to Chapter-7, Q.No.-4

Q5. Discuss how the environmental question have been understood in the Indian philosophical traditions?

Refer to June-2007, Q.No.-1

Q6. Explain the process through which various mountains were transformed into hill stations.

Ans. The transformation of hill stations from mountains is first related to the hills. Hills may be formed by a buildup of rock debris or sand deposited by glaciers and wind. Hills may be created by faults. Faults are a slight crack in the earth which can cause earthquakes. Hills are formed when these faults go slightly upward. Thus, there is not any specific process (in nature) entitled through which various mountains were transformed into hills. Hills may form through geomorphic phenomena: faulting, erosion of larger landforms, such as mountains and movement and deposition of sediment by glaciers (e.g. moraines and drumlins or by erosion exposing solid rock which then weathers down into a hill.) Many settlements were originally built on hills, either to avoid or curb floods, particularly if they were near a large body of water, or for defence, since they offer a good view of the surrounding land and require would-be attackers to fight uphill. But for attracting various tourists, government made various hill stations, which add not only beauty to the place but also enhance economic opportunities.

The hill stations are the endowment of European travellers, who were attracted by the scenic delights of the Indian mountains, no efforts were spared to create hill-resorts-cum-summer capitals.

More than 200 hill settlements came up on the hill tops during the course of nineteenth century. From Simla and Landaur in the North to Darjeeling in East and Ooty and Kodaikkanal in the South, innumerable hill resorts sprang up to cater to the needs of the weather weary English elite.

Aspirations of the English populace led to the modifications of the natural local habitat of the mountains. Gradually a spatially-differentiated urban system developed to erode the natural landscape of the mountain beauty to a large extent.

The development of some prominent hill stations during the course of nineteenth century to understand the environmental impact upon the mountains is discussed as follows:-

Simla: Simla in the Punjab province (31.6 degree North, 77.1 degree East) lies on a spur of Central Himalayas at a height exceeding 7000 feet. A fin hill 'Jacko' rising 1000 feet higher and clothed with deoder, oak and rhododendron occupies the east side of the station Shimlah or 'Shumlah', (from the temple of Goddess Shyamli) as pronounced by the hill-tribes, is the actual word from which the station takes its present name. Prospect Hill and observatory hill lie along the western part of the ridge. Annandale, the beautiful glen and the centre of Simla social life under the Raj, witnesses the sprouting of yellow primroses from the dripping rocks in April

According to Gazetteer of 1904, Simla was a wild tract, a portion of which was retained at the close of Gorakhpur of 1816 by the treaty of Sugauli. Afterwards the whole of the present station of Simla was bought from Rajas of Keonthal and Kothi and Maharaja of Patiala. From the time it was declared the summer capital of the British Empire in India in 1864 under the Viceroyalty of Sir John Lawrence, the development of Simla accelerated.

Between 1868 and 1881, the population of district rose by about 32.9%, the increase being almost entirely in the Simla town. The population further rose from 13,034 in 1891 to 13,960 in 1901 in Simla proper alone.

In 1878, under Lord Lytton, the first impetus to good roads in Simla was given, for in that year two wide roads under Gorton Castle estate and 'Ladies Mile' at the back of the Jacko were constructed. By degrees the whole of Mall stretching from the Viceregal Lodge to around Jacko, some 10 miles in length, was widened and improved into a carriage drive. In 1879, consequent on the improved condition of the Mall, which admitted of the wheeled traffic, the 'jinrickshaw' commenced to supersede both the 'Jhampans' and 'dandy'. By the early twentieth century, motor cars made their entry into the hills.

Trade and commercial activities also increased in Simla. 'Native' bazaars like the Bara Bazaar, Lakkar Bazaar, Sanjauli Bazaar etc. rapidly developed.

Mall was scientifically planned along the regularly aligned rows with the better planned shops mostly owned by the Europeans.

Simla also emerged as an important entrepot where foreign trade was registered. Chief articles of commerce in the Simla hills were opium, potatoes, wool, borax, fur, woollen cloth, semiprecious stones, goats and horse.

Twentieth century brought about an intrusion into the mountains' environment. Kalka-Simla railway, a narrow gauge line was started in 1900. It was opened to traffic in 1903. It reduced the duration from the plains to Simla hills to seven and a half hour.

As a result the thirty house 1830 increased to about 2000 houses by the early twentieth century.

Darjeeling: Darjeeling, the summer capital of the Lieutenant Governor of Bengal, during the British Raj was under the Rajshahi division. Darjeeling lies between latitude 26 degree 30' 50" and 27 degree 12' 44" and longitude 88 degree 1' 30" and 88 degree 56' 35". It is situated at the height of 7500 feet above sea level. It is a crescent shaped loop in the area of 1234 square miles. In 1901, population of Darjeeling was 94,772.

The name 'Darjeeling' is a corruption from Dorje-ling, which in Tibetan language means the mystic thunderbolt of the lamaist religion, a designation formerly given to the Buddhist monastery which used to stand on top of the Observatory Hill. Technically this territory belonged to the Raja of Sikkim, as it was on his behalf that the East India Company had intervened. In 1835, the Sikkim ruler formally handed over the territory to the East India Company under the Governor General Lord William Bentinck. A Darjeeling gazetteer described the situation of Darjeeling as "singularly beautiful as it stands on a narrow ridge that just out into a vast basin in the heart of Himalayas."

The year 1866 may be taken as marking an epoch in the history of Darjeeling. Peace was established within its borders and the Darjeeling gazetteer of 1908 wrote: "thenceforward began the march of progress and civilisation" into the terra incognito.

The construction of Darjeeling Car Road began in 1861, from Tarai Foothills to the Virgin forests. There are various developments that took place in the interest of wheeled traffic and development of the frontier trade.

In 1881, the construction of Darjeeling-Himalayan Railways brought Darjeeling within day's journey from Calcutta. A piece of engineering skill which adds to the attraction of the railways is that the railway line near Darjeeling makes a U-shaped loop called the Batasia loop. The population of Darjeeling doubled between 1881 and 1891.

Darjeeling was introduced on the international scene for its green-leaved and delicately flavoured tea which has a unique blend all its own. Tea gardens were laid out under the encouragement give by Dr. Campbell. The humid climate of Darjeeling ensures the success of the plantations.

Q7. What do you understand by wetlands? What major ecological function do they play? Also mention with example their role in tourism development.

Ans. First Refer to Chapter-9, Q.No.-1

Wetland tourism has benefits both locally and nationally for people and wildlife – benefits such as stronger economies, sustainable livelihoods, healthy people and thriving ecosystems. Wetlands fulfil a variety of ecological functions in the life cycles of numerous plants and animals, usually on a local scale, but often on a regional or even global scale. For example, wetlands may function as a summer range, migration stopover, wintering area and/or breeding site for migratory waterbirds such as geese, terns and waders.

The birds' migration routes may cover thousands of kilometres, and this emphasises the need for the conservation and wise use of wetlands – whether protected areas or not – along the route. Their long migrations and tendency to concentrate in large numbers in certain wetlands make water birds both visible and attractive. They are important indicators of the ecological condition and productivity of wetland ecosystems, and their presence is widely valued by numerous stakeholders, including local people, tourists and associated enterprises.

Q8. Define Multiplier Effect. Discuss its role in the local economy.

Refer to Dec-2007, Q.No.-6

Q9. How would you identify pressure and assess thresholds of environment in the context of tourism?

Ans. (1) Wildlife: National parks of wildlife and conservation increase the levels of tourism and recreation. The regulating authorities of tourism sector believe that with proper regulations a delicate balance can be retained between nature and tourism. But the facts suggest otherwise. The increase in tourism has decreased the number of birds (& Wetland species) in Kashmir. This has scared away the birds to higher altitudes. Entertaining the tourists has also affected the arrival of 'Whiskered tern' and the 'Indian Great seed warbler' around Dal Lake. The same is the situation due to tourist pressure in the national parks near Delhi - Corbett, Sariska and Ranthambore.

Even forest resorts have caused a lot of damage. Cottages for the tourists have resulted into forest clearance - Mollem - 'Mahavir Wildlife sanctuary is a case in sight. The same is the case with Pichavaram mangrove forests at the mouth of Vella river in Tamil Nadu. This can result into take over by the common forest plants & the dealth of the mangrove. The mangrove which acts as resistant to coastal erosion, tidal erosion and cyclones, has already disappeared (about 40%) on the eastern coast which is rich in different species of flowers and fishes. All this bring villages closer to water front due to commercialisation. Close to water they might lead to dumping of waste in the water in turn affecting the trees. Lack of planning and management is a crucial factor.

(2) Beaches and Seas: The ecology of Seas and Beaches is very fragile because here two ecosystems-land mass and water mass-interact. The balance between these two should be maintained as cultures surviving along sea coasts are very delicate. Tourism developed along sea coasts is basically luxury tourism. This could be explained by the following example: Aguada as a seaside village in Goa was a peaceful place where toddy tappers, fishermen and farmers lived a self-sufficient life till some Hotels and Resorts came on the scene.

The projection of Andaman and Nicobar Islands as a tourist paradise is an ecologically disastrous project. The islands are being provided with free port, shopping complexes, hotels, casinos, race courses, deep diving facilities, water sports and scuba diving. These developments endanger the safety of exquisite rain forests and untapped gene pool of medicinal and herbal plants. Most of the islands still have a forest cover of nearly 85%. The number of flowering plants on the islands are estimated at 2300, and about 100 plant species have already disappeared. A few pockets have endangered species of animals and birds. The most exquisite feature of the Andamans is it's coral, glistening white and pink in the blue waters. Howsoever controlled the development be it will eventually destroy the coral reefs.

The disruption of any of the sub-systems - the forested hills or coastal mangroves - will jeopardise everything else. Ecology apart, there is an acute shortage of drinking water on the islands. The already existing tourism has done plenty to destroy the coral in Lakshadweep.

(3) Mountains: Mountains are not exempt from the tourist devastation. Ladakh especially has all its trails choked in garbage and filth, left by trekkers. It is found that mountains and valleys are strewn with skins of potatoes and fruits, cooked and uncooked vegetables, shells of eggs, packings of medicines and noodles, tins and try food, and worst of all, stinking human waste uncovered at various places. In Nepal, 200 kilos of garbage was removed from the Everest alone. A massive deforestation accompanies each of the expeditions up the peaks: only seven per cent of the tourists use fuel other than wood. As such vegetation is sparse in upper altitude.

Dal Lake is another example that is dying slowly due to the sewage and grins in its waters.

A sanctuary for numerous wild life and birds, it is also the catchment area of the Dal Lake.

Another place where tourism has meant direct devastation is in kumaun and Garhwal Himalayas- vast hectares of good forest and grasing land have been appropriated for tourism development.

As a perfect example of the saying "Tourism destroys tourism", we can see the plight of hill stations. Building construction in addition to denuding the forest cover, has brought the mono-culture of urban sprawl to these much loud townships. Apart from these short-term social, economic problems, uncontrolled tourism is taking the environment to the thresholds of destruction.

The environment thresholds include the following:

(1) Pollution: It is claimed that "tourism industry" is uniquely benign, ins that it is an industry without smoke stacks and that each dollar spent has a fertile "multiplier effect". This is simply special pleading by those with a vested interest. Tourism emits no smoke-it is true but pollution comes in many forms and tourism has evolved general special forms of its own.

Unfortunately the experience hitherto says that it has a proven ability to spoil the unspoilt. Tourism can no longer be separated from other man-made disruptions of the ecology such as mining and deforestation.

Many of the types of impacts considered can result from various types of development and most are not unique to tourism.

The pollution is of different kinds in tourism industry. If a proper sewage disposal system has not been installed for hotels, resorts and other tourist facilities, there may be pollution of ground water from the sewage, or if a sewage outfall has not been adequately treated, the effluent will pollute the water area. Air pollution is also the result of growing tourism. It can come from excessive use of internal combustion vehicles (cars, buses & motor cycles) used by and for tourists in particular areas, especially at major tourist attraction sites that are accessible only by roads.

Noise generated by Aeroplanes motor boats and some times certain types of tourist attractions such as amusement parks reaches uncomfortable and irritating levels for nearby residents and other tourists.

These pollution are of lesser harm to human being as we can use the safeguards. But from these the rest of the bio-sphere suffers.

(2) Population: Population has got a very important bearing over our ecosystem as for its various requirements of basic survival. Food is basically provided or grown over Earth/land which needs protection from over exploitation.

Technology provided a better living through Chemistry in the form of synthetic fibers, plastics, inorganic pesticides, leaded fuels, and many other products that sooner or later caused the introduction of toxic and biologically active materials into Environmental. To this explosive of industrial technology was added that of the human population in the post - war "baby-boom". The result was an exponential growth in the pollution of air, land and water by chemicals and chemical wastes. Soon natural mechanisms of detoxification of pollutants and of adjustment to their effects were overwhelmed by these inputs.

The activities of increasing humanity are now approaching a new set of limits set by the overall regulatory capabilities of the biosphere. Basic atmospheric processes are being modified by massive urban industrial discharges of greenhouse gases that produce lower atmospheric warming, chlorofluorocarbons that affect the stratospheric ozone layer and Sulphur and Nitrogen oxides that lead to acid deposition.

(3) Exploitation of Natural Resources: Nature has its own methods of survival and too much of human interference disturbs the mechanism which sustains ecology. Tourism developed in environmentally fragile and vulnerable areas necessitates exploitation of locally available resources to provide basic amenities to the tourists.

On the industrial side, machines and sources of energy were harnessed to enable resources to be processed on new scales and with increased efficiency. With the steam engine came railroads and steamships that opened new regions to exploitation. On the scientific side, discoveries led to a revolutionary change in the basic concept of nature: a world in which all was created and overseen by God was replaced by the world that functioned according to the operation of basis laws of physics and chemistry. The industrial and Scientific Revolution gave individuals an enormously expanded ability to exploit resources and create material wealth.

The western system of environmental exploitation was thus spread widely, so that it became operational, even in areas where the basic philosophical view of humans and nature was quite different.

Ironically Environment is of far greater concern for a poor country because a large proportion of its people prefer life close to the Earth. Most of them have to trudge to a spring, a tank or an open well, or at best a public borewell serving hundreds of families for water to drink, to bathe, to wash. Hence it is often told that exploitation of environment in a poor country is a luxury which it can ill afford.

Q10. Write short notes on any two of the following:

(a) Impact of tourism on wildlife

Refer to Chapter-8, Q.No.-3

(b) Hotels and Resorts

Refer to June-2007, Q.No.-9

(c) Abiotic Environment

Refer to June-2006, Q.No.-1

(d) Visitor Behaviour

Refer to June-2008, Q.No.-8

TS–5 : ECOLOGY, ENVIRONMENT AND TOURISM
December-2013

Note : Attempt any five questions in about 600 words each.

Q1. Explain two major types of Food chains? How they are different and similar?

Refer to Chapter-1, Q.No.-5

Difference

	Grazing food chain	Detritus food chain
1.	It starts from the living green plants i.e. producers occupying the first trophic level.	It starts from the dead organic matter and decomposers called detritivores as the first trophic level.
2.	A much less fraction of energy flows through this type of food chain.	A much larger fraction of energy flows through this type of food chain.
3.	It binds to inorganic nutrients.	It releases the inorganic nutrients bound in organic matter
4.	It is directly dependent on the influx of solar radiation.	Energy for the food chain comes from the organic wastes, exudates and dead matter termed as detritus.

Similarities

- Both food chains are invariably linked to one another in nature.
- The food chains are mostly sequential in nature.

Q2. Explain the main features of environmental conservation?

Refer to Chapter-2, Q.No.-1

Q3. "The tourism industry be structured to maximise the economic benefits. While reducing social and environmental impact"? Explain the statement.

Refer to Chapter-4, Q.No.-11

Q4. Discuss the problems relating to the financing and management of the tourism infrastructure.

Refer to Chapter-5, Q.No.-7

Q5. Explain how tourism has been an instrument in protecting historical sites.

Refer to Chapter-5, Q.No.-1(ii)

Q6. Discuss the major circuits/destinations that have been identified for concentrated tourism development in India.

Refer to Chapter-6, Q.No.-8

Q7. What is eco -tourism? Explain the impact of such tourism development?

Refer to Chapter-2 Q.No.-2&3

Q8. Discuss the pressures on the environment of a destination created by tourism.

Refer to June-2006, Q.No.-10(iv)

Q9. Explain the term vegetation and wildlife. How wildlife is so important to human beings?

Ans. First Refer to Chapter-8, Q.No.-1

Importance of Wildlife to Human Beings: Biodiversity includes the wild as well as the cultivated species. Since the number of wildlife species is much more than the cultivated ones, the discussion in the above cited reference can be construed for the wildlife. To briefly recapitulate, biodiversity is of tremendous economic significance. A large number of products derived from forests including timber, gum, resins, oils, waxes, dyes, and rubber are of immense commercial value. The people residing in forests such as many tribes, depend largely on the wildlife for food, fodder and even recreation. Importantly, many wild species have medicinal value and the potential of innumerable species is yet to be tapped. The wildlife genepool is also of utmost importance in the field of agriculture. Many such genes from the wild have been utilised in crop improvement. It goes without saying that wildlife is a source of beauty, wonder, joy and recreational pleasure for a large number of people. Observing leaves change colour in autumn, smelling the aroma of wild flowers, watching an eagle soar overhead are some of the pleasurable experiences that are unexplainable and even not bought with money. Above all, the wildlife is of immense ecological significance. Each species interacts with other species and plays a role in the transfer of energy and materials within and between ecosystems. Hence, each one in its own way contributes to the stability of ecosystems. If a number of species disappear, the diversity diminishes and the number of checks and balances on plant and animal populations decreases. As species are lost, the stabilising influences of predation, parasitism and competition are disrupted and the ecosystem become vulnerable to disturbances that in some cases threaten to destroy it.

Thus, the importance of wildlife is unquestionably immense and so is the need for conserving it in its natural state. It is difficult to imagine the existence of human beings without wildlife. If one glances at the history of India, one would be amazed to know that even 2000 years ago, people were aware of the importance of wildlife.

Q10. Write short notes on the following:

(a) Adventure sports

Refer to Chapter-9, Q.No.-7

(b) Function and importance of wet lands.

Refer to Chapter-9, Q.No.-1

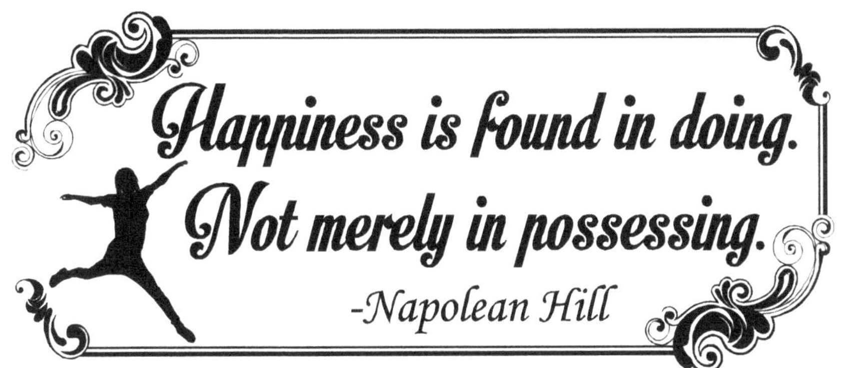

TS–5 : ECOLOGY, ENVIRONMENT AND TOURISM
June-2014

Note : Attempt any five questions in about 600 words each. All questions carry equal marks.

Q1. Explain two major types of food chains. How are they different and similar?

Refer to Dec-2013, Q.No.-1

Q2. Discuss flow of energy in ecosystem and highlight the implication of energy transfer through trophic levels.

Ans. The capacity to do work is called energy. We required and utilise energy for our various works. Energy used for all life processes is derived from solar energy, which also caters to the need of our ecosystem. It is absorbed by green plants during photosynthesis, and then, food is transferred from the producers to decomposers. Thus, all living things need food for energy. The ultimate source of all this food and all ecosystems on earth starts with the Sun.

However, in the interior of the sun, a thermonuclear reaction is continuously going on at a temperature of about 108 K wherein hydrogen is converted into helium. This is accompanied by a release of huge amount of energy, which manifests itself as heat and light.

Flow of energy through the ecosystem is a fundamental process, which can be easily quantified if the energy input to the ecosystem and its subsequent transformation from one trophic level to another can be expressed in terms of calories. Study of ecosystem energetics gives a sound basis for energy budget at individual, population and ecosystem level. We can get a scientific basis for evaluating efficiency of different trophic levels in an ecosystem and comparing diverse ecosystems by quantifying the energy flow.

Observations made from artificial satellites indicate that nearly 30% of the total solar radiation entering our atmosphere is reflected by the earth-atmosphere system. The remaining 70% of the radiation is absorbed by the earth's atmosphere. Of this, 19% is absorbed directly by the atmosphere and the rest by the earth's surface. The blue and red component (400-500 nm and 600-700 nm band respectively) of solar radiation are strongly absorbed by chlorophyll, the green pigment, present in vegetation and are converted into chemical energy. That is how energy for the ecosystem is trapped.

The energy captured by the autotrophs will never revert back to the sun. Similarly, the energy, which passes to the herbivore, does not revert back to autotrophs and so on. Thus, we can say that the flow of solar energy is unidirectional. Its immediate implication is that an ecosystem would collapse if the sun stops giving out energy.

The second important fact is that the amount of energy decreases at successive trophic levels. When any organism dies, it is converted to detritus or dead biomass that serves as an energy source for decomposers. Organisms at each trophic level depend on those at the lower trophic level for their energy demands. Each trophic level has a certain mass of living material at a particular time called as the standing crop. The standing crop is measured as the mass of living organisms (biomass) or the number in a unit area. The biomass of a species is expressed in terms of fresh or dry weight. Measurement of biomass in terms of dry weight is more accurate.

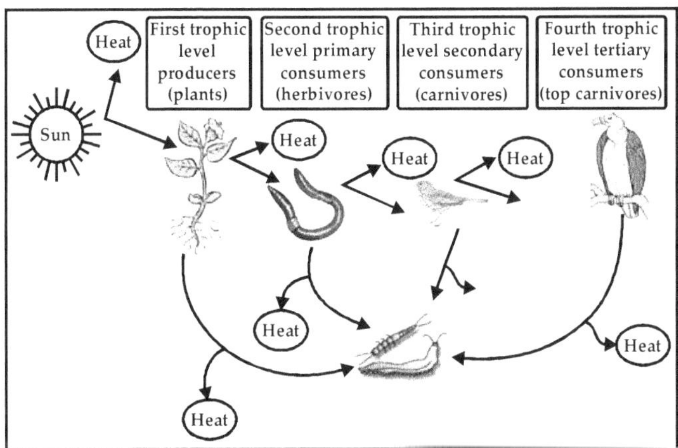

The number of trophic levels in the grasing food chain is restricted as the transfer of energy follows 10 per cent law only 10 per cent of the energy is transferred to each trophic level from the lower trophic level. In nature, it is possible to have so many levels, i.e. producer, herbivore, primary carnivore, secondary carnivore in the grasing food chain.

Q3. Define the concept of conservation of nature. Recreate the history of conservation of nature in brief.

Ans. Conservation of nature does not have a universally accepted definition. Infact as the human concern about nature has grown so have the definitions evolved. For our purpose, however, and especially with respect to a specific inter-relationship that seemingly exists between tourism and environment

Now Refer to Chapter-2, Q.No.-1 and June-2007, Q.No.-1

Q4. Discuss the role of tourism in the development and conservation of resources.

Ans. Another form that is widely used in connection with tourism is conservation. It refers to the planned management of specific sites and places and natural resources in general and not necessarily categorical preservation which is used to mean no change of the site, place or resources. Sometimes, it includes restoration to its original condition. Conservation implies that some use and controlled change can take place if the basic integrity of the site, place or resource is maintained.

Major categories of natural environmental attractions for tourism include following types.

(i) Climate: A warm, sunny, dry climate is typically considered desirable by most tourists from cold winter areas. To this are added certain other attractions such as seasonal festivals or added physical attractions that provide opportunities for recreation activities. Conservation of a desirable climate through control of air pollution or retaining the architectural styles suitable to the climate is, therefore essential for tourism.

A long climatically desirable season is obviously an advantage for development of tourism so that investment made in facilities, services and infrastructure is maximised. For example, generally the tourist season for a destination like Goa used to be September-March and now it is promoted for June-August also as "monsoon on golden beaches."

(ii) Scenic Beauty: The overall natural scenic beauty of an area may be a major motivation to visit the area, especially if conservation measures have been applied to maintain the cleanliness and natural character of the environment. Remote scenic areas may offer opportunities for nature or adventure oriented tourists engaging in such activities as river rafting, rock climbing and long distance trekking.

(iii) Beaches and Marine areas: Beaches and associated marine areas for sunbathing, swimming, boating, wind and board surfing, water skiing, parasailing, snorkeling and scubadiving, sport-fishing and other water recreation activities are major attractions in many places in the world. Beach and marine areas should also have conservation measures application in the form of banks, reserves and development controls.

(iv) Flora and Fauna: Unusual and interesting flora and fauna can be very important attractions, especially when combined with scenic landscapes. Game parks of East Africa and Redwood parks of California fall under this category. Zoos, aquariams and botanic gardens are also specialised attractions as far as the features of flora and fauna are concerned. Adequate conservation measures are thus an absolute necessity for the promotion of tourism in such areas.

Conversely the development of tourism can be one of the techniques used to accomplish environmental and cultural conservation and maintain an area's unique sense of place. However, there are situations where development of special types of features, such as theme parks or gambling casinos, not already related to the character of the local area, is justified because of profitability. This type of tourism should be developed in the manner that the country believes to be the most appropriate for its own environment and socio-cultural benefits.

Q5. Explain the significance of planning for tourism and its impact on economy.

Refer to Chapter-5, Q.No.-3 and Chapter-6, Q.no.-4

Q6. "The culture of a country can be an important asset for it can be marketed to foreign tourists." Comment.

Refer to Chapter-4, Q.No.-6

Q7. Analyse the problems which can arise out of unplanned or badly planned tourism.

Ans. Planning is concerned with anticipating and regulating change in a system to promote orderly development so as to increase the social, economic and environmental benefits of the development process. To do this, planning becomes an ordered sequence of operations, designed to lead to the achievement of either a single goal or to a balance between several goals.

Tourism planning involves many aspects: sites and itineraries, tour groups and transport, safety, sewage treatment, health and security, guides, finance and accounting, booking and advertising, equipment.

It is widely acknowledged that unplanned or badly tourism may lead to severe ecological and social problems in tourist destinations.

Unplanned or badly-planned tourism can have various negative impacts on nature reserves: on rocks, minerals and fossils; on soils; on water resources; on vegetation; on animal life; on sanitation; on aesthetic features of the landscape. Unplanned or badly-planned tourism can damage the local scenery and have gigantic impact on the environment as well as day to day life of the local community.

Negative impacts can be minimised and mitigated through good planning (e.g. controlling the number of visitors, and the type, timing and extent of their activities), environmental impact assessment, and preparation.

Now Refer to Chapter-5, Q.No.-4

Q8. What is eco-tourism? Explain the impact of such tourism development.

Refer to Dec-2013, Q.No.-7

Q9. Explain the cause of pollution. How is it harmful to our environment?

Refer to Chapter-4, Q.No.-12

Q10. Prepare an account of the wildlife species that occur in the different Biographic Zones of India.

Refer to Chapter-8, Q.No.-2

"It doesn't matter who you are, where you come from. The ability to triumph begins with you – always".

-Oprah Winfrey

TS–5 : ECOLOGY, ENVIRONMENT AND TOURISM
December-2014

Note : Attempt any five questions in about 600 words each. All questions carry equal marks.

Q1. Define abiotic environment and discuss its important factors that are crucial for life.

Q2. If you have to take eight people on a tour to show a tropical forest, where in India would you take them? Explain the process of taking these people and highlight the salient features of the selected tropical forest.

Q3. The Indian philosophical explanation considers nature as composition of five elements. Comment on it.

Q4. What is the role played by the Government and the local people in protecting the environment while expanding the tourism industry?

Q5. What are the direct and indirect economic benefits of tourism? Explain with illustrations.

Q6. Explain how tourism has become an instrument in protecting historical sites.

Q7. Explain the important measures for balanced tourism development in a country.

Q8. Discuss the major circuits/destinations that have been identified for concentrated tourism development in India.

Q9. Give your comment on the statement:
"Wildlife is considered a valuable resource for mankind."

Q10. Analyse how water sports and golf damage the environment.

TS–5 : ECOLOGY, ENVIRONMENT AND TOURISM
June-2015

Note : Attempt any five questions in about 600 words each. All questions carry equal marks.

Q1. Define the concept of Ecosystem. Discuss the components of an Ecosystem.

Q2. Write a note on major terrestrial biomes of the world.

Q3. What is Biodiversity? Discuss the importance of Bio-Diversity.

Q4. Describe important measures to decrease environment degradation to be taken up by the public sectors in tourism.

Q5. What is responsible tourism? Describe the ways in which responsible tourism helps in preserving the environment.

Q6. Explain the concept of multiplier effect. Describe the positive socio-economic benefits of tourism.

Q7. Discuss the advantages of national and regional level tourism planning.

Q8. Discuss the major circuits/destinations that have been identified for concentrated tourism development in India by the Ministry of Tourism, GOI.

Q9. What is "Chipko Movement"? Discuss the arguments of the environmentalists against the building of big dams.

Q10. Discuss the impact that tourism industry has had on the wetlands and describe its implications.

TS–5 : ECOLOGY, ENVIRONMENT AND TOURISM
December-2015

Note : Attempt any five questions in about 600 words. All questions carry equal marks.

Q1. Discuss the inter-relationship between tourism and environment. How can responsible growth of tourism be ensured without causing damage to the environment?

Q2. What is resource partitioning? What is the ecological significance of resource partition?

Q3. How is biodiversity related to the balance in an ecosystem? Also explain how can the stratum of tourism industry contribute in the conservation of biodiversity?

Q4. Write a brief note on any two in about 300 words each:
(a) Tourism carrying capacity
(b) Responsible Tourism
(c) Politics of Environment
(d) Biodiversity

Q5. Discuss the impact of tourism activities on environment and suggest some possible solutions to check/mitigate these impacts.

Q6. What do you mean by regional imbalances? Explain the importance of regional planning in tourism.

Q7. "Alternative tourism provides an alternative answer to the problem of tourism". Justify with an example.

Q8. Point out the problems of responsible tourism. Why do the developing countries have to face more problems in tourism than the developed countries.

Q9. What is Multiplier effect? What are the impacts of tourism multipliers?

Q10. Visitor behaviour can play a crucial role in the preservation or the destruction of the environment. Discuss.

TS–5 : ECOLOGY, ENVIRONMENT AND TOURISM
June-2016

Note : Attempt any five questions in about 600 words each. All questions carry equal marks.

Q1. Differentiate between biotic and abiotic components of ecosystem? Also write few principles of ecosystem function.

Q2. Visitor behavior can play a crucial role in the preservation or the destruction of the environment. Discuss.

Q3. How is biodiversity related to the balance in an ecosystem? Also explain how can the stratum of tourism industry contribute in the conservation of biodiversity?

Q4. Write a brief note on any two in about 300 words each:
(a) Tourism infrastructure
(b) Alternative Tourism
(c) Master Plan in Tourism
(d) Biodiversity

Q5. Discuss the impact of tourism activities on environment and suggest some possible solutions to check/mitigate these impacts.

Q6. What do you mean by regional imbalances? Explain the importance of regional planning in tourism.

Q7. How has the environment been understood in the Indian philosophical traditions?

Q8. Suggest the role of host and guest population in environmental conservation and protection?

Q9. Write a note on the Politics of Environment? What are the problems and benefits associated with the same?

Q10. What is resource partitioning? What is the ecological significance of resource partition?

TS–5 : ECOLOGY, ENVIRONMENT AND TOURISM
December-2016

Note : Answer any five questions in about 600 words each. All questions carry equal marks.

Q1. Name the three basic characteristics of a living community. Describe how species interact within a community.

Ans. Refer to Chapter-1, Q.No.-13

In a community, the populations of both plants and animals live together, share common resources, depend on each other and meet their requirements through mutual cooperation and interaction.

Kinds of Interactions: Things do not remain quiet and static, after different plant and animal populations have inhabited an area. Each individual organism actively interacts with the biotic and abiotic components of the habitat. Basically three types of interactions namely, predation, symbiosis and competition exist in a living community. These are discussed as follows:

(1) Predation: In any ecosystem, only the producers are capable of manufacturing their own food whereas all the consumers-be the herbivoures, carnivores or omnivores, or even the scavengers and decomposers depend on other sources for their food. Some of the consumers are also known as predators. A predator is an organism that feeds directly upon another organism, and the prey may or may not be killed in the process. This definition, while separating the live-feeders from dead-feeders, includes a wide spectrum of organisms. The herbivores, carnivores and omnivores are predators. So are the various kinds of parasites.

(2) Competition: It is another kind of interaction within the species of a community. This interaction is mainly of antagonistic type as the organisms compete with each other for basic environmental resources required for their survival. These resources are mainly energy and matter in usable forms, space and specific sites for various life activities. The plants compete with each other for space for spreading roots and shoots to ensure maximum absorption of sunlight, water and nutrients. Animals too compete for space for living, reproducing and feeding purposes. An organism whether plant or animal faces basically two kinds of competition. One from the members of the same species - intraspecific competition, and second with the members of other species - interspecific competition.

(3) Symbiosis: All the interactions among members of communities are not always antagonistic. The non-antagonistic interactions exhibited by organisms are known as symbiotic interactions. The symbiotic relationships are those in which two species of organisms live together in close association. This association is the result of co-evolution of the symbiotic species over the geological time scale. Three major kinds of symbiotic relationships are seen amongst organisms: commensalism, mutualism and parasitism.

Q2. Discuss the various causes of Biodiversity loss and their impact on human lives.

Refer to Chapter-1, Q.No.-16

Q3. How has the notion of conservation in modern times evolved? Explain the Indian philosophy of conservation.

Refer to Chapter-2, Q.No.-1 and June-2007, Q.No.-1

Q4. Define Sustainable development. Enumerate its relevance and practice in modern day tourism development.

Refer to Chapter-3, Q.No.-7

Q5. Explain the basic framework for developing a Tourism Master Plan and the various components which can be included.

Refer to Chapter-4, Q.No.-1

Q6. Explore relevant examples related to the potential of tourism as a tool for conservation.

Refer to June-2008, Q.No.-8

Q7. Write short notes on the following in about 150 words each:

(a) Ecosystem

Refer to Dec-2006, Q.No.-10(i)

(b) Difference between Food web and Food chain

Refer to Chapter-1, Q.No.-6

(c) Aquatic Biomes

Refer to Chapter-1, Q.No.-11

(d) Impact of Ozone layer depletion

Ans. Thinning of ozone layer means getting direct in touch with ultra violet rays which can cause skin cancer or skin irritation which can lead to death. A decrease in 1% of ozone layer can cause 5% increase in cases of skin cancer. Exposure to UV rays has also increased the cases of cataracts which in turn affects people's vision and could also cause an increase in people becoming blind.

Depletion of ozone layer and increase in UV rays can also cause DNA damage which can also be catastrophic. Aquatic plants and animals are not even safe. UV rays can penetrate through water and can kill small plants and animals. If ozone hole keep on expanding, there would be very few plants which means less food in the whole world.

The effect of the ozone hole and the damage done to the layer is still not very well understood. Apart from the gradual decrease of the ozone layer all over the world, there is little quantifiable evidence of new holes appearing any time soon. Even so, a number of countries have been working towards mitigating the damage.

Q8. How does tourism activity deteriote the ecology of the following?

(a) Sea and Beaches

(b) Mountains

Refer to June-2007, Q.No.-8

Q9. In what ways do visitors' behaviour affect the environment? Cite appropriate examples.

Refer to June-2008, Q.No.-8

Q10. Discuss initiatives which hotel properties can take up to minimise environmental degradation.

Refer to Chapter-9, Q.No.-12

TS–5 : ECOLOGY, ENVIRONMENT AND TOURISM
June-2017

Note : Answer any five questions in about 600 words each. All questions carry equal marks. Marks are allotted against each question.

Q1. Highlight the importance of Biodiversity and explain how is it related to the balance in an ecosystem.

Q2. How many Biogeographical regions are there in India? Briefly describe each of them.

Q3. Discuss the significance of the concepts of Preservation and Conservation in tourism development.

Q4. What do you understand by 'Responsible tourism'? How can the Government, Industry and Locals contribute to its success?

Q5. Discuss the various considerations in planning for development of a coastal settlement as a tourist resort.

Q6. Describe the impact of increasing pollution and population on the environment. Suggest concrete steps to minimise the negative impacts.

Q7. As an Eco-friendly tourist, how would you conduct yourself during your travel?

Q8. Write short notes on the following in about 150 words each:
(a) Social cost of Tourism
(b) Effect of tourism on Local customs
(c) Multiplier Effect
(d) Tourism Master Plan

Q9. How do hotel operations impact the environment? Enumerate steps being taken up by the Hoteliers to counter them.

Q10. Discuss the adverse effects of tourists' behaviour on the physical, socio-cultural and economic environments of hosts' destinations.

TS–5 : ECOLOGY, ENVIRONMENT AND TOURISM
December-2017

Note : Attempt any five questions in about 600 words each. All questions carry equal marks.

Q1. The environment consists of Biotic and Abiotic components that are inter-related in an Ecosystem. Explain it with suitable examples.

Q2. By explaining the concept of eco-tourism, discuss how eco-tourism plays a positive as well as negative role on environment. Give suitable examples.

Q3. What do you understand by development? What are the social and ecological problems that are encountered in relating development with environment?

Q4. What do you mean by regional assets? Highlight the changes which came about in the life of traditional communities as a result of the contact with colonial power.

Q5. Discuss how tourism development creates regional imbalances. Substantiate your answer with suitable examples.

Q6. Explain how tourism has been an instrument in protecting historical sites? Substantiate your answer with suitable examples.

Q7. What is chipko movement? Discuss the arguments of the environmentalist against the building of Big Dams.

Q8. Prepare an account of the wildlife species that occur in the different Biographic Zones of India.

Q9. Trace the development of some prominent hill stations during the course of nineteenth century to understand the environmental impacts upon the mountains?

Q10. Write short notes on the followings in about 300 words each:
(a) Functions and importance of Wetlands
(b) Scope of water sports in India

TS–5 : ECOLOGY, ENVIRONMENT AND TOURISM
June-2018

Note : Attempt any five questions in about 600 words each. All questions carry equal marks.

Q1. Define the concept of Ecosystem. Discuss the components of an Ecosystem.

Q2. What do you understand by conservation of nature? Recreate the history of conservation of nature in brief.

Q3. Critically analyse the role of Government and the local people in protecting environment while expanding the tourism industry. Substantiate your answer with suitable examples from travel and tourism field.

Q4. Explain the concept of multiplier effect. Give suitable examples from travel and tourism field.

Q5. What do you mean by tourism infrastructure? Discuss the initiatives taken by the Government for the development of tourism infrastructure with reference to any state.

Q6. Discuss the major circuits/destinations that have been identified for concentrated tourism development in India.

Q7. Discuss the impacts of tourism development on culture.

Q8. Give your comment on "Wildlife is considered a valuable resource for mankind".

Q9. Write a detailed note on summer capital of British Raj.

Q10. Write short notes on the followings in about 300 words each:
(a) Functions and importance of wetlands
(b) Condition of Adventure sports in India

TS–5 : ECOLOGY, ENVIRONMENT AND TOURISM
December-2018

Note : Attempt any five questions in about 600 words each. All questions carry equal marks.

Q1. Differentiate between the terms Ecology and Environment. Explain how Environment changes with time.

Ans. Refer to Chapter-1, Q.No.-1 (Pg. No.-2)

Environment changes with time: The history of our solar system or planet earth provides us enough evidences that there have been gradual but continuous changes in our environment. Some changes are slow whereas some are fast.

(1) Slow Changes: Slow changes cannot be seen in a lifetime or even in a span of 100-200 years. We can study such changes through fossil records. For example, the rocks brought back from the moon were found to be about 4000 million years old and the oldest rock recorded on earth is about 3000 million years old. From the fossil records, we can study the slow change in the environment and organisms of a particular region.

The first organisation of earth system took place when it melted within 800 million years of its formation. Iron and other heavy metals sank towards the centre or core of the earth and lighter metals were expelled as gases to form its first atmosphere. At that time there was no free O_2. When the planet cooled, the outer surface of the mantle solidified into a crust. After that many changes took place through falling meteorites which not only punctured the primitive earth crust but caused it to heat up. This drove away most of the atmosphere's original gases. The earth became geologically active and volcanoes threw up huge quantities of lava ash composed namely of gases. Evidence suggests that at that time and even nowadays gases like carbon-dioxide, nitrogen and water vapour are important constituents of volcanic emmision, (released from hydrated minerals). On cooling of water vapours clouds were formed and due to the rains that followed, formation of oceans, rivers, etc., on this planet took place. There was a significant role of thunderstorms, that accompanied these rains, in conversion of elements of primitive atmosphere into complex molecules which are the building blocks of life.

Over a period of time, earth's crust became more and more thick. Sunlight provided heat to the earth's surface and uneven heating of earth's surface and change in the temperature caused flow of gases and water in the atmosphere. The complex molecules of carbon, hydrogen, nitrogen forged by lighting discharges in the atmosphere, accumulated into the ocean to form the first living organism (life started for the first time in the ocean). There were gradual changes in the nature and atmosphere. A new organism appeared containing a compound chlorophyll which could trap sun-energy and utilize carbon-dioxide and water of the sea to form carbohydrates giving out free oxygen as a by product. Before that the atmosphere was made up of nitrogen, carbon-dioxide and hydrogen.

Today, we cannot imagine that in the early life of the earth there was no oxygen in the atmosphere. In fact early organisms were extremely prone to oxidation. As oxygen started accumulating in the atmosphere due to photosynthesis by green plants, carbon-dioxide correspondingly started decreasing. Some of the newly formed oxygen was siphoned off by the iron dissolved in the oceans. In this new combination of gases along with oxygen, new organisms might have evolved, having higher tolerance for oxygen and ability to use it to drive life process much more efficiently. This way oxygen became the second most abundant gas after nitrogen in the atmosphere, and the concentration of carbon-dioxide reduced significantly.

Addition of oxygen in the atmosphere made another significant change when some of the oxygen was converted into ozone. As you know, the ozone layer in the stratospheric zone of atmosphere is a protective layer for a number of organisms against ultraviolet radiation emitted by sun. Around 600 million years ago, through the process of slow changes our atmosphere reached the stage we are living in now. This is the most comfortable state of' atmosphere for life. But by increasing activities of man, this state of atmosphere is also changing rapidly.

Changes in land-mass or continental movement: According to the German Scientist, Alfred Wegener, about 200 million years ago there was a single continent called 'Pangaea'.

Scientists believe that the continents do drift slowly, about 15 cm every year. This gradual shift in 400 million years has shaped the earth as we see it today. there are scientific evidences that the indian plate also drift from 'Gondwanaland' met 'Laurasia' to give the present shape to this continent. The formation of Himalayas took place because of the impact of this union of the two continents.

There are many slow activities and events taking place inside the earth too. The core or interior of the earth is composed of a dense intensely hot mass of molten metal. Surrounding the core is the mantle - a hot, pliable layer of rock. Vast flow of convection currents circulate in this region. These are responsible for volcanic erruptions, earthquakes, formation of mountains, etc.

Hence, it is clear that there has been a continuous change in the atmosphere, within and outside the earth. The entire evolution of species on this planet depends on adaptation of organisms to the environmental conditions. These changes have obvious implication on climate which has changed drastically since the origin of the earth.

(2) Fast Changes: There are certain human activities which have brought about fast changes in our environment as well as in the climate. Since the industrial revolution, technological progress and economic achievements have made tremendous contribution to modern civilisation and brought the human society unprecedented prosperity. But they have also led to unprecedented risks and crisis which must be solved quickly for safeguarding the future of the mankind. If you visit some industrial towns like Bombay, Delhi, Kanpur (U.P.), Mandi Gobind Garh (Punjab), Korb(aM .P.), Surat (Gujarat), Vishakhapatnam (A.P.), etc., you will observe that the environment of these cities is changing. In metropolitan cities the vehicular pollution is increasing day by day and is mainly responsible for atmospheric pollution. If you ask your parents and grand parents, they will tell you how fast the environmental conditions have changed in rural and urban areas. Some global environmental issues like climatic changes, are mainly caused by human activities such as burning cod, oil and other fossil fuels, large scale deforestation and mining, etc. This is one example of fast changes in our environment, which can be seen not only within a generation but even in one or two decades.

Now, Refer to Chapter-1, Q.No.-3 (Pg. No.-6)

Q2. Write a detailed note on Biomes in the world.

Ans. Refer to Chapter-1, Q.No.-9, 10 & 11 (Pg. No.-14, 15 & 17) and June-2008, Q.No.-2 (Pg. No.-211)

Q3. Elaborate the factors which may lead to loss of Biodiversity and their possible consequences.

Ans. Refer to Chapter-1, Q.No.-16 (Pg. No.-29)

Q4. Explain the dynamics between environmental conservation and economics of tourism.

Ans. Refer to Gullybaba "download section"

Q5. Discuss the various issues involved in planning for tourism in the hilly regions from the environmental sustainability viewpoint.

Ans. Physical Planning: Hill Tourism:

Today most of the hill stations are over crowded and all types of scarcities have emerged because of the unplanned growth of tourism. It is time to realise that tourism can play a positive role in the socio-economic development of the hill areas and hill towns of the Himalayan and Sub-Himalayan region. However, this is possible provided resource planning and management is done on scientific lines. Tourism planners must recognise that the models applicable to the plains would not fit the Himalayan terrain, nor would the experience of European and American mountain resorts be necessarily ideal in the Indian context.

A hill environment presents ideal conditions for outdoor recreation, and tourism, if scientifically exploited. Tourism has been a major factor in the development process of many Alpine countries of Europe, and has been an agent of economic changes in many developing societies and island economies. It has also been observed that the most backward regions offer the most exotic resource base for tourism promotion. This holds true without any reservation for the Himalayan and Sub-Himalayan districts and regions of the country.

The Himalayan region offers some of the rarest 'tourism' products of nature with a wide ecological range and diversity. Apart from the many-splendored natural attractions and scenic beauty, the religious and socio-cultural dimensions of the tourist resource assume significance in the context of the hill districts lying in the lap of the lower Himalayas. Tribal life, ethnic culture, folk traditions, folklore and the innumerable religious shrines and sanctified spots seem to have grown with the splendor of nature as an organic whole.

Accelerated pace of development since the 1950s, gradual socialization and broad basing of tourism, educational awareness, and improved transport and infrastructure facilities, have all contributed to enormous proliferation as well as concentration of tourism related infrastructure in the popular hill-stations like Simla, Nainital, Mussoorie and Darjeeling, to name a few. In the absence of advance planning in a systematic manner, relentless influx of tourists to such centers has disturbed the demand and supply equilibrium. This has given rise to:

1. acute problem of land use,
2. environmental pollution and degradation,
3. stress condition on infrastructure, transport and services, and
4. creating conflicting conditions.

All these have been described as negative impacts of tourism. Keeping in view of the distinctive physical, socio-economic and environmental setting within which hill-tourism as a popular mufti-faceted activity should be able to function optimally, following imperatives should guide tourism planning policies and programmes at macro and micro levels.

Planning Imperatives: A scientific approach to tourism planning in the hill regions and the habitat, would require analytical studies relating to:

- likely impacts of development on the local environment and the hill habitat,
- valuating the tourist resources and infrastructure needs,
- establishing certain developmental thresholds consistent with the carrying capacity of the area and similar aspects.

The focus in all development programmes, particularly tourism related development, should be primarily on:

- the upgradation of the quality of life,

• safeguarding and maintaining their socio-cultural identity, and
• a general improvement in the town's economy.

In fact tourism should be considered as a means to achieve this end rather than an end in itself. It is in this context that the concept of carrying capacity mentioned earlier acquires significance.

It is also imperative to arrive at a consensus on the policy of resource use in the Himalayas. Equally important is to identify and conserve the sensitive eco-systems in the higher Himalayas. This could be done by designating them as biosphere reserves with buffer and core zones. Tourism activity should thus be pursued with care and sensitivity in such zones.

Hill districts and regions are characterized by a dispersed settlement pattern. Here individual settlements and settlement clusters exhibit a low structural profile. The built form is characterized by traditional hill architectural styles and motifs, intimate social spaces, interplay of levels and gradients, and an ever-changing street scope. The design of the tourist complex, and facility clusters should be sensitively dealt with and should not result in a loud imposition of an alien, cosmopolitan massive looking built mass in a low profile traditional setting. Maintaining a design continuity according to the architectural heritage in tourism complex development should be a prime concern.

A dispersed locational pattern of tourist amenities and facilities in a hill-tourism region, linked to select nodes will enable development of a hierarchy of tourist village complexes. This can also be catered to, by non-conventional sources of energy, and thus economise on conventional energy consumption. Moreover, such a spatial pattern of tourist complexes will help diffuse tourism related activities and its concomitant benefits over a wider area, rather than concentrating at one or two spots in hill districts. This will avoid causing conditions of conflict and the threat to the hill environment.

Tourist village concept on a reduced scale, should also be incorporated while planning for additional tourist infrastructure in an existing resort. This shall enable planned dispersal of tourist related infrastructure wherever necessary.

Now, Refer to Chapter-4, Q.No.-3 (Pg. No.-68)

Q6. How has tourism development been instrumental in protecting the physical features and wildlife of tourist destinations?

Ans. Refer to Chapter-3, Q.No.-5 (Pg. No.-54)

Q7. Write short notes on the following in about 150 words each:

(a) Greenhouse Effect

Ans. Refer to Chapter-1, Q.No.-3 (Pg. No.-6)

(b) Carrying Capacity

Ans. Carrying Capacity: Tourism is a resource based industry and resource evaluation is important to identify areas for resource conservation to promote tourism vis-a-vis other demands. It is also imperative to identify and designate the resource under various competing uses and further to arrive at the capacity which will be matched by the supply location wise and activity wise. The concept of carrying capacity is significant for scientific planning of tourism facilities and infrastructure, particularly in relation to sensitive tourist destination areas like the hill areas. It is the threshold of tourist activity, beyond which facilities are saturated (physical capacity), the environment is degraded (environmental or ecological capacity), or visitor enjoyment is diminished (perceptual or psychological capacity). These concepts are now generally accepted but difficulties in measuring the thresholds (except perhaps physical capacity) have restricted the use of carrying capacity as a planning tool. A blend of factors determining physical and ecological capacity of recreational areas with those that determine the social (perceptual) capacity, makes it possible to determine optimum capacity guidelines. In nature reserve areas and ecologically sensitive areas namely the hilly environment more reliance has to be given to ecological capacity guidelines and these would need to be formulated with respect to the environment of which the habitat is an integral part. Very often this is ignored because of immediate profit motives of developers. This is not a healthy trend and needs to be curbed.

(c) Chipko Movement

Ans. Refer to Chapter-6, Q.No.-18 (Pg. No.-12)

(d) Demonstration Effects in Tourism

Ans. When the people of developing countries come into contact with superior goods and more extravagant spending patterns, they are stimulated into emulation. This can lead to tension, restlessness and increased consumption. This is demonstration effect. Wide spread imitation of American consumption patterns lead directly to increased or even conspicuous consumption rather than savings and investments. In India as else where in the third world, the pattern is set and ensured by the luxury hotels islands of conspicuous consumption. A misuse of limited capital is made to buy superior or imported goods.

The 'demonstration effect' of tourists from different cultural background on residents, especially on young people, may completely or partially alter their value system and beliefs. It may also drive a wedge and create friction between different generations in a community. It may also result in loss of cultural character, self respect, and an overall social identity because of submergence of local society by outside cultural patterns brought by affluent and seemingly successful tourists. It must have become fairly evident to you by now that social costs outweight the little economic benefits that are derived from a growth of tourism unmindful of the host cultures.

Q8. Why do hotels and resorts form an important component of touristic infrastructure? How can their development be made more environment-friendly?

Ans. Refer to Chapter-9, Q.No.-10 and Q.No.-14 (Pg.No.-164 and 171)

Q9. Write notes on the following in about 300 words each:

(a) Involvement of community for sustainable tourism development

Ans. Refer to Chapter-4, Q.No.-7 (Pg. No.-74)

Community and Sustainable Tourism : The onslaught of colonialism and the rising pressures of commercial and consumer demand which wrecked havoc upon the indigenous community are poignant reminders for more careful utilization of the regional assets. It is of salience that World Tourism Report senses the alienation of local inhabitants and takes into consideration the various sensitive issues while evolving the strategies of sustainable tourism. It realises the sense of deprivation and marginalisation of the local inhabitants. In its principles for sustainable tourism the Report focuses upon the broader vision which incorporates following guidelines:

(1) Tourism planning, development and operations should be in the spirit of sustainable development in being cross-sectoral and integrated, involving different government agencies, private corporations, citizens groups and individuals so as to provide for the widest possible benefits.

(2) Agencies, corporations, groups and individuals should follow ethical principle which respect the culture and environment of the host area, the economy and traditional way of life, the community and traditional behaviour, leadership and political patterns.

(3) Due regard should be given to the protection and appropriate economic use of the natural and human environment in the host areas.

(4) Tourism should be undertaken with equity in mind, with the idea of access to a fair distribution of benefits and costs among tourism promoters and host peoples and their areas.

(5) Good information, research and communication on the nature of tourism and its effects on the human and culture environment should be available prior to and during development. This information should be known to all parties, including the local people, so that they are in a position to participate in and influence the direction of, development in their area. This would reinforce the community spirit and negate the sense of alienation.

(6) Local people should be encouraged to undertake leadership roles in the planning and development of their regional assets with the assistance of

government, financial, business and other interests.

(7) There should be integrated environmental, social and economic planning to link with existing uses, ways of life and environmental considerations.

(8) Careful monitoring should be done to allow local community to take advantage of opportunities offered by new changes.

(b) Environmental conservation in Indian philosophy.

Ans. Refer to June-2007, Q.No.-1,(Pg. No.-197)

Q10. Critically examine the concept of Responsible Tourism in terms of benefits, problems and solutions.

Ans. Refer to Dec.-2007, Q.No.-4, (Pg. No.-205) and Chapter-3, Q.No.-9 (Pg. No.-61)

Role of Industry: It was mentioned earlier that the tourism industry has been using eco-tourism or responsible tourism as a slogan or market ploy only to maximize its profits. This is not to say that there are none in the industry who are bothered about ecological destruction or environment degradation, though the voices may be few. Next to the government the industry has a major role to play in this regard if those managing the industry want their future generations to be in the same business. The government frames laws and regulations and it is for the industry to implement them. The role that the industry should play includes:

• sensitising their customers (tourists) on environmental issues and providing them all types of information regarding rules, etc. at the time of selling their package.

• educating and training their own staff and employees towards responsible tourism. Tourism sector being one of the largest employer (120 million employees the world over) imagine that by doing so a strong movement for responsible tourism will emerge on its own,

• ensuring that their own construction or other infrastructure development activities will be governed by environment friendly attitude. For example eco-friendly architecture, waste recycling, use of renewable energy, etc. can be inbuilt in a resort development or any project plan,

• Undertaking environmental audits for assessing their own business performance in that area, and

• Having business relations with those who adopt similar approaches towards environment, etc.

TS–5 : ECOLOGY, ENVIRONMENT AND TOURISM
June-2019

Note : Answer any five questions in about 600 words each. All questions carry equal marks.

Q1. Define a Biotic community. Explain the various types of interactions among the members of a biotic community.

Ans. The biotic community is defined as a collection of different populations which reside at one place. They interact with one other in many ways. It includes pond community, lawn community, forest and grass land community. In some cases plants, animals and the microbes are studied separately. They are known as plants, animals and the microbe community respectively. The biotic community is dominated by one of the character. It determines the nature of community. It can be biotic or abiotic. There is a frugivorous community which is also known as the fruit eating community. It includes the fruit eating animals such as insects, rodents and bats.

The population cannot be isolated. One population depends upon the other population for survival. The food, shelter and oxygen are provided by the plants to animals. The animals get carbon dioxide, food and pollination from the plants. There are certain features of the biotic community which include trophic organisation, stratification, dominance, variety of species and the interactions between different species. A trophic organisation is a chain of producers, consumers and decomposers. One of the species dominates out of all the different species. The population of each species has a particular stratum which is defined as a grouping of plants in well defined layers. The members of different species also interact with each other.

There are a lot of differences between a genus and community. The different species constitute a genus. They have a common ancestory and occur in different geographical areas. They do not have a functional relationship. The different populations constitute a community. They do not have a common ancestory and occur in the common geographical areas. They do not have a functional relationship which may be direct or indirect.

Various types:

(1) Dominant Plants Define the Conditions: The organisms of a community are either producers or consumers based on their food procuring mechanisms. The producers exert a dominant influence on the community. Think of any terrestrial community with which you are familiar, say for example a forest? The community in a forest is dominated by trees. Some forests even have specific names depending on the dominating species of tree, e.g., Sal forest, Pine forest and so on. The dominant plant species are usually the largest in size or are in highest numbers amongst the other life forms. You may recall that plants fu solar energy and make up the largest proportion of biomass in a community. They not only constitute the food base of the community but also modify the environment, determining by their presence what kind of organisms can live in that area. In a forest, for example, the different kinds of trees modify the local environmental conditions under their canopies. The microclimatic modifications 'create' new conditions enabling the survival of different kinds of plants and animal species which may not survive in the absence of the microclimate created by the canopies. The dominant plants have a controlling influence in the area and govern the community composition.

(2) Kinds of interactions

Refer to Dec-2016, Q.No.-1 (Pg. No.-267)

Q2. Elaborate citing relevant examples the importance of environmental conservation for the growth and development of tourism.

Refer to Chapter-2, Q.No.-1 (Pg. No.-33)

Q3. Discuss how various tourism activities contribute to environmental degradation and suggest possible ways to mitigate them.

Refer to Chapter-2, Q.No.-3 and Q.No.-4 (Pg. No.-35, 39)

Q4. Write short notes on the following in about 150 words each

(a) Photosynthesis

Ans. Photosynthesis is a process used by plants and other organisms to convert light energy into chemical energy that can later be released to fuel the organisms activities. This chemical energy is stored in carbohydrate molecules, such as sugars, which are synthesized from carbon dioxide and water – hence the name photosynthesis, from the Greek öõò, phôs, "light", and óýíèåóéò, synthesis, "putting together". In most cases, oxygen is also released as a waste product. Most plants, most algae, and cyanobacteria perform photosynthesis; such organisms are called photoautotrophs. Photosynthesis is largely responsible for producing and maintaining the oxygen content of the Earth's atmosphere, and supplies all of the organic compounds and most of the energy necessary for life on Earth.

Although photosynthesis is performed differently by different species, the process always begins when energy from light is absorbed by proteins called reaction centres that contain green chlorophyll pigments. In plants, these proteins are held inside organelles called chloroplasts, which are most abundant in leaf cells, while in bacteria they are embedded in the plasma membrane. In these light-dependent reactions, some energy is used to strip electrons from suitable substances, such as water, producing oxygen gas. The hydrogen freed by the splitting of water is used in the creation of two further compounds that serve as short-term stores of energy, enabling its transfer to drive other reactions: these compounds are reduced nicotinamide adenine dinucleotide phosphate (NADPH) and adenosine triphosphate (ATP), the "energy currency" of cells.

(b) Food Chain and Food Web

Refer to Chapter-1, Q.No.-5 and Q.No.-6 (Pg. No.-8, 10)

(c) Ozone Layer Depletion

Refer to Dec-2016, Q.No.-7(d) (Pg. No.-268)

(d) Green House Effect

Refer to Chapter-1, Q.No.-3 (Pg. No.-6)

Q5. What do you understand by Responsible Tourism? Enumerate how government, industry and the local community can contribute to its development.

Refer to Dec-2007, Q.No.-4 (Pg. No.-205)

Role of Industry: The tourism industry has been using eco-tourism or responsible tourism as a slogan or market ploy only to maximize its profits. This is not to say that there are none in the industry who are bothered about ecological destruction or environment degradation, though the voices may be few. Next to the government the industry has a major role to play in this regard if those managing the industry want their future generations to be in the same business. The government frames laws and regulations and it is for the industry to implement them. The role that the industry should play includes:

- sensitising their customers (tourists) on environmental issues and providing them all types of information regarding rules, etc. at the time of selling their package.
- educating and training their own staff and employees towards responsible tourism. Tourism sector being one of the largest employer (120 million employees the world over) imagine that by doing so a strong movement for responsible tourism will emerge on its own,
- ensuring that their own construction or other infrastructure development activities will be governed by environment friendly attitude. For example eco-friendly architecture, waste recycling, use of renewable energy, etc. can be inbuilt in a resort development or any project plan,
- Undertaking environmental audits for assessing their own business performance in that area, and

• Having business relations with those who adopt similar approaches towards environment, etc.

MacGregor has suggested that "Environmental responsibility can become a common goal that reflects all participants in the travel industry (clients, managers, investors, shareholders, employees, policy makers). This will result in a sustainable resource base that will remain intact for future generations of tourists and travel industry operators, as well as improved bottomline for individual business."

Q6. Discuss the various environmental issues involved in the development of coastal areas for tourism purpose.

Ans. Refer to June-2007, Q.No.-8 (Pg. No.-201) and Refer to June-2013, Q.No.-9(2) (Pg. No.-251)

Q7. How has tourism been instrumental in the protection of the cultural and historical sites at destinations.

Refer to Chapter-5, Q.No.-1(4) and (2) (Pg. No.-84)

Q8. Define a wetland. Explain the impact of tourism on the functioning and conservation efforts of wetlands in India.

Refer to Chapter-9, Q.No.-1 and Q.No.-2 (Pg. No.-152, 153) and Refer to June-2008, Q.No.-10 (Pg. No.-215)

Q9. Discuss the various initiatives taken up by hotel industry, to minimise wastage and environmental degradation.

Ans. A number of hotels are now taking environmental issues seriously and are embarking on activities like recycling, water and energy conservation, environmental education, waste management and afforestation (the planting of trees). The growing environmental consciousness in the industry can be attributed to government regulation, changing consumer demand, advocacy and initiatives by Non-governmental Organisations (NGOs) and ethics by professional associations. Studies conducted by the International Hotels Environment Initiative (IHEI) and Accor revealed that 90 per cent of hotel guests preferred to stay in a hotel that cared for the environment. Environmental management in hotels also reflects a paradigm shift in the industry from mass tourism to sustainable tourism. It is a continuous process adopted through management decisions, through which an organisation's activities are monitored and appropriate programmes devised to reduce the negative environmental impacts.

There are many examples of hotels taking specific initiatives to reduce the impacts of their operations on the host community. An EU funded hotel construction project in Western Samoa used traditional designs and techniques and only imported materials where local substitutes could not be produced. The hotel sites are owned by local villagers, local people are employed and local agricultural produce are consumed by tourists. Also Grecotel, the largest hotel chain in Greece uses only local styles and materials in architecture and facilities design. The hotel also sustains the local economy, serves local dishes and encourages environmental conservation, as well as encouraging guests to visit smaller villages. Moreover, one of the NOVOTEL and Hotel Ibis initiatives at Homebush Bay in Sydney, Australia is the reduction of portable water by 50 per cent through a dual piping system. At the Kingfisher Bay and Village (KBRV) in Queensland Australia, architectural design and use of fluorescent bulbs allow for minimal energy consumption.

It is recommended that the GTB, Environmental Protection Agency (EPA), Accra Metropolitan Assembly (AMA) and other institutions tasked with enforcing environmental standards should organise training programmes for hotel managers on sound environmental management practices. The training should cover areas like hotels purchasing policies, recycling of waste, government's environmental requirements, national environmental policy and the benefits to be derived from sound environmental practices among others. Such programmes will adequately inform hotel managers about their responsibilities and help them to pursue suitable environmental management programmes.

Secondly, education of guests and staff on environmentally responsible behaviour should be a major preoccupation of hotels. Laudable efforts of managers could come to nothing if guests and workers, who are major players in the hotel environment are not included. Guests could be educated through brochures, posters and signs into efficient water and energy conservation; respect for local cultures; and proper waste disposal. Hotel workers should also be educated on environmentally responsible management and marketing practices as part of their induction. They should also be constantly updated on current environmental management trends in the industry.

Finally, recycling of waste must be an important environmental management programme of hotels. Hotels must recycle the thousands of tons of wastewater that goes down the drain each day. Wastewater could be used to water ornamental plants around the hotels or to flush toilets. Food leftovers can be used for composting as manure or to feed animals. Recycling of solid waste demands some form of technology, which should not be beyond the collective scope of these hotels. They should in their own small way have, however, separate dustbins for collecting papers, plastic and bottles to make easier, the work of waste management companies involved in recycling.

Q10. What is the role and importance of tourism policies in the development of tourism? Discuss this in the context of Indian tourism industry.

Refer to Chapter-6, Q.No.-1 (Pg. No.-99)

TS–5 : ECOLOGY, ENVIRONMENT AND TOURISM

June-2020

Note : Answer any five questions in about 600 words each. All questions carry equal marks.

Q1. Explain two major types of Food Chains? What are their points of similarities and differences?

Q2. Discuss the concept and components of an Ecosystem. How does energy flows in an eco system.

Q3. What is Biodiversity? Elaborate the importance of Biodiversity?

Q4. Comment on the statement, "Environment has been perceived as a living being which breaths, feels and protects".

Q5. Discuss the concept of nature and its use in travel and tourism. Support your answer by giving suitable examples.

Q6. What is the role played by the government and local people in protecting environment while planning for the growth of tourism industry?

Q7. What is Tourism Master Plan? Elaborate its importance in the development of regional tourism infrastructure.

Q8. Critically analyse the role of Tourism in the overall process of conservation of our resources?

Q9. What is Eco-Tourism? Describe the impacts of Eco-Tourism on environment and ecology.

Q10. What are the adverse visitor behaviors that affect the socio-cultural environment of a tourist site? Give suitable examples.

TS–5 : ECOLOGY, ENVIRONMENT AND TOURISM
December-2020

Note : (i) Answer any five questions in about 600 words each. (ii) All questions carry equal marks.

Q1. Discuss the flow of energy in Ecosystem and highlight the implications of energy transfer through tropic levels.

Q2. "The philosophical explanation considers nature as a composition of five elements." Comment on the statement.

Q3. Discuss the role of tourism in the conservation and preservation of natural resources. Substantiate your answer with suitable examples.

Q4. What do you mean by regional assets? Highlight the changes which came about in the life of traditional communities as a result of contact with the colonial power.

Q5. Discuss how tourism development eradicates regional imbalances. Give suitable examples.

Q6. What is 'Chipko Movement'? Discuss the arguments of the environmentalists against the building of big dams.

Q7. Critically analyze the immediate environmental impacts on any tourist destination of your choice.

Q8. Write short notes on the following:
(a) Wildlife of India
(b) Summer capital of British Raj

Q9. Discuss the importance of Islands and Beaches in the tourism industry. Give suitable examples.

Q10. Write short notes on the following:
(a) Components of Ecosystem
(b) Responsible Tourism

TS–5 : ECOLOGY, ENVIRONMENT AND TOURISM
December-2021

Note : Answer any five questions in about 600 words each. All questions carry equal marks.

Q1. What is Biodiversity? Discuss the importance of Biodiversity.

Q2. "Environment has been perceived as a living being which breathes, feels and protects." Comment.

Q3. What do you mean by Development? What are the social and economic problems that are encountered in relating development with environment? Discuss.

Q4. Discuss the significance of the tourism master plan for the development of tourism.

Q5. How does tourism development create regional imbalances? Discuss how created imbalances can be minimized. Give suitable examples.

Q6. Analyse the problems which can arise out of unplanned or badly planned tourism.

Q7. Explain the causes of pollution and state how it is harmful to our environment. Substantiate your answer with suitable examples.

Q8. Explain the causes of immediate environmental impact on any tourist destination of your choice.

Q9. "Wildlife is considered a valuable resource for mankind." Comment.

Q10. Write short notes on the following:
(a) Conservation of Wetland
(b) Potential of Adventure Sports in India

Note : Answer any five questions in about 600 words each. All questions carry equal marks.

Q1. Discuss the flow of energy in ecosystem and highlight the implications of energy transfer through trophic level.

Q2. "The philosophical explanation considers nature as composition of five elements.? Comment on the given statement.

Q3. Discuss the problems associated with responsible tourism and their possible solution. Substantiate your answer with suitable examples.

Q4. Explain the significance of planning for tourism and its impact

Q5. What are the direct and indirect economic benefits of tourism? Explain with illustrations.

Q6. "The culture of a country can be an important asset for marketing of tourism to foreign tourist." Comment on the given

Q7. Elaborate the features of the Tourism Policy, 1982 and National Action Plan for Tourism, 1992.

Q8. Analyse the causes of pollution and state how it is harmful to our environment.

Q9. Write a detailed note on the Himalayas in the North and the Nilgiris in the South of India.

Q10. Write notes on the following :

(a) Importance of wetlands

(b) Adventure sports

Note : Answer any five questions in about 600 words each. All questions carry equal marks.

Q1. Define the concept of Ecosystem. Discuss the components of

Q2. Describe important measures to decrease environmental

Q3. "The local residents of a destination must share the responsibility of promoting responsible tourism." Describe the role of locals in promoting responsible tourism.

Q4. Discuss the problems relating to the financing and management of the tourism infrastructure. Give suitable examples.

Q5. Discuss how tourism development, creates regional imbalances. How can the same be minimized?

Q6. Write short notes on the following:

(a) Importance of Wetlands

(b) Adventure Sports

Q7. Explain any three important Environmental Legislation Acts of India. Also elaborate on the association of legislation with travel and tourism phenomenon.

Q8. What are the adverse visitor behaviours that affect the socio-cultural environment of a tourist site? Give suitable examples.

Q9. Critically analyse the impact of tourism development on the mountains in India.

Q10. Write short notes on the following:

(a) Convention Tourism

(b) Destination for Concentrated Development

www.ingramcontent.com/pod-product-compliance
Ingram Content Group UK Ltd.
Pitfield, Milton Keynes, MK11 3LW, UK
UKHW021932200726
13853UKWH00010B/446